THE MORAL ECONOMY OF WELFARE AND MIGRATION

The Moral Economy of Welfare and Migration

Reconfiguring Rights in Austerity Britain

LYDIA MORRIS

McGill-Queen's University Press
Montreal & Kingston · London · Chicago

© McGill-Queen's University Press 2021

ISBN 978-0-2280-0662-6 (cloth)
ISBN 978-0-2280-0663-3 (paper)
ISBN 978-0-2280-0758-6 (ePDF)
ISBN 978-0-2280-0759-3 (ePUB)

Legal deposit third quarter 2021
Bibliothèque nationale du Québec

Printed in Canada on acid-free paper that is 100% ancient forest free
(100% post-consumer recycled), processed chlorine free

Library and Archives Canada Cataloguing in Publication

Title: The moral economy of welfare and migration : reconfiguring rights
in austerity Britain / Lydia Morris.

Names: Morris, Lydia, 1949– author.

Description: Includes bibliographical references and index.

Identifiers: Canadiana (print) 20210169117 | Canadiana (ebook)
20210169222 | ISBN 9780228006626 (cloth) | ISBN 9780228006633
(paper) | ISBN 9780228007586 (ePDF) | ISBN 9780228007593 (ePUB)

Subjects: LCSH: Welfare state—Moral and ethical aspects—Great Britain. |
LCSH: Public welfare—Moral and ethical aspects—Great Britain. |
LCSH: Immigrants—Civil rights—Great Britain. | LCSH: Great Britain—
Moral conditions. | LCSH: Great Britain—Social policy. | LCSH: Great
Britain—Economic policy.

Classification: LCC JC479 .267 2021 | DDC 361.6/10941—dc23

This book was typeset by Marquis Interscript in 10.5/13 Sabon.

Contents

Acknowledgements   vii

Abbreviations   ix

Introduction   3

1   The Moral Economy of Austerity: Analysing UK Welfare Reform   28

2   Welfare, Migration, and Civic Stratification: The Shifting Terrain of Rights   51

3   Moralizing Welfare and Migration: A Backdrop to Brexit   73

4   Reconfiguring Rights: Boundaries, Behaviours, and Contestable Margins   96

5   Moral Economy from Above and Below: Contesting Contraction of Migrant Rights   119

6   Activating the Welfare Subject: The Problem of Agency   142

7   The Topology of Welfare–Migration–Asylum: Britain's Outsiders Inside   167

Conclusion: The Moral Economy of Welfare and Migration   189

Notes   213

References   219

Index   257

Acknowledgements

This work was made possible by the award of a Major Research Fellowship (MRF-2015-012) from the Leverhulme Trust, whose support is gratefully acknowledged. As well as releasing me from teaching and administrative duties at the University of Essex for three years, the award funded part-time assistance from Philippa Reeve, who helped to organize, store, and classify the very large amount of electronic material collected in the course of the research. She also helped prepare this manuscript for submission, and I am grateful for her hard work and commitment. I am also grateful for the comments of three anonymous reviewers, and to Richard Baggaley at MQUP for help in the whole process, from finalizing the manuscript to its ultimate publication. Thanks are also due to Matthew Kudelka, for his polished and patient work as copy editor, and to Celia Braves, for a thoughtful index produced under tight time constraints.

The main chapters (1 to 7) of this book are based on previous articles that have been updated, interlinked, and often extended. I gratefully acknowledge the original outlets as follows:

'The Moral Economy of Austerity: Analysing UK Welfare Reform', *British Journal of Sociology*, 2016, 67(1): 97–117, copyright London School of Economics and Political Science. Updated and reused with the permission of John Wiley and Sons Ltd.

'Welfare, Migration, and Civic Stratification: Britain's Emergent Rights Regime', in *Capitalism in Transition*, edited by A. Andreotti, D. Benassi, and Y. Kasepov, 111–26 (Manchester: Manchester University Press, 2018).

'Squaring the Circle: Domestic Welfare, Migration, and Human Rights', *Citizenship Studies*, 2016, 20(6–7): 693–709. A portion of

viii   Acknowledgements

this article is reprinted with permission of the publisher (Taylor and Francis Ltd, http://www.tandfonline.com).

'Moralising Welfare and Migration: A Backdrop to Brexit', *European Societies*, 2019, 21(1): 76–100, doi.org/10.1080/1461669 6.2018.1448107.

'Reconfiguring Rights in Austerity Britain: Boundaries, Behaviours, and Contestable Margins', *Journal of Social Policy*, 2019a, 48(2): 271–91.

'Moral Economy from Above and Below: Contesting Contraction of Migrant Rights in Austerity Britain', *Journal of Ethnic and Migration Studies*, doi.org/10.1080/1369183X.2018.1538774.

'Activating the Welfare Subject: The Problem of Agency', *Sociology*, 2020, 54(2): 275–91.

'The Topology of Welfare–Migration–Asylum: Britain's Outsiders Inside', *Journal of Poverty and Social Justice*, 2020, 28(2): 245–64, republished (with additions and adjustments) with permission of Policy Press, an imprint of Bristol University Press, UK.

Abbreviations

AIP I	Article 1 Protocol 1 (of the ECHR)
AIRE	Advice on Individual Rights in Europe
APPG	All-Party Parliamentary Group
ASAP	Asylum Support Appeals Project
BAME	Black, Asian, and minority ethnic
BME	Black and minority ethnic
CAB	Citizen's Advice Bureau
CAP	Church Action on Poverty
CESCR	Committee on Economic, Social, and Cultural Rights
CPAG	Child Poverty Action Group
CTB	Council Tax Benefit
CTC	Child Tax Credit
DSS	Department for Social Security
DWP	Department for Work and Pensions
ECHR	European Convention on Human Rights
ECJ	European Court of Justice
EEA	European Economic Area
ESA	Employment and Support Allowance
EU	European Union
EWCA	England and Wales Court of Appeal
EWHC	High Court of England and Wales
FtT	First-Tier Tribunal
GDP	gross domestic product
HB	Housing Benefit
HL	House of Lords
HO	Home Office
HOC	House of Commons

Abbreviations

HRA	Human Rights Act
ICESCR	International Covenant on Economic, Social and Cultural Rights
IFS	Institute for Fiscal Studies
ILPA	Immigration Law Practitioners Association
IS	income support
JAM	Just About Managing
JCHR	Joint Committee on Human Rights
JCWI	Joint Council for the Welfare of Immigrants
JR	judicial review
JRF	Joseph Rowntree Foundation
JRS	Jesuit Refugee Service
JSA	Job Seekers Allowance
LA	local authority
LHA	Local Housing Allowance
LASPO	Legal Aid Sentencing and Punishment of Offenders Act
MAC	Migration Advisory Committee
MIR	minimum income requirement
NAO	National Audit Office
NASS	National Asylum Support System
NEET	not in education, employment, or training
NHS	National Health Service
NIESR	National Institute of Economic and Social Research
NPI	New Policy Institute
NRPF	no recourse to public funds
OBR	Office for Budget Responsibility
ONS	Office for National Statistics
PAC	Public Accounts Committee
PESA	Public Expenditure Statistical Analysis
PSED	Public Sector Equality Duty
RC	Refugee Council
S17	Section 17
SJPG	Social Justice Policy Group
SMCPC	Social Mobility and Child Poverty Commission
SSAC	Social Security Advisory Committee
SSWP	Secretary of State for Work and Pensions
TC	tax credit
TCN	third country nationals
TUC	Trades Union Congress
UC	Universal Credit

Abbreviations

UKSC	United Kingdom Supreme Court
UNCRC	United Nations Convention on the Rights of the Child
UT	Upper Tribunal
WCA	Work Capability Assessment
WPC	Work and Pensions Committee
WRAG	Work Related Activity Group
WTC	Working Tax Credit

THE MORAL ECONOMY OF WELFARE
AND MIGRATION

Introduction

This book was being finalized as Britain entered a new decade, and 2020 opened with a Conservative government returned to power by a strong majority, heralding a new era that promised to unite the country. The incoming regime was able to boast a record 32.8 million people in work and unemployment at only 3.8 per cent (Partington 2019), a level not seen since the 1970s, alongside a restructured welfare system dedicated to 'making work pay'. The then chancellor of the exchequer, Sajid Javid, declared a readiness to 'turn the page on austerity' (Inman 2019b) – the deficit reduction policy that had dominated the previous decade – while a further feature of the new dawn was a commitment to make withdrawal from the European Union (Brexit) a reality. With Brexit came the claim that Britain would be able to 'take back control' of immigration, ending free movement for workers from countries of the European Economic Area (EEA) and with it their associated social rights.

Behind this narrative lie record rates of homelessness and an unravelling of the welfare safety net under a punitive system of welfare conditions and sanctions,[1] with no indication that cuts and erosions would be restored by a 'turning of the page' (*Observer* 2019; Partington and Inman 2020), despite some modification in response to COVID-19. Meanwhile, child poverty has risen to the unprecedented level of over 4 million; and in-work poverty, underemployment, and economic inactivity have all been growing (Barr, Magrini, and Meghnagi 2019). Migration from EEA countries fell in the wake of a referendum result that favoured leaving the European Union (EU), but migration from outside Europe continued to rise (Grierson 2019) despite stringent controls and was even argued by some to have saved the country from recession (Inman 2019a). Nevertheless, employers have raised concerns about a recruitment and skills gap, while the creation of a hostile environment for undocumented migrants led to a scandal in which long-established migrants with a right of abode were wrongfully denied employment, health care, and welfare benefits, and some even suffered deportation. Meanwhile, unaccompanied child refugees with relatives in Britain have been stranded in Europe, and asylum-seekers survive on £5.40 per day.

It has often been argued (e.g., Hutton 2020) that the deficit reduction driving the austerity decade was far from being an economic necessity, given that borrowing costs were low and that the national debt had represented a much higher share of UK output for most of the preceding three hundred years. In fact, the first budget following the 2019 general election saw the biggest fiscal boost to the British economy in almost thirty years, combined with an interest rate reduction, and including an additional £12bn package to alleviate the impact of COVID-19. Ironically, the latter sum mirrors the £12bn George Osborne sought from the second round of welfare cuts in his own 2015 budget (bringing the total to just under £40bn), but it was dwarfed six days later by a sum almost thirty times as large (Rawnsley 2020). By the beginning of April 2020, a Universal Credit system that was already struggling faced nearly 1 million new claims over a two-week period – claims that could not plausibly be written off as the product of a 'dependency culture'. Although the circumstances are unprecedented, the scale of state intervention to manage the crisis serves to demonstrate that what appears as economic necessity at any given moment is subject to political will and that a level of spending viewed as impossibly high in one context can seem catastrophically low in another. At the very least, we are confronted with the question of 'which economic constraints are real and which imagined?' (Tooze 2020), and a key theme of the present study is the power and the contestability of political discourse in shaping a perceived 'reality'.

AN EMERGENT MORAL ECONOMY?

A complex tangle of claims and counterclaims has been one consequence of the decade of austerity. The policy was first announced by David Cameron in 2009 (Cameron 2009) in the run-up to his premiership in the 2010 Coalition government. 'Austerity' was to become pivotal to a political discourse that advanced a distinctive conception

Introduction

of 'fairness' and 'responsibility', linked to protection of the 'hardworking taxpayer' and having a particular focus on welfare expenditure. Day-to-day spending by government departments fell 10 per cent between 2010 and 2018; but meanwhile, the welfare budget was on track for a 25 per cent reduction in real terms by 2021 (Inman 2019b), and a freeze on working-age benefit rates from 2016 to 2020 reduced the value of payments by 6 per cent (Partington 2019a). These developments were accompanied by an attack on migration as a welfare drain and a cause of domestic unemployment (Cameron 2011a; 2013).

This book focuses on the moral economy of welfare and migration that characterized the austerity decade. It analyses not just *what* happened but *how*. The notion of 'moral economy' was advanced by Edward Thompson (1971) to analyse a moral consensus that legitimized protest against rising food prices in eighteenth-century England. The idea refers to a communal assertion of rights and customs that sought to constrain the rigours of an emergent market economy, and it found some support in the paternalist traditions of authority. However, the concept has aroused renewed interest in contemporary analysis (e.g., Sayer 2007, 2000; Fassin 2005, 2009; Clarke and Newman 2012; Booth 1993, 1994) through the recognition that all socio-economic systems rely on a supporting 'moral' framework of some kind. In this reconfigured usage, the term refers not simply to resistance from 'below', but to a discourse that may be imposed from 'above' and thus deployed in a strategic reshaping of key features of socio-economic life.

A focus on the decade of austerity opens a window onto the dynamic unfolding of a period of concentrated change that dramatically intensified tendencies long apparent in the welfare–migration–asylum complex. It allows us to trace political discourse through to policy formulation and implementation and to examine concrete effects that at every stage have been challenged and contested. The decade from 2010 to 2019 saw an ambitious programme of welfare reform driven by claims to fairness and responsibility but based on more stringent conditions for benefit receipt, increased financial sanctions for failure to comply, benefit caps and frozen rates, and destitution by design in the flagship Universal Credit (uc) system, which imposes a five-week wait before receipt of a first payment. At the same time, David Cameron's campaign to remain in the eu was couched in terms of a need for reform, particularly in relation to free movement and its welfare guarantees (Cameron 2013), and it conceivably contributed to the success of the Leave campaign. In addition to a referendum result that favoured withdrawal, and the subsequent drive to 'get Brexit done', there have been increasingly stringent controls on non-EU migration, often designed to forestall, remove, or reduce access to welfare rights.

Before outlining the framework of this book, and the purpose of the analysis to follow, I should concede that a case might be made that the measures just detailed did in fact succeed. However, some major reservations should also be noted. Though the official unemployment rate had fallen to its lowest level in more than forty years, regional disparities remained,[2] and there was evidence of considerable 'hidden' unemployment. An OECD report (Barr, Magrini, and Meghnagi 2019) found high levels of involuntary economic inactivity that increased the 'real' rate of unemployment from 4.6 to 13.2 per cent of the UK working-age population. This involuntary inactivity was reportedly three times higher among the young than the middle-aged. It was especially high for marginalized youth not in employment, education, or training (NEETs) (ONS 2020) and showed wide variation between cities and regions (e.g., 31 per cent in Blackburn, but 11 per cent in Crawley), with a clear North/South divide. In fact, half of all new jobs in England since 2010 have been in the South East (Walker 2020).

Furthermore, there are official expressions of concern that people have been driven away from claiming benefits. Indeed, the Department of Work and Pensions (DWP) fears that potential claimants were being deterred by 'scaremongering' (WPC 2019c) led to advertised claims for the UC system that were ruled misleading and unlawful (Advertising Standards Authority 2019). The UN Special Rapporteur on Extreme Poverty has condemned the administration of UC as a digital-by-default system in which one third of all claims did not progress to final payment; meanwhile, the WPC (2015, 2019c) has criticized a failure to monitor outcomes for claimants. Changes to welfare policy have resulted in less support for those in low-paid work, and the much-lauded high employment rate is being buoyed up by a precariat (Standing 2011) formed of the 'reluctant' or 'false' self-employed,[3] zero-hours contractees, and part-time workers who would like more hours (Inman 2019). Indeed, the UC system has been designed to facilitate 'flexible' employment, and households with someone in work now make up well over half of those in both relative and absolute poverty (Full Fact 2019).

Introduction

According to Taylor-Gooby (2016), such changes are a feature of the strategic development of a 'divisive welfare state', one that is geared not to the achievement of social cohesion but rather to social division, with the government directing its highly visible cuts to non-supporters at no electoral cost. A picture emerges of a marginal fringe driven out of the benefits system, sanctioned, or subject to the five-week wait rule. Many claimants are making repayments against advances from or debts to official bodies (Webster 2019), while non-standard working has worsened poverty rates. The conditions imposed on UC claimants permit sanctions for refusal of zero-hours work, and job search or work preparation requirements have been extended to ever more groups. There is a growing consensus that the welfare safety net has all but disappeared (e.g., WPC 2019, 2019C; NAO 2018).

All of this has been thrown into stark relief by the official response to COVID-19. With the prospect of sudden job losses among previously secure workers, and with unemployment predicted to reach 4 million, it has now been formally acknowledged that working-age benefits are inadequate. There has been an increase (for one year)[4] of £1,000 per year for the personal allowance under UC (a near 25 per cent rise), and comparable increases to the Working Tax Credit (WTC), as well as a rise in Housing Benefit (HB) for private renters. But familiar dividing lines remain: the cap on the total amount of benefits a household can receive is unchanged, and claimants who have not made the move to UC but receive the older (legacy) benefits are not covered by the increase. In fact, the rise favours those only recently unemployed, who have a nine-month grace period before the cap on household benefits applies, provided they had previously earned £570 or more per month (Simpson 2020). The rise is anyway dwarfed by a state subsidy of up to £2,500 per worker per month to shore up the incomes (by 80 per cent) of hitherto secure employees (*Guardian* 2020). Protections for self-employed workers were initially lacking beyond a newly granted entitlement to £94.25 per week in sick pay (Inman 2020), and their plight was only addressed after widespread criticism and a threat of legal action on the grounds of discrimination (Booth 2020). They nevertheless face a three-month wait before relief that for many will be 80 per cent of what was already a poverty wage.

The welfare reforms that characterized the austerity decade also unfolded alongside a drive to reduce net migration that has relied on a similar array of disciplinary conditions and requirements, and a related discourse of fairness and responsibility. The run-up to the referendum on EU membership featured an attack on the free movement of workers and their associated welfare rights, as well as a statutory time limit placed on benefit entitlements. This was despite official sources showing that EEA migrants were not claiming in disproportionate numbers (Keen and Turner 2016), paid in more to the exchequer than they took out (Oxford Economics 2018), and had a negligible impact on jobs and pay for the domestic population (MAC 2014; Metcalf 2016). Migration policy and Brexit have now come under question in the context of the coronavirus pandemic, given that 13 per cent of all NHS staff were born overseas: in 2015–16, EU nationals accounted for 19 per cent of nurses joining the NHS, but only 7 per cent in 2018–19, while in 2017–18 a record number left (totalling 12.8 per cent of all leavers) (Baker 2019, 6). The first eleven doctors to die in the pandemic were from BME backgrounds, as are 44 per cent of NHS medical staff (Siddique 2020).

Calculations of the overall fiscal impact of migration reveal only very narrow margins of difference (+/–1 per cent of Gross Domestic Product [GDP]), though non-EEA migration has historically yielded a more negative balance than EEA migration (Vargas-Silva and Sumption 2019). This is largely because of the costs attributed to educating the children of migrants, many of whom are British citizens[5] – and note that when the government is running a deficit the fiscal impact of the average UK resident will also present as a cost. Yet over the austerity decade, skill and income requirements for both the entry and settlement of non-EEA migrants have been tightened in order to forestall future resource demands. However, concerns have been expressed about the gap between perception and reality in relation to both the scale and the effects of migration (e.g. MAC 2014; European Commission in the UK 2013; Wadsworth 2015). Furthermore, many migrants are present on the basis of human rights claims, and there is scope for a rights-based approach to augment more narrowly framed fiscal calculations. Yet the past decade has also seen a notable tightening of requirements for family unification, as well as an erosion of support for asylum-seekers and failed asylum-seekers unable to leave. These changes have been put in place in the context of a 'hostile environment' for undocumented migrants that has been shown to rebound on *all* migrants and on some British citizens.

The overall effect has been a regime dedicated to deterrence and control, and a message for public consumption that sets domestic welfare claimants (that is, citizens and established residents) in opposition to migrants, and in which immigration and welfare dependency are portrayed as competing drains on welfare spending (Cameron 2013), with tailored strategies of constraint deployed in both policy areas. So the starting point for the present study was the idea that there is something to be learned from viewing domestic welfare and migration/asylum through the same analytical lens – that of an emergent moral economy of welfare and migration. Not least, we find that the interface of these different policy areas reveals concentrations of minority disadvantage in the experience of the domestic welfare regime, aspects of racialization in patterns of differentiated entitlement by immigration status (Yuval-Davis, Wemyss, and Cassidy 2017), and what Anderson (2019) terms a 'migrantization' of the experience of citizen welfare claimants.

MIGRATION AND SOCIAL RIGHTS

There is of course a rich and extensive literature on the social rights of migrants, but taken together it points to the advantages of a unified approach that also includes the position of domestic claimants. So, for example, in examining what progress has been made toward sanctionable global norms that establish social rights beyond national state borders, Faist (2009) shows how such rights are institutionalized within national states and are not secured as distinct objective rights. He therefore argues (2009, 16) that full membership of a political system is the key determinant of social inequality, upholding social exclusivity to create and consolidate unequal life chances. Elsewhere, Faist (2013) outlines the need for an approach to social protection that goes beyond national regimes, and his work has elaborated what such a system might entail. He notes, however (Faist 2009), that for the past thirty (now forty) years welfare states have stagnated, and while he argues that they have *not yet* been subject to fundamental deconstruction the point does invite a further consideration of this side of the picture.

Other work, including my own (Morris 1997, 2002), has addressed the management of migration through the construction of an elaborate hierarchy of legal statuses with differential rights attached. This approach has been taken up by Kofman (2002), who emphasizes the increasing complexity of such projects of status differentiation. The result is argued to pose a challenge to construals of a post-national expansion of rights, but such work implicitly takes national citizenship as the marker of full membership in society. Morrisens and Sainsbury (2005) make the comparison explicit in showing disparities between migrant and citizen households in terms of how they fare within national welfare systems, noting that these disparities widen for migrants of colour. They emphasize the stratifying effects of conditions of eligibility that govern access to benefits, as well as the resultant inequalities suffered by migrants with respect to adequate living standards. They therefore highlight the need to consider the dynamics at play between welfare and immigration regimes, but they do not take the next step of interrogating the impact of conditionality and control on the differential treatment and experience within the category of citizenship.

In pointing to the system of 'nested citizenship' that emerged from EU law on free movement for citizens of EEA countries, Faist (2009) notes that this has been established without seriously endangering the status of national social citizenship, though in Britain at least this has started to change. There is a wealth of work that looks at welfare inequalities that have developed *within* the operation of equal treatment guarantees for the free movement of workers, and Amelina (2020) has documented the hierarchical boundaries of partial inclusion experienced by different categories of 'movers'. In a similar vein, Bruzelius (2019) has shown how access to welfare can depend on various national construals of habitual residence, and she notes that the European Court of Justice has found these construals to be acceptable even when they have discriminatory effects. The court has also shown some readiness to uphold time limits placed on (non-contributory) social assistance claims by unemployed EU citizens who had exercised free movement as workers, as in the Alimanovic case in Germany (*Jobcenter Berlin Neukölln v Nazifa Alimanovic et al.* (C-67/14)).

However, of particular interest for the present study is the contraction of EU migrants' social rights in Britain (see O'Brien 2015; Shutes 2016), which reduced entitlement and access even prior to the decision to withdraw from EU membership and also accelerated moves toward an individualized rather than collectivized approach to social entitlements. Notably, Shutes (2016) recognizes that the latter development has also had implications for British citizens, apparent in the intensification of work-related conditionality that has constructed and extended exclusions both from within and from without, and thus

Introduction

moves beyond the citizen/non-citizen binary. Analysing conditionality in both areas in terms of category, circumstance, and conduct (Clasen and Clegg 2007), she argues that the effect is to establish a continuum in relation to social security that operates across the designations of migrant and citizen.

Soysal (2012) suggests that European welfare regimes more generally have been reconfiguring notions of 'good citizenship' in a manner that moves away from collectivized solidarity toward individualized responsibility. This, she says, has had negative effects for both non-EU migrants and 'lesser Europeans', including national citizens, while Düvell and Jordan (2002) earlier highlighted the mesh between controls on migration and attempts to 'activate' claimants within the national welfare regime. Anderson (2013) makes an interesting contribution in considering citizen claimants and migrants side by side in her analysis of exclusionary devices that turn on distinctions between 'us and them'. One striking insight of her book is that the non-citizen and the 'failed citizen' are both constructed as categories of the undeserving poor, and although she stops short of a more fully integrated frame of analysis, like Shutes (2016) she opens up a space for its development.

A distinctive contribution from Guentner and colleagues (2016) sets out the possible contours of such a framework with respect to social rights. They outline two forms of 'welfare chauvinism' – 'ethnic or national welfare chauvinism' based on the view that migrant access to state welfare should be either wholly or partially limited, and 'class-based welfare chauvinism' based on the view that recipients of welfare, whatever their national status, are of lower value than non-recipients. Carmel and Sojka (2020) caution that notions of ethnic or national chauvinism can simplify a complex picture of differentiation, which operates according to varied 'rationales of belonging', and Guentner and colleagues point to the multiple means by which formal and informal exclusions occur. However, of particular interest is the parallel they draw between chauvinism based on ethnicity/nationality and that based on class, and hence between the treatment of migrants and that of domestic welfare claimants. Central to their argument is that such treatment is not simply the expression of a public mood; it also functions as a mode of governance, and the authors note a circular process whereby policies simultaneously respond to and encourage negative public perceptions of both migrants and domestic welfare claimants. They also suggest that 'measures imposed on migrants

The Moral Economy of Welfare and Migration

frequently serve as a de facto 'pilot' for sanctions that may in due course be deployed against the least influential British nationals' through a form of 'social bordering' – a view also advanced by O'Brien (2015) – and the mutual influence can presumably run both ways.

CONTINUITY OR CHANGE?

This argument provides an entry point for my own study, though there are inevitable questions about periodization. The contraction of welfare rights for domestic claimants and attempts to control inward migration each have a long history, and it could be argued that the 'austerity decade' is simply a continuation of practices that have long been in play. Indeed, Neville Harris's (2008) review of continuity and change in British social security law opens by stating that 'the notion that worklessness is immoral was inherent in the English Poor Law's tradition of setting the poor to work' (49).

Provision for the poor has always been bedevilled by a concern to maintain the incentive to work. This is apparent in the concept of 'less eligibility' in the 1834 Poor Law and is reflected in the setting of the benefit rates under the National Assistance Act of 1948 (Morris and Llewellyn 1991). Financial penalties for non-compliance with requirements (sanctions) have also been a recurrent feature of provision; these were set at six weeks' disqualification under the 1911 Act, with the maximum penalty rising to twelve weeks in 1986 and twenty-six weeks in 1988. Conditions continued to tighten under various Conservative governments: the requirement to be actively seeking work was established in 1989, and this was followed by a stricter approach to allowable limitations on availability under the Job Seekers Act of 1995 (Harris 2008). That act represented a shift in the balance between state and individual responsibility; it took a strong contractarian approach and promised a better deal for taxpayers, though note that the obligation to take up employment required a job offer of at least forty hours per week. The use of sanctions intensified under the Job Seekers Allowance (JSA), and attention began to shift to the activation of those with a 'looser attachment' to the labour market (notably the disabled and lone parents).

New Labour launched its own responsibilities agenda with its New Ambitions for Our Country (Department of Social Security, 1998), which promised an expansion of opportunity that would 'alter the contract' between the state and those capable of work (Morris 2007).

A range of New Deal training programmes were established, the age of the youngest child as related to job-search requirements was lowered from sixteen to ten in 2009 (Millar 2018), and a new two-tier benefit, the Employment and Support Allowance (ESA), replaced the Invalidity Benefit, requiring 'work related activity' from those with limited capacity for work (the Work Related Activity Group – WRAG). The number of sanctions started to climb around 2007 (Adler 2015), and so it might seem that the welfare reforms introduced by the Alliance government of 2010, and further advanced by its Conservative successors, therefore reflected a trend of intensified conditionality that was already well established.

The argument that the Alliance government and its Conservative successors represent a new order of control and constraint rests in part on the intensity of the change they have overseen, which is more fully documented in the chapters to follow. Among those changes has been a 'striking increase in the scope and severity [of sanctions], and in their incidence' (Adler 2015, 1), with increases for most categories and a maximum three-year sanction at the highest level of conditionality. The total number of sanctions jumped from 471,476 in 2009 to more than 1 million in 2013; moreover, the UC system as it is now unfolding requires thirty-five hours active job-search per week, and claimants can be required to accept zero hours' employment. An extension of conditionality to in-work benefits is being piloted, the age of youngest child for lone-parent job search was lowered in stages to age three by 2017 (Millar 2018), and an income supplement was removed from the WRAG. In addition, we have seen a four-year freeze on benefit rates, a five-week waiting period for UC payments, the introduction and further lowering of a benefit cap on the total benefit a household can receive (regardless of size), and a two-child limit on the Child Tax Credit (CTC).

All of these measures have been part of a declared 'moral mission' to reform the welfare system, a mission that marks a clear departure from the principle of a guaranteed minimum of support and has gone some way beyond previous interventions. The JSA's introduction is correctly viewed as a turning point, and one that New Labour would also embrace. Fletcher and Wright (2018) nevertheless identify a 'punitive turn' after 2012, pointing to a 'wholesale roll-out of conditionality, never seen before in the British system' (329). The same authors (Wright, Fletcher, and Stewart 2019) depict a 'new' form of symbolic violence, inseparable from material domination and featuring what Adler terms a 'secret penal system' (Adler 2016). Within this system, they argue, the Job Centre has emerged as a site of symbolic and material suffering on a self-administered 'jobsearch treadwheel' under threat of destitution, in a return to the failed forms of punishment of the eighteenth and nineteenth centuries.

Further distinctiveness is apparent in the explicit linkage of welfare dependency and migration as 'two sides of the same coin' (Cameron 2011a), which brought with it a related package of changes to migrant rights. Elements of continuity are apparent in the details of immigration regulation, in that Britain has gradually extended its traditional reliance on control at the borders to an increasing elaboration of internal controls (Morris 1998). After the introduction of 'employment vouchers' for Commonwealth Immigrants in 1962, a patriality requirement[6] in the 1971 Immigration Act placed restrictions on their right of abode, notoriously discriminating against black Commonwealth citizens. The 1971 act also introduced a 'no recourse to public funds' (NRPF) condition for arrivals lacking this right, thus illustrating an argument made by Bhambra and Holmwood (2018) that racialized hierarchies have been integral to the development of Britain's welfare state. After further changes in the routes of access to citizenship (the British Nationality Act of 1981), policy attention shifted toward internal controls and entailed a closer alignment between benefits regulations and the immigration rules.

There had been no statutory immigration constraint on access to Supplementary Benefit under the 1966 Social Security Act (Shutes 2016), though there was a discretionary element, but as of 1980 those defined as 'persons from abroad' were deemed ineligible. In 1985, public funds were formally defined for the first time in the Immigration Rules, and this was followed by a drive to write the 'no recourse to public funds' (NRPF) condition for entry to Britain into the administration of benefits and services (Morris 1998). In October 1993 the Home Secretary set up a study on interagency cooperation for the enforcement of immigration laws (HC Hansard, 18 July 1995, col. 1027), thus setting in train a process now apparent in the huge expansion of internal controls in the 2014 and 2016 Immigration Acts. This was also the period in which the notion of 'benefit tourism' first appeared, principally in relation to EU jobseekers (Allbeson 1996,4), along with a growing assumption that asylum requests were fuelled by economic motivation (see debate, HC Hansard, 11 December, 1995, col. 268). There were long-running efforts to end supports for those who applied for asylum after entry into the country, which were

Introduction

eventually defeated when the House of Lords ruled against the Home Office under New Labour (*Adam, Tesema and Limbuela v SSHD* [2005] UKHL 66).

Clearly, then, these concerns were not confined to the Conservative government; under New Labour, asylum-seekers were seen as a threat to the aim of a managed migration system. They were removed from the mainstream benefits system through a newly created National Asylum Support System (NASS), which would provide support at 70 per cent of standard benefit rates. But at the same time, efforts were made to harness the economic benefits of migration through a tiered system of immigration controls that established preferential treatment for highly skilled workers along with tighter controls and more limited rights for other categories (Flynn 2005). And it was a Labour government that allowed unfettered labour market access to East European migrants following the expansion of EU membership in 2004 (Favell 2014), though these migrants were denied access to welfare rights for the first twelve months of their stay. The British response to the accession of Romania and Bulgaria to the EU in 2007 was more constrained: for a transition period of seven years, prospective employers would be required to secure permits, and again, a twelve-month wait was imposed for full welfare entitlements.

So despite occasional sharp contrasts, key features of the measures adopted during the 'austerity decade' had clear precursors, notably the expansion of internal controls, concerns about benefit tourism, and attempts to drive down asylum applications. Most of these measures carried an implicit moral message linked to conceptions of desert and assumptions of abuse, but as the chapters to follow will show, subsequent developments can justifiably be viewed as a very significant intensification of these trends. They have included the first specified target to reduce net migration (by more than 50 per cent), significantly increased income thresholds for entry and settlement, dramatic reductions in maintenance for asylum-seekers, an extension of the NRPF condition to new groups, a vast expansion of internal controls, the decision (albeit unplanned) to withdraw from membership of the EU, and a distancing strategy in relation to the Syrian refugee crisis.

PURPOSE AND AIMS OF THIS STUDY

I have therefore suggested that the decade of austerity represents a qualitative leap in the nature of the measures imposed and a quantitative leap in their extent. Some of these measures were unprecedented

– most notably, the abolition of a guaranteed minimum within the welfare system, an aggressive target for reducing net migration, and the explicit creation of a 'hostile environment' for undocumented migrants. In sum, Britain's incoming Coalition government of 2010 ushered in an 'age of austerity' and a 'moral mission' of welfare reform as part of a drive for deficit reduction that rested on greatly expanded welfare conditionality. This policy focus was then extended to the management of migration and asylum in such a way that domestic welfare and international migration were presented as inextricably linked (Cameron 2011), and policy in the two areas unfolded more or less in tandem. A stepping back from any engagement with or endorsement of a post-national orientation thus accompanied the fuller elaboration of a conditional, contractarian model of social rights for the domestic population. As a result, citizenship can no longer stand as the notional yardstick of guaranteed social inclusion, and rather, developments in both areas have engaged a moral message of earned entitlement. This invites a sociological approach that examines such policies in combination, alongside their associated value frame or underpinning 'moral economy'. While this moral economy did not spring newly fashioned 'from nowhere', its explicit elaboration in political discourse, and the intensified nature of the measures that followed, with all of their far-reaching ramifications for both migrants and welfare claimants, amount to distinctive features of the decade of austerity.

Claims and counterclaims about the fiscal impact of migration are only part of the picture. There is scope for a broader approach that addresses the discursive presentation of welfare and migration, and its related policy initiatives, within a unified frame of analysis. We can also look to how developments in each area have been contested and how civil society and other actors have adopted various means of challenging the rationale, legal basis, and moral messages of the policy developments noted above. Hence, the reform of domestic welfare, viewed alongside the management of trans-national migration, and taken together with civil society advocacy and institutional critique, opens up the need and the scope for research into the reconfiguration of rights both inside and outside of citizenship, and their inter-relations. Taking the UK as a case study of this reconfiguration, the aims of the present study were:

(a) to build a conceptual framework for analysing the policy developments shaping both domestic welfare and transnational migration in the austerity decade;

Introduction

(b) to map the dominant political discourse and emergent pattern of rights and controls in both fields, and explore their inter-relations;

(c) to document critical commentary and contestation, as promoted by civil society and institutional actors; *and*

(d) on this basis, to assess how far the reconfiguration of domestic welfare and migrant rights may be understood as the expression of a refashioned moral economy for legitimizing the governance of these fields, and how far its ethical underpinnings have been challenged or reshaped by civil society and other actors in their policy critiques, legal action, and public campaigning.

THE POLICY FRAME

Domestic welfare systems and patterns of migrant entitlement have traditionally occupied separate fields in both policy making and academic research, the former being the terrain of social policy analysis, and the latter more commonly viewed through the lens of mobility or ethnicity. As we have seen, this is beginning to change (Guenter et al. 2016; Anderson 2019; Shutes 2016), and some reflection on what is to be gained by viewing developments in these areas through the same analytical frame is therefore warranted. This question will be addressed at a number of levels in the chapters to follow, but one starting point is the fact that there have been parallel legislative interventions in both areas. The restructuring and contraction of welfare rights in the 'age of austerity' began with the 2012 Welfare Reform Act, which passed into law under a coalition government (2010–15); this was followed by stronger measures in the 2016 Welfare and Work Act under the subsequent Conservative government (2015–16). Similarly, some of the control measures of the 2014 Immigration Act introduced by the Coalition were strengthened by the Conservatives' 2016 Immigration Act.

These acts, all of which were passed into law under David Cameron's premiership, led to the policy measures that are the central focus of this study. For this reason, the political discourse analysis that follows concentrates on speeches from Cameron and his team that announced and justified the measures, with additional attention to speeches in the run-up to the referendum on EU membership, which focused on migrant benefits. In the aftermath of the vote, Theresa May seemed to signal a change in relation to those 'just about managing', but this had little real impact, and her position on this promise is considered in relation to Brexit. The most significant welfare developments under Boris Johnson have been in relation to the coronavirus, discussed above and in the conclusion.

However, changes introduced between 2010 and 2016 have continued to unfold beyond this period – the lower benefit cap came into force in November 2016, the two-child limit on the Child Tax Credit (CTC) was implemented in 2017, the UC system is still unfolding, conditionality for in-work benefits is still being piloted, and the freeze on working-age benefits lasted into 2020. In relation to immigration, a challenge to the family reunification regulations was not resolved until 2017, the end of free movement for EEA citizens was enacted in June 2018 with the withdrawal from the EU, the implications of the hostile environment were only fully revealed in 2018, and elements of the limitations on support for failed asylum-seekers are not yet in place. Third-sector campaigning, parliamentary scrutiny, and legal challenges to many of the measures continue to unfold into the present, so we find ongoing critical interventions from NGOs, statutory bodies, and judicial decisions, which have informed the present study's analyses of contestation.

The discursive presentation of policy in the fields of welfare and immigration has set them in opposition through the argument that migrants are both a drain on welfare resources and a cause of domestic welfare dependency, though official sources show reasons to doubt this claim. It is also interesting that policy in both areas has engaged a similar discourse of fairness, responsibility, and protection of the hard-working taxpayer while also deploying similar devices of conditionality and control. The contraction and enhanced policing of welfare resources has been a central feature of welfare reforms and is also reflected in the purpose and design of immigration legislation, and meanwhile, both areas have seen the administration of benefits being harnessed as a mode of control. This brings the experience of citizens and migrants closer together, and though the two groups are often counterposed in political discourse, the treatment of each has increasingly prompted court action through recourse to domestic, universal, and/or EU guarantees, all themselves under challenge. The result has been a system of stratified entitlements, analysed in the following chapters as a form of 'civic stratification' (Lockwood 1996) that not only operates through the elaboration of different immigration statuses but also extends into the structuring of citizens' social rights.

Introduction

THE ANALYTICAL FRAME

The intellectual challenge in analysing this complex is inevitably multilayered and requires both the development of a unified conceptual framework and its empirical application. The concept of 'moral economy' has been a central reference point for this study, prompted in part by the injection of moral parlance into political discourse – as with Cameron's 'moral mission' of welfare reform, and present less directly in references to 'benefit tourism', 'non-genuine' asylum claims, and 'abuse' of the immigration/asylum system. All are linked in different ways to conceptions of 'fairness' and 'responsibility', and analysis must therefore look to the discursive construction and deployment of such terms. The related process of embedding a supporting ethical framework can be informed by Freeden's (1996) approach to political ideology, which he views as an attempt to decontest the meaning and substance of key principles, thereby shaping and legitimating a particular form of social structure. A distinct but complementary argument may be found in Laclau's (2014) explication of the rhetorical foundations of society; he sees political discourse as an attempt to close off meaning, constructing chains of equivalence and difference through discursive links between some categories and behaviours, which are then set in opposition to others.

In more concrete terms, connections can be drawn between fairness, rights, and responsibilities as they have featured in Conservative discourse, and the way a particular understanding of these notions has been embedded in policy design. Here we can look to the role rights play in shaping the contours of society, an approach that has its source in T.H. Marshall's (1992[1950]) classic essay *Citizenship and Social Class*. That essay famously outlines the development of British citizenship through the chronological unfolding of civil, political, and social rights, which are expected to secure equal social standing and to guarantee 'the life of a civilised being' (8). The model has been found wanting for its uncritical acceptance of the national framing of rights and was seemingly undermined by the argument that (in Europe at least) we were witnessing the development of a post-national society in which citizenship would be superseded by rights of universal personhood (Soysal 1994, 1), or by an emergent cosmopolitanism (Beck 2006). Beck argues for a decentring of the state as the taken-for-granted 'container' of society and envisages a universalist challenge to state sovereignty (Beck and Sznaider 2006). This has informed a call for 'methodological de-nationalism' (Anderson 2019), which goes even further in deproblematizing migration and making a case for 'no borders' (see also Anderson, Sharma, and Wright 2009). However, neither the Marshallian nor the cosmopolitan ideal has ever been fully realized, and both are now under challenge, while the normative guarantees of citizenship are further undermined when devices of management and control in the granting and delivery of rights are increasingly applied to both migrants and citizens.

The empirical expression of these arguments can be traced from the boundary drawing implicit in political discourse through to policy design and implementation, informed by Douglas's (1986) argument on 'how institutions think'. Its outcome can then be captured through a mapping of the formal entitlements granted to different categories within and outside of citizenship in an instance of what Lockwood (1996) terms civic stratification. This concept refers to a system of inequality by virtue of the rights that are granted or denied by the state. Lockwood's analysis turns on two axes: the presence or absence of rights, and the possession of moral or material resources. The former denotes the granting or denial of formal entitlement while the latter refers to informal advantage or discrimination in the delivery of a right.

This idea was first developed in relation to the inequalities generated within citizenship and is thus an advance on Marshall, but the model admirably lends itself to analyses of transnational migrant rights, and the elaboration of formal legal statuses that this entails. The informal dimension of civic stratification is of particular interest and has been captured in work that traces 'bordering' practices (Guenter et al. 2016; Yuval-Davis, Wemyss, and Cassidy 2019) through to micro-level decisions that extend the reach of internal controls. However, this informal dimension also has a dynamic influence: just as the accrual of moral resources can enhance a claim to rights, their absence or erosion can undermine such a claim, filtering through to an individual's experience at the hands of authority. We can readily see how this same influence may be built into the dynamic of political discourse and feeds into an associated perspective emerging from work on the notion of moral economy. This perspective examines the construction and promotion of the legitimizing principles that underpin the functioning of a socio-economic system, thus offering an approach increasingly applied to analyses of contemporary society (Sayer 2000, 2007; Fassin 2005, 2009; Clarke and Newman 2012).

Introduction

CONTESTATION

The policy developments under austerity and the analytical argument set out above inevitably suggest the possibility of challenge or contestation. If political discourse is so significant in the construction of social categories and their subsequent treatment in policy, then surely this discourse invites deconstruction by bodies seeking to advance an alternative 'moral economy' – or in Fassin's (2009, 18) terms, seeking to replace a moral *economy* with a *moral* economy. Much of the challenge to welfare and immigration policy has been driven by civil society organizations active in specific areas (e.g., the Child Poverty Action Group [CPAG], the Joint Council for the Welfare of Immigrants [JCWI], the Refugee Council [RC]), and this is reflected in the analysis to follow. However, it should also be noted that institutional bodies exist whose the explicit purpose is to scrutinize policy formulation and implementation (e.g., Parliament's Joint Committee on Human Rights, the Work and Pensions Select Committee, the National Audit Office, and the Social Security Advisory Committee), often informed by the work of third-sector organizations.

All such entities engage in what Munch (2012) terms 'battlefields of change' in relation to the formulation, design, and implementation of policy. Close study of the output of these sources reveals that contestation does not necessarily amount to a fully formed counterdiscourse, and the chapters that follow identify three different types of contestation with reference to their modes of argumentation, or forms of reason. These are termed rationality, legality, and morality, and viewed as forms of reasoning, they can sometimes be supplemented by academic commentary, especially when this enters the terrain of public debate. However, of the three modes of argument identified, it is only 'morality' that amounts to an overtly normative riposte, though moral argument is often implicit in critiques based on rationality and legality. Hence:

- A *rationality* critique considers the degree to which policy is coherent and effective in its own terms, and therefore identifies inconsistencies or contradictions within a specific policy, or between different areas of policy. It also considers how far the underlying assumptions of policy are convincing and whether its implementation or practical outcomes undermine its key objectives.

- A *legality* critique looks at the degree to which policy is consistent with established legal commitments – whether through existing legislation governing domestic policy (e.g., the Public Sector Equality Duty), human rights commitments enshrined in domestic law (e.g., the Human Rights Act), or obligations incurred by signatories to international treaties (e.g., the Convention on the Rights of the Child), all of which feature in litigation and public campaigns.
- A *morality* critique takes a normative position, usually expressed in opposition to the dominant political discourse. While there is often a moral dimension to rationality and legality critiques, it is much more explicit in this category and more commonly designed to engage public interest or sympathy. This is most immediately apparent in relation to poverty and welfare, but there is also moral content to arguments about the contributions migrants make to the national economy and public services, to accounts of injustice through administrative error (e.g. the Windrush scandal), and to the nature and extent of obligations to asylum-seekers and refugees.

As the chapters to follow will show, each of these forms of contestation has had some purchase, but it also becomes apparent that the most crucial struggle is often over the hold that conceptions of a policy 'problem' have on public understanding. Munch (2012) terms this the symbolic (or rhetorical) battlefield, and as we will see, the dominant discourse is only partly dislodged by rationality and legality critiques. In fact, in driving policy design such discourse may succeed in establishing what Munch describes as a paradigm shift – and one indication of an emergent policy paradigm comes when devices and techniques of governance spill over from one area to another. A final dimension of the present study has therefore been the endeavour to identify these 'crossover' aspects of the entire welfare–migration–asylum complex, as apparent in policy design, implementation, and effects, but also therefore in the ways that policy has been challenged. The various analytical layers set out above are combined in different ways in the chapters to follow, to paint a cumulative picture of the moral economy of welfare and migration, the way that its underlying assumptions have been scrutinzed and contested, and its concrete effects on the experience of target groups.

Introduction

CHAPTER OUTLINE

Chapter 1, 'The Moral Economy of Austerity: Analysing UK Welfare Reform', introduces the concept of moral economy with reference to Thompson's (1971) analysis of the popular protest that erupted in eighteenth-century England in response to rising prices. Contemporary applications of the term (e.g., Booth 1994) have broadened its scope to argue that all economies are moral economies in that all rely on an underpinning value frame. The moral mission of welfare reform is thus described here as an attempt to embed the wider economy within a particular conception of 'morality' that seeks to replace a culture of dependency with a culture of responsibility and that deploys 'fairness' as a pivotal justificatory device. These developments are outlined with reference to Freeden's (1996) account of ideology as the attempt to impose substantive meaning on abstract concepts and Laclau's (2014) conception of equivalential chains. The chapter then moves on to consider how the ideological message underpinning a contraction of social rights for the working-age domestic population has been challenged, not necessarily in ideological form, but with reference to the three-pronged critique of rationality, legality, and morality.

Chapter 2, 'Welfare, Migration, and Civic Stratification: The Shifting Terrain of Rights', considers shifting conceptualizations of the relations between citizen rights, migrant rights, and human rights and their reconfiguration in light of recent policy changes. The dominant political discourse presents migration as displacing domestic labour and causing unemployment, and promotes a solution based on more forceful 'activation' of the unemployed and tighter controls on immigration. This represents a reversal of both the Marshallian model of social citizenship and the cosmopolitan ideal of expanding transnational recognition, which are now simultaneously under challenge. Cosmopolitan writers (e.g., Beck 2006) have envisaged a blurring of the boundaries between citizens and migrants, and this has indeed occurred – though not in the manner anticipated by pronouncements of an emergent post-national society. Rather, the devices of governmentality that have long operated in the administration of migrant rights are being turned increasingly on benefit-dependent citizens, and vice versa. The chapter shows how the concept of civic stratification can offer a unified frame through which to analyse these developments with respect to both the designation of formal entitlements and the associated erosion of informal 'moral standing'.

Chapter 3, 'The Moral Economy of Welfare and Migration: The Backdrop to Brexit', offers a particular instance of the dynamic noted above and looks more closely at government discourse on welfare and migration in the years preceding the referendum on membership of the EU. It outlines the discourse of morality and fairness in the speeches of David Cameron, then traces its operationalization through related policy changes, notably the aggressive curtailment of welfare rights for both domestic claimants and EU nationals. Combined with an attack on the 'abuse' of free movement, a claimed displacement of British workers, and a policy of deficit reduction, the effect was to place a denigrated and disadvantaged domestic population in a zero-sum relationship with EU migration, though the driving rationale was unsupported by available empirical evidence. Again there are grounds for critique in terms of rationality, legality, and morality, but an account of the divisive nature of political discourse in terms of the formal and informal dimensions of civic stratification reveals a perverse effect of the discursive and policy package. Though intended to shore up support for Remain, it set domestic welfare recipients and migrant groups in opposition, thus providing the context for a strong degree of Brexit support in the deprived areas most affected by welfare reform.

Chapter 4, 'Reconfiguring Rights: Boundaries, Behaviours, and Contestable Margins', addresses the entire welfare–migration–asylum complex in a mapping exercise that documents and analyses policy development in terms of a unified system. It reviews policy change in Britain since 2010 across the fields of domestic welfare, migration, and asylum and analyses the association between welfare, conditionality, and control through the lens of civic stratification. Informed by the work of Richard Munch (2012) on 'battlefields of change' and of Mary Douglas (1986) on 'how institutions think', it moves beyond existing literature in this area to show that the more complex the classifications in play, and the more severe their boundary implications, the more likely it is that contestable margins will emerge. The chapter identifies the key boundary problems that are apparent in each field, discusses the ensuing contestable margins, and outlines the nature and source of challenges that have arisen on the 'institutional battlefield' in terms of their nature and sources. The chapter then reflects on what is revealed by viewing welfare, migration, and asylum within

Introduction

the same conceptual frame, identifying an emergent welfare paradigm that displays recurrent problems across all three fields.

Chapter 5, 'Moral Economy from Above and Below: Contesting Contraction of Migrant Rights', returns to the concept of moral economy and considers its extension to the management of non-EEA migration and asylum, viewed here in the context of Fassin's (2012) conception of moral economy and related debate. The chapter argues that the ensuing policy regime can be analysed as a moral economy 'from above' in terms of its underlying objectives and rationale, which is then challenged and contested by a moral economy 'from below', as advanced by civil society actors. The chapter again engages the concept of civic stratification, but looks more closely at the arguments contesting contraction. As with the analysis of domestic welfare, it shows how contestation is framed in terms of a threefold critique based on rationality, legality, and morality, which is examined in four areas of recent policy change – migration and family life, welfare provision for asylum-seekers, support for those without status, and the creation of a 'hostile environment' for undocumented migrants. A concluding section reflects on the implications of all this for our understanding and application of the notion of moral economy and assesses the scope for and impediments to an emergent moral economy from below.

Chapter 6, 'Activating the Welfare Subject: The Problem of Agency', looks in more detail at civil society challenges to the welfare reform in its varied manifestations, given the behavioural focus of much of the policy relating to both domestic welfare and migration. Engaging conceptual argument about the nature of human agency, it looks in particular at how agency becomes apparent in unsettled times (Emirbayer and Mische 1998), when the master frames of political discourse collide with the lived experience of claimants. It then outlines the assumptions at play in a range of domestic welfare measures, alongside analysis of how they are undermined in the course of legal argument. Examining a series of legal judgements, it shows how such argument is informed by the impact of each measure as grounded in the claimants' varied life situations, and how a mismatch between such experience and the design and implementation of policy provides a basis to compel official adjustments. A later section of the chapter elaborates a possible extension of such argument to the fields of immigration and asylum, where much policy has been driven by assumed motivations of gain or abuse, but where claimant context again complicates official representations and undermines the master frames in play.

This book's final substantive chapter, Chapter 7, 'The Topology of Welfare–Migration–Asylum: Britain's Outsiders Inside',[7] looks at the common issues that emerge in relation to the treatment of domestic welfare recipients and the management of migration and asylum, to consider the 'topology' of the entire welfare–migration–asylum complex. The notion of topology refers to a process of folding and filtering that undermines rigid distinctions of inclusion and exclusion (Mezzadra and Neilson 2012) to reveal commonalities in the approach and effects of policy across distinct fields. Key 'crossover' issues include the creation of a hostile environment in both the welfare system and the immigration/asylum system, which also entails high rates of administrative error and failures of access to justice. Conditionality, deterrence, and discrimination are shown to be common to all fields, as is the prejudicial treatment of children in attempts to enforce behavioural change from their parents. Reference is made to Agamben's (1998) conception of 'bare life' in the designation of an apparently rightless zone on the outskirts of society. However, within the welfare–migration–asylum complex of austerity Britain, this zone is not a physical location but a legal and experiential space, at whose extremes we find enforced destitution and despair, and the creation for some of a life that is not worth living.

In this book's conclusion, I bring together the empirical and theoretical insights generated by the study as a whole and make some concluding comments about the nature and application of the concept of moral economy, its discursive construction, its relation to civic stratification, and the scope for an alternative stance. While registering the force of rationality and legality critiques in the piecemeal erosion of much of the policy at issue, I also note their limitations and the scope for a more fundamental shift in the underlying ideological framework. Political discourse plays a prominent role in shaping public perceptions of policy problems, as well as the moral standing of target groups, but there have been powerful public responses to some of the more extreme effects of policy design and administration. The theoretical arguments advanced in the present study, together with the various elements of critique, point to the logical possibility of a different paradigm, one that would change the way institutions think through a moral economy based on a fuller recognition of the constraints on human agency, such that humanity and compassion could take a more central role.

The need as well as the moral case for such an approach is starkly illustrated by the experience of a pandemic unleashed on a society in which a health system dependent on migrant labour has been stretched beyond its limits; in which millions of workers are in insecure work, only one pay packet away from destitution; and in which the welfare system no longer delivers a guaranteed minimum, homelessness is at unprecedented levels, and some migrant groups are debarred from accessing public funds. The collective benefits of caring for every individual have never been more apparent, but are as yet some way from being realized.

I

The Moral Economy of Austerity: Analysing UK Welfare Reform

A SOCIOLOGY OF MORALITY?

In our intellectual division of labour, treatment of the normative aspects of social life has traditionally been the terrain of moral philosophy, both in abstract determinations of right and wrong and in their potential application to concrete ethical dilemmas. However, in recent years sociologists have begun to make the case for an approach to morality that is concerned less with the generation and application of normative principles and more with the sources and consequences of varied moral frameworks present in society. Such an approach could rest on an examination of the social dynamics at play in competing conceptions of social worth (e.g., Sayer 2005; Skeggs 2014), on an interrogation of socially patterned frameworks of meaning (Hitlin and Vaisey 2013), on the role of dominant interests and moral entrepreneurs in drawing moral boundaries (Lukes 2010), or on analysis of the boundary work involved in formulations of and justifications for social policy (Atkins 2010; Steensland 2006). Given this background, Hitlin and Vaisey (2013, 53–4) argue that the sociological import of the study of morality lies in the fact that while 'morality can bind groups together ... it can also be the subject of negotiation, contestation, and exclusion'.

One aspect of the implied agenda for research must therefore be a consideration of the dominant uses of the concept of morality in public life, their implications for (re)shaping the social order, and the form and content of challenges to the meanings and judgements they entail. It is perhaps unsurprising that these reflections and developments in sociological thinking have run parallel to the emergence of an explicit rhetoric of morality in contemporary political parlance. One example can be found in the Conservative Party's *Responsibility Agenda* (2008, 12), with its assertion that 'ending Britain's welfare culture is a *moral duty* for any progressive government', reinforced by David Cameron's (2012) later statement that the ensuing welfare reforms were part of a 'moral mission' for the country. The present chapter considers the rationale underpinning this claim, the conceptual tools that can be brought to bear on its analysis, and the form and content of the challenges and critique it has provoked.

MORAL ECONOMY REVISITED

As a preliminary to this exercise, we should note that the idea of 'moral economy' was taken up by E.P. Thompson (1971) to address the ways in which behaviour in the face of hunger is modified by custom, culture, and reason. Analysing the crowd reaction to food shortages in eighteenth-century England, Thompson argued that in almost every case there was a 'legitimising notion' at work, 'informed by the belief that they were defending traditional rights or customs ... supported by the wider consensus of the community' (1971, 78). This belief was grounded in norms and obligations supported by a paternalist model of production and distribution, as well as by the common law, which in combination constituted the moral economy of the poor. Thompson's analysis was concerned with the disturbances that erupted as this paternalist model began to break down, and the same conceptual framework has been applied in James Scott's (1976) study of rebellion and subsistence in Southeast Asia.

The idea of 'moral economy' has since been subject to considerable debate. It has been taken up and applied to contemporary circumstances by a number of writers (Sayer 2007, 2000; Fassin 2005, 2009; Clarke and Newman 2012), and Booth (1993, 1994) provides a helpful discussion of what is involved in this transposition. Drawing on Polanyi (1957), he sees the core conception of a pre-industrial moral economy as resting on the notion of embeddedness, through the non-market integration of economic activity within broader social relations and their underpinning values. The model of the modern market economy then implies the reverse arrangement, whereby society itself becomes embedded in the economy and is fashioned accordingly, even to the extent of reshaping individual behaviour and motivations. Booth views these characterizations as based on a false dichotomy: he rejects any implication that there is no calculative, maximizing behaviour in pre-market societies, while also arguing that the market itself is embedded in both a normative and an institutional framework. He does, however, depict the transition to market society as entailing a normative shift in the social order, away from (pre-given) status toward (negotiated) contract, and he crucially suggests that what is involved in this move is 'a moral redrawing of the community and of the place of the economy within it ... a new form of moral embeddedness' (Booth 1994, 661).

Based on these reflections, Booth (1994, 662) offers the idea of moral economy as both a prompt and a language for thinking normatively about the economy, to argue at 'all economies ... are moral economies, embedded in the [ethical] framework of their communities', and so to focus attention on the role of the economy in the 'architecture' of community (1994, 663). This revised sense of 'moral economy' entails a holistic view of society and the moral presuppositions that underpin its inter-relations, while 'moral' in this context is not an evaluative descriptor of a given arrangement, but an element of all socio-economic systems. Explicit references to morality (as in Conservative discourse) are not, therefore, a *necessary* marker of a moral economy at work. However, the appearance of such references at a given moment is a likely indication that some significant development is afoot, to be supported by the embedding of an associated value frame. Indeed, while the term 'moral economy' was developed to address the breakdown of reciprocal arrangements in pre-industrial economies, and its possible linkage to protest and rebellion, moral economy investigation can equally turn its attention to the refashioning of public sentiment in support of a distinctive moral foundation for reconfiguring economic relations.

It is in this sense that all economies are moral economies, or more accurately that all economic systems imply and to some degree depend upon, a particular moral form. Other contemporary moral economy writers have arrived at similar conclusions, and they have in common a wish to recognize the internal moral underpinnings of any economic system, while also holding out the possibility of evaluating such systems from the outside, with reference to independent criteria of value. We need, however, to distinguish these two different strands in contemporary applications of the term moral economy. They are therefore treated separately in this chapter, taking first an illustrative example of the claim that all economies are moral economies, and coming later to the question of standards and means of contestation. The first strand examines the *process* whereby re-embedding happens, the second, the appropriate criteria for *judgement*.

RE-EMBEDDING THE ECONOMY: PROCESS

The moral economy of austerity Britain serves well as an illustrative example. The following description is derived from policy documents and speeches generated by the Conservative wing of the Coalition government in pursuit of its proclaimed 'moral duty' to end Britain's welfare culture. The resulting policy agenda took legislative form in the Welfare Reform Act of 2012 and was later advanced under an incoming Conservative government by the Welfare Reform and Work Act of 2016. The precursors to these initiatives were detailed in this book's introduction, but the more recent political argument may be seen as part of a programme to further embed (or re-embed) the British economy in a supporting morality. This was enforced by a drive for radical reform of the welfare system, given early expression in two papers from the Centre for Social Justice[1] (SJPG 2006, 2007), which have helped shape subsequent policy.

Concerns addressed in the first of these documents included growing social security costs in the face of successive failures to 'get tough on fraudulent claims' (SJPG 2006, 13); the alleged causes of dependency – family breakdown, educational failure, indebtedness, and addiction; the emergent tax credit (TC) economy, itself seen as a form of entrenched (worker) dependency; and a need for closer monitoring of the economically inactive (single mothers and the disabled). The solution to these problems centred on a drive to 'make work pay' by means of an integrated welfare system (SJPG 2007; Conservative Party 2008; DWP 2010a; Duncan Smith 2012) designed to combine benefits for the workless with the TC system, improve work incentives, and increase childcare support while enforcing tighter conditionality for all groups. This policy programme promised to replace a culture of dependency with a culture of responsibility and to construct a more efficient system of delivery and enforcement through payment by results to private providers operating an intensified and incremental system of conditions and sanctions (Conservative Party 2008; DWP 2010a; Finn 2011). The force of these proposals is captured by the statement that 'at present over 80 per cent of the system remains rights based, placing no real demand on its recipients' (SJPG 2007, 32).

The Universal Credit (UC) system as it is currently unfolding has blurred the distinction between in-work and out-of-work claimants, integrating six main means-tested benefits,[2] with other reforms to these benefits established in the meantime, almost all entailing losses for claimants. Key changes have included the following: a freeze for elements of the Working Tax Credit (WTC) since 2011; a lowering of working-age benefit upratings to 1 per cent per year as of 2013 (McInnes 2014a), with a complete freeze from 2016 to 2020 (Osborne 2015); a cap on the total amount of benefit per household, introduced in 2012 and reduced in 2016;[3] a two-child limit on Child Tax Credits (CTCs), effective from 2017; a cut in the housing benefit (HB) for those 'underoccupying' a social rented property; a cap on the Local Housing Allowance; a reduction in disability support and increased conditionality for the disabled in receipt of Employment and Support Allowance (ESA); a job-search requirement for single mothers whose youngest child is aged five or over (lowered to three or over in 2017); abolition of the discretionary social fund; and replacement of Council Tax Benefit (CTB) with locally based schemes, many requiring a minimum contribution from claimants. Taken together, we see a number of deterrents to reliance on benefits through cuts, caps, freezes, and conditionality in the name of a 'make work pay' policy that has broadened the target population for conditionality, extended the category of dependence to the working poor, and by implication eroded public conceptions of desert.

Cameron's first prime ministerial conference speech (2010) offered some clues as to the nature of the associated re-embedding process, expressed through his intention to 'change the way we think about ourselves and our role in society'. The rhetoric of his key speeches conveys the nature of that change. There are explicit references to an underpinning morality, especially concerning reform of the welfare system, as in Cameron's (2011c) response to the urban riots that were sparked by the police shooting to death of a black British man, Mark Duggan. That speech warned against a 'moral collapse' and pointed to the risks attendant on 'moral neutrality' in relation to the 'moral hazard of welfare'. His conference speech of 2012 asserted his 'moral mission' to cut dependency, citing increased conditionality as the means (Cameron 2012), while his reply to a rebuke from the Archbishop of Westminster made a 'moral case' for welfare reform along similar lines (Cameron 2014b). The content of this morality seems best translated in Conservative parlance as 'fairness', and Cameron added 'unfairness' to Beveridge's 'five great evils' (Cameron 2012).

The notion of fairness was broached repeatedly in Conservative Party speeches following the 2010 election and was often paired with 'responsibility'; it was 'not just about who gets help' but 'who gives that help through their taxes' (Cameron 2010). A variety of speeches from the then prime minister and the chancellor as well as the secretary of state for work and pensions repeated the need to ensure that the out-of-work population would never be better placed than 'hardworking families/people' and that the welfare system would be fair to 'the taxpayer' (Osborne 2012), 'the abused taxpayer' (Duncan Smith 2013), or 'the hardworking taxpayer' (Duncan Smith 2014). There were associative links to the aims of deficit and debt reduction (e.g. Cameron 2010a) as well fraud reduction (e.g. Duncan-Smith 2012, all of which carried an implied moral message.

This policy approach is largely behavioural – it assumes a culture of dependency and seeks to correct choices 'skewed' by the welfare system – yet its objectives are structural, insofar as 'Britain cannot run a modern flexible economy, if at the same time, so many of the people who service that economy are trapped in dependency on the state' (Duncan Smith 2014). This then has been the moral economy of austerity under the Coalition government and its Conservative successor, and it is noteworthy that the UC scheme permits the sanctioning of claimants for refusing a zero-hours contract.[4] The changes are not simply a retread of traditional moralizing about welfare claimants; rather, they are using welfare to refashion economic and social relations on a grander scale. Undermining support for the vulnerable is thus one means of embedding a particular kind of economy while enabling a change in the balance of power between workers and employers and a worsening of the terms and conditions of work at the lower end of the employment spectrum. Taylor-Gooby (2016, 718) argues that the overall effect has been to direct public attention downwards toward stigmatized outgroups and away from the unequal impact of policies that benefit those already advantaged. We saw this echoed in a response to the coronavirus crisis, when the prospect of welfare dependency for previously secure workers was averted for many by government provision of an 80 per cent wage subsidy.

THE RHETORICAL FOUNDATIONS OF SOCIETY?

To understand what was happening in the 're-embedding' process of austerity Britain, we can look to some key figures in political theory, especially to Michael Freeden (1996, 2003) on the study of ideology.

In his argument, diverse ideologies offer competing interpretations of facts, and each ideology imposes a pattern of meaning that is amenable to substantive analysis. Much of the political work involved is to render contestable meanings incontestable, and to give 'core' concepts substance by building a close association with 'adjacent' concepts, and a looser link with 'peripheral' concepts. So Freeden's argument contains an invitation to think in a contextual and indeed sociological way about the role of ideology and political rhetoric in shaping society, through a more embedded reading than is offered by the abstractions of political philosophy. In the sources cited above, morality is translated into fairness, which then assumes its content through reference to welfare dependency and the hard-working taxpayer, in loose association with fraud and deficit reduction. So here we have some of the tools for Cameron's (2010) quest to 'change the way we see ourselves' and to 'shape Britain' in the course of a shift from irresponsibility to austerity (Cameron 2009).

Another theoretical resource for thinking about this process comes from a different tradition, as outlined in the work of Ernesto Laclau (2014) and his exploration of *The Rhetorical Foundations of Society*. Laclau and Freeden share the view that the role of ideology in social and political life is not so much to mask reality as to shape the way we see it, and in so doing to (re)order aspects of the social world. While Freeden looks at how the contestable is decontested through core and adjacent concepts, Laclau writes of the quest to secure an absent sense of completion in the very idea of society, 'projecting into something that is essentially divided the illusion of a fullness and self-transparency' (2014, 15). In his account, this is achieved through the construction of a chain of equivalential meanings, whose purpose is to give substance to an unachievable promise – as in the moral pursuit of fairness in the name of hard-working taxpayers, set against dependency, deficit, and fraud. In Laclau's terms, such a discursive configuration should be understood as an attempt to close off meaning, in effect stabilizing an illusory sense of cohesion and incarnating the impossible 'fullness' or completion of society. In practice, however, the logic of equivalence requires constant negotiation, and for Laclau this reaches its limit in the face of a clear contradiction, or a 'resistance of meaning' (Laclau 2014, 36) – as for example through competing conceptions of 'fairness'.

These arguments may seem rather distant from the constitution and ordering of the social world, but there is one further framework that makes the process more sociologically accessible, and that is David Lockwood's (1996) concept of civic stratification. This notion is implicitly concerned with the construction of 'moral standing' in society and explores the relation between possession or absence of rights and access to 'moral and material resources'. Briefly put, the argument is that a regime of rights can both shape and be shaped by the moral standing of a given group in society such that an erosion of standing can undermine the enjoyment of, or claim to, rights (civic deficit or civic exclusion); while the denial of rights further erodes moral standing. The converse could also apply, in that the accrual of moral standing in society, perhaps through the intervention of civic activists, can lead to an expansion of rights or to enhanced enjoyment of a right (civic expansion or civic gain). In the case of welfare reform, we see an erosion of moral standing for a social category of 'dependence', its extension to include the working poor, and its use to question the validity of 'inactivity' as a basis for support, all set against the moral ascendancy of the hard-working taxpayer and harnessed in the cause of legitimizing cuts to welfare spending and entitlements.

The three figures mentioned above come from very different traditions of social and political thought; they are cited here for the way each works at a distinct level and offers different tools for understanding how ideology and rhetoric can operate as social forces. Freeden provides a key to understanding the internal mechanics of a political ideology through the claim to bring definitive, substantive meaning to abstract principles; Laclau's focus is on how political forces build their constituencies by forging patterns of equivalence and difference, and hence lines of opposition, which then shape the nature and structure of society itself; Lockwood traces the moral sentiment generated by such political manoeuvres back to the dynamic construction of moral standing. So there is a certain complementarity among the three approaches sketched out here, in that each highlights how moral and political sentiment can influence the functioning of social relations, but each also contains scope for movement in the form of challenges to the emergent moral and social order. The fallout from the coronavirus may itself prove such a challenge, as the position of previously secure strata of society suddenly begins to look more precarious.

Norval (2000) has argued that ideologies are struggles over socially legitimated meanings of political concepts and that the scholar's task is to investigate why one decontestation prevails over another at any

36   *The Moral Economy of Welfare and Migration*

given time, thus illuminating the process by which a moral economy is embedded, or undermined. With regard to the latter, Lockwood notes the role of civic activists in enhancing the moral standing of certain groups and pushing for an expansion of their rights, while Freeden recognizes that new sources of ideological creativity are likely to be found in pressure group activities. Freeden notes that such activities may be fragmented, to produce only a patchwork of alternative thinking, whereas Laclau argues that specific claims may fuel more general confrontations, especially if equivalential connections can be made between different subject groups. Of course, while demonstrating in their different ways how ideologies work, none of these approaches draws conclusions or offers guidance as to whether they are good or bad, right or wrong. So it may be instructive at this point to consider the challenges to the Conservatives' moral mission – their nature, their form and foundations, and their implications for an alternative conception of a moral economy.

CHALLENGING AUSTERITY: JUDGEMENT

If ideology, discourse, and rhetoric serve to decontest key concepts and close off meaning, how are they to be challenged, and must a challenge necessarily take the form of a counter-rhetoric? Freeden (2003) argues that ideologies are illusory wholes, composed of fragmented facts and competing values; Laclau sees ideological closure as impossible yet also necessary to politics; Lockwood envisages social struggles over the moral standing of groups that are targeted by specific policy measures. These elements together suggest spaces of (re)contestation, which need not be expressed as a fully formed counter-rhetoric. A strategy for research is then implicit in Luke's (2010) call for us to focus on both dominant elites and moral entrepreneurs and their role in shaping and sustaining moral codes. Hence his interest in the 'manifold ways in which individuals and social groups escape and resist' (Lukes 2010, 554) dominant influences.

In fact, the attempt by political ideology to control representation and interpretation does not rule out the possibility that evidence could be brought to bear in evaluating rhetorical positions – indeed, in constructing alternative orientations. Freeden, Laclau, and Lockwood all hint at how this might happen, whether through recontesting the substantive meaning of key concepts, challenging equivalential chains, or revalorizing vulnerable groups; each also gestures toward a likely

The Moral Economy of Austerity

role for third sector/civil society actors in such a process. With this in mind, we can explore the form and content of challenges to the UK austerity agenda that have emerged from these sources. A close reading of third-sector responses, supplemented by academic, press, and institutional scrutiny,[5] yields three broad categories of critique that I identified in this book's introduction. Defined by the form and content of their argument, these are based respectively on rationality, legality, and morality (my terms), which also carry echoes of the theoretical possibilities outlined above.

Rationality

Though ideology represents an attempt to control meaning, it can be judged with reference to both its internal coherence and its areas of neglect. This possibility is supported by Freeden's (2003, 95) view of ideologies as 'illusory wholes' and by Laclau's recognition that chains of equivalence will eventually encounter a 'resistance of meaning'. A rationality critique therefore challenges the rhetoric of welfare reform as fairness and morality on its own terms – with reference to its targets, objectives, outcomes, and internal logic, and this is apparent in the commentary that accompanied the reforms as they unfolded.

One critique examined the presentation of the reform agenda and its focus of emphasis. The roll-out of that agenda provoked comment on the classification and calculation of 'welfare' spending itself (Hood and Johnson 2014; Mason 2014; *Economist* 2014). Thus, the introduction of a Treasury statement of account to taxpayers (HM Treasury 2014) was criticized for folding the 14 per cent of government spending dedicated to working-age benefits (the target of reforms) into the 25 per cent designated as *total* welfare spending (including personal care services and public service pensions not normally classed as welfare, but excluding state pensions). The Child Poverty Action Group (CPAG) placed these numbers in fuller perspective by circulating figures to show that unemployment benefits accounted for only 0.7 per cent of total public expenditure on services, with HB at 3.8 per cent, TCS at 4.3 per cent, and Sickness/Disability at 6.8 per cent (see HM Treasury 2014, Table 5.2).

Others challenged as misleading any pairing of concern about welfare spending with references to fraud (as in SJPG 2006, and Duncan Smith 2012), in that the £2.4bn overpaid to benefit claimants[6] was less than one third of total unclaimed benefits (see Finn and

Goodship 2014), and paled to insignificance against the (growing) £34bn of unpaid tax (Kaleeli 2014; see also Sikka 2015). Here, then, is a rationality critique that highlights distortion in the focus of attention and effort in welfare reform, and that greatly weakens the chain of association from fairness to benefit cuts to deficit reduction. Even references to the 'hard-working taxpayer' are obfuscating, in that Taylor-Gooby (2016, 719) notes a shift from income tax to value-added tax (VAT) as a major source of revenue, which shifts the burden from the rich to the poor.

Fairness has been placed in contention by the Centre for Welfare Reform (Duffy 2014), which showed that despite a government commitment to make cuts fairly, 36 per cent fell on people in poverty, who made up 20 per cent of the population and were less able to bear them (see also De Agostini, Hills, and Sutherland 2014), with a greater skew against the disabled and social care users. Indeed, it has been argued that many cuts have been perverse in generating new social costs and that their likely outcomes are increased personal debt and family breakdown – the very 'pathways to dependency' the government was seeking to address (SJPG 2006). Other bodies – for example, the Social Security Advisory Committee (SSAC 2014a) – have noted that a significant number of claimants are affected by multiple cuts, and there have been calls for a cumulative impact assessment that would further undermine claims to 'fairness' (e.g., WPC 2019c). Thus, Oxfam (2014) has pointed out that changes to CTB and HB have meant that some families were making payments from subsistence benefits already undermined by reduced upratings, and several organizations, such as the Joseph Rowntree Foundation (JRF 2014), Church Action on Poverty (CAP/Oxfam 2013); Oxfam (2014), and the WPC (2019c), have questioned whether a guaranteed subsistence level any longer existed – again, an issue that has been thrown into relief by the urgent increase in UC allowances prompted by COVID-19.

More detailed argument (Oxfam 2014) has examined the *perverse effect* of specific measures, which may collide with other aspects of policy. For example, several bodies have shown that the first round of reform had a deleterious effect on child poverty figures (IFS 2011; SMCPC 2014). This left projections far short of statutory goals for reducing child poverty to which the government was legally committed, though this commitment was removed by the Welfare Reform and Work Act of 2016, which also brought a further deterioration. Implementation of the under-occupancy penalty (bedroom tax)

The Moral Economy of Austerity

encountered difficulties, in part because of the dearth of smaller alternative properties (JRF 2014a; Jenkins 2013); this created problems for local authorities and had a particularly severe impact on disabled tenants.[7] The cap on the overall amount of benefits a household can receive[8] is also flawed in that one rationale for this policy was to incentivize employment. Yet the WPC (2019a) reports that only 18 per cent of those affected were claiming Jobseekers Allowance (JSA), but 51 per cent were on Income Support (IS) because they were caring for young children, and 13 per cent had been assessed as having limited capability for work. Indeed, the Work Capability Assessment (WCA) has itself been discredited (Gentleman, 2012; Stone, 2016), while performance of the Work Programme has fallen far short of expectations for this group (Disability Rights UK 2019).

Work incentives have a central place on the welfare reform agenda, but even in its early stages, the SSAC (2014a) pointed to a perverse effect – such incentives were undermining the aim to 'make work pay', in that 59 per cent of reductions fell on households with someone in employment. A JRF (2014b) study reported that half of all adults in poverty were living in households where someone was working, and the situation was set to worsen with the announcement in 2015 of a two-child limit on CTC (effective from 2017) and a planned reduction of the work allowance.[9] The DWP's position was that people should therefore work more hours (Mason 2015), but in the face of widespread criticism of this seeming contradiction of the 'make work pay' policy,[10] work allowances were eventually restored for those with limited capability for work and for families with children (CPAG 2018). However, the two-child limit for CTCs remains in place, and increases in the personal tax allowance have offered little gain for the lowest-paid (Collinson 2018).

Indeed, the ambiguous promise to 'make work pay' has been promoted in the context of what the Trades Union Congress (TUC) terms the longest pay squeeze since Victorian times (Collinson 2017), and a number of organizations have questioned its credibility when viewed against deteriorating labour market conditions (e.g., Oxfam 2012). Commentators have noted the persistence of zero-hours contracts, increased temporary work, and reluctant self-employment (Clark 2014; Monaghan 2014; Inman 2019); the latter reached its then highest-ever level of 4.8 million in 2017 (Pyper 2018) and is still rising. ONS figures for September 2019 show employment rates at an all-time high of 76 per cent, yet there is a 10-percentage-point difference in regional employment rates (ONS 2019a). ONS figures also report 890,000 part-time workers who would like full-time work, as well as levels of real pay still below 2008 levels (ONS 2019), while the Resolution Foundation (Clarke and Cominetti 2019) notes a concentration of atypical employment among already disadvantaged groups. They see this as a structural shift that is unlikely to be reversed, and the UC system is designed in part to accommodate the 'flexible' labour market that has emerged (see Dean 2012). The SMCPC (2014) has expressed concern that children will simply move between low-income workless households and low-income working households, with little change in their living standards. Child poverty in working households is now a growing concern (e.g., CPAG 2019).

One feature of the 'make work pay' approach seems to rest on eroding supports for the unemployed. In that regard, much critical comment relating to rationality and perversity has focused on heightened conditionality and tougher sanctions in the delivery of benefits. Both have been increasing steadily since the 1980s (Finn 2011; Wiggan 2012; Dwyer and Wright 2014; Fletcher and Wright 2018), but such increases have been driven with particular intensity under the welfare reforms of austerity Britain (WPC 2018). In October 2012, a minimum sanction withheld benefits for four weeks, and the maximum sanction for three years (DWP 2013), while some clients ceased their claims for the relevant period. By 2018, 31 per cent of sanctions were for a period exceeding three months and one in eight was for more than six months (Alston 2018), though after repeated criticism (e.g., National Audit Office 2016; WPC 2018) the three-year sanction was abolished in October 2019 (Butler 2019). A common reservation regarding the punitive approach is that it has generated a tension between advising and coercing (Grant 2013). Payment of providers by results is also argued to have perverse effects, in creaming off the most employable and 'parking' the hard-to-help, many of whom have complex mental or social problems (Grant 2013; Finn 2011; Manchester Citizen's Advice Bureau 2013; Viney 2014). The SSAC (2006) had previously questioned how far claimants fully understand how the system functions, while a report from Manchester CAB (2013) found that one quarter of those sanctioned did not know why and that 40 per cent had not received written confirmation.

The rationale for the sanctions system was undermined by the finding (Oakley 2014) that one primary provider reported one in three clients having health issues, mental health problems, or a learning

The Moral Economy of Austerity

disability. Some claimants, especially those from more vulnerable groups, lacked a clear understanding of the requirements being placed on them, and correspondence was overly long and legalistic. Considering that the aim was to change behaviour, it is no surprise that the same report found that poor communication could render this endeavour ineffective, while some go further, and speak of knowingly tormenting the poor (Webster 2013). There has been concern that families could become cut off both from work and from state support (Oakley 2014; JRF 2014c), while the system is also thought to produce a high degree of recycling of claimants, who move on and off benefits (SMCPC 2014; New Policy Institute 2013), sometimes vanishing from the system entirely (WPC 2015). UC aims to accommodate such movements, but in so doing it is supporting insecurity and poor pay, while also planning to bring an additional group of low paid workers under the stigmatizing effects of conditionality and sanctions, thus eroding their moral standing.

In sum, the 'rationality' critique undermines government rhetoric not with an explicit counter-rhetoric but by confronting policy rationales with evidence and experience, to show that underlying assumptions may be poorly grounded and that measures may be self-defeating or in conflict with other established objectives. So while an ideological position and its supporting rhetoric are about shaping the way we see the world, their associated policies can nevertheless be assessed in terms of coherence and 'rationality'. While these arguments do not constitute a full-blown counter-rhetoric, they do point to another way of seeing, one that highlights the flaws internal to the welfare reform rhetoric and alerts us to the illusory nature of some of the claims being made, thus recalling Laclau's 'impossible fullness' and Freeden's 'illusory wholes'.

Legality

A 'legality' critique adopts a similar form of argument but goes further than the 'rationality' approach by questioning the degree to which policy is consistent with established legal obligations, which means the courts often play a determining role. This critique places government policy within a framework of institutionalized commitments that may have accumulated over time. But note that legality is itself an uncertain field, especially in unfolding areas of the law such as universal human rights, which is one of Freeden's (1996, 59) fields of contestability.

In relation to welfare reform and austerity politics, one element of contestation lies in attempts to give a stronger role to the International Covenant on Economic, Social and Cultural Rights (ICESCR) and bring concrete meaning to existing formal obligations. The UK is a signatory to this covenant but has resisted signing the optional protocol that would secure a mechanism for individual complaints. ICESCR includes the right to an adequate standard of living, as well as a range of associated rights, all of which should be exercised without discrimination (CESCR 2009, General Comment 20). In particular, Article 2 requires a signatory state to 'take steps ... to the maximum of its available resources, with a view to achieving progressively the full realization of the rights recognized'. There is a strong presumption against retrogression, which must be justified by reference to the totality of rights and full use of available resources (CESCR 1990, General Comment 3). This in itself offers a basis for challenge (see Elson 2012), but also scope for varying interpretation.

Much contestation has focused on the non-discrimination requirement under ICESCR and the European Convention on Human Rights (ECHR), as a route to challenge the fairness agenda by showing that the burden of cuts has fallen disproportionately on women (Elson 2012), black and minority ethnicity (BME) groups (Women's Budget Group 2017), and people with disabilities (Butterworth and Burton 2013). It has also been argued that reforms have been introduced 'to pursue a moral agenda of individual initiative' and that the government is in breach of obligations imposed by the international human right to food (Justfair 2014). Yet as Palmer (2010, 306) notes: 'There remains a deeply embedded conviction that matters of public finance and resource allocation ... are the preserve of the elected branches of government and not of the courts.' Despite government resistance to accepting the justiciability of social and economic rights, several cases have challenged elements of the welfare reform by recourse to domestic law and to rights protected by the ECHR (enshrined in the Human Rights Act [HRA]). Several such cases will be discussed in Chapters 4, 6, and 7; here, it is also worth noting that Scotland's new Social Security Agency explicitly recognizes social security as a human right and has modified the English system in a number of ways (Scottish Government, 2019), while in Northern Ireland there have been various attempts to mitigate the effects of the reforms (see Evason and Higgins 2019).

Legal judgements offer an underexploited source for studying contestation over the implementation of policy, as the courts provide a

The Moral Economy of Austerity

forum for contextual interpretation of the law through the lived experience of its subjects (read more about this in Chapter 6). For the purposes of the present chapter, two early cases have been selected for comment, given their engagement with core elements of the welfare reform, the 'fairness' issues thereby raised, and the significant role played by third-sector organizations. The case of *s g and Ors v s swp* [2015] uksc 16, with interventions from cpag and Shelter, challenged the benefit cap on behalf of two single parents, each of whom had a child under five and both of whom had suffered sexual abuse and domestic violence. The case rested on the discriminatory effects of the cap on single parents and victims of domestic violence, with respect to rights under the echr/hra.[11] This was the first of several challenges to the cap, which will be detailed in later chapters, but is of particular interest here in that much of the deliberation turned on a consideration of 'fairness'. The intervention by cpag (2014) offers a clear instance of Freeden's (1996) argument about contestable concepts, and deliberation over their substantive meaning.

The position set out by cpag on behalf of the appellants was that 'fairness' had been *emptied of content* (cpag 2014, para 15), given that the comparison between capped benefit income and that of an average earner disregards the benefits available to the latter. The cap applies regardless of family size and includes within its scope benefits paid on behalf of children, thus contravening the idea of a level playing field between working and workless families (cpag 2014, para. 12). Furthermore, the aim of incentivizing employment through income differentials was anyway weakened by the existence of such differentials *prior to* the imposition of a cap (cpag 2014, para. 40). The government sought to place 'fairness' beyond contention, defending the cap's legitimate objectives, which were to introduce fairness to taxpayers into the welfare system, make financial savings, tackle a culture of dependency, and incentivize employment. However, this position was advanced despite the fact that mothers of children under five were not normally expected to seek work.[12] The government argued that possible exemptions had been discussed and rejected by Parliament (*s g and Ors*, paras. 40–33) and that exclusion of child-related benefits would 'emasculate the scheme' (*s g and Ors*, para. 127). Giving considerable weight to the will of Parliament (*s g and Ors*, paras 92–6), the Supreme Court (with two judges dissenting) found the discriminatory effects of the cap to be justified. However, three of the five judges expressed concern about non-compliance with the UN Convention on the Rights of the Child (UNCRC), one observing that the cap 'breaks the link between benefit and need' (*SG and Ors*, para. 180).

A rather different case concerned the sanctions regime and eventually led to an overriding of Parliament in relation to implementation of the Coalition government's Employment Skills and Enterprise Scheme, under which claimants could be required to participate in work-related schemes, including unpaid work. The case was brought with the support of Public Interest Lawyers and succeeded in the Court of Appeal (*Reilly and Wilson v SSWP* [2013] EWCA Civ 66) on the basis that the 2011 governing regulations were *ultra vires* in that they failed to provide details of the relevant schemes or the requirement of participation. Thus, fairness was at issue, and the regulations were quashed, though the judge found against the claim of forced labour. The case was appealed to the Supreme Court by both respondents and appellants (Reilly and Wilson v SSWP [2013] UKSC 68), but Parliament meanwhile retrospectively validated the 2011 regulations, while also adding descriptions of the seven schemes in operation. The Supreme Court found that the 2011 regulations had provided insufficient information about the relevant schemes, that the first respondent had been given no written notice, and that the details given to the second respondent were inadequate, even though he had been sanctioned with loss of benefits for failure to participate.

Again the issue turned on a question of 'fairness'. This point was made repeatedly in the judgement, both in relation to the claimants and as a matter of public interest (e.g., *Reilly and Wilson*, paras. 64 and 66), though the court again found against a claim of forced labour. However, there was follow-up litigation (*Reilly and Hewstone v SSWP* [2014] EWHC 2182 (Admin)) on the fact that the 2011 regulations governing the scheme had been validated retrospectively by Parliament while the case was ongoing, pre-empting decisions on 2,512 pending appeals against unlawful sanctions,[13] in favour of the DWP (*Reilly and Hewstone*, paras. 49 and 102). The High Court found this retrospective validation to be incompatible with the right to a fair trial for the respondents (as protected by Article 6 of the HRA), with the result that any pending appeals against sanctions were likely to succeed (as illustrated by Hewstone). The judge took issue with descriptions of the claimants in background parliamentary debate, noting: 'It would be unjust to categorise the claimants in Reilly

The Moral Economy of Austerity

No.1 as claimants "who have not engaged with attempts made by the state to return them to work" and who should therefore "face the appropriate consequences rather than receiving an undeserved windfall", as Lord Freud put it' (Reilly and Hewstone, para. 126). The entire saga took as a central concern conceptions of fair treatment, and the judgement gave prominent place to what we can term the 'moral standing' of the claimants.

While these illustrative cases fell short of complete success, both are significant in that they turned to the legal process to give content to the concept of fairness, elaborating an alternative interpretation and rendering its meaning contestable. They also, in different ways, sought to establish the moral standing of the claimants involved against a discourse of dependency and dis-merit, and so to correct the negative dynamic at play in relation to civic stratification.

Morality

The rationality critique is clearly limited in that it functions within the terms of a given policy or set of policies and thus poses no challenge to the wider context in which such policy functions. Legality goes a little further: it contests key issues and principles but nevertheless operates within given social and institutional constraints. However, the rationality and legality arguments outlined above do have an implicit moral content, as becomes more apparent in third-sector documentation that takes its force from experience and that recontests morality as the prevention of human suffering. Thus, in a letter to the *Daily Mirror* (Beattie 2014), twenty-seven Anglican bishops and sixteen other faith leaders stated that the prime minister had 'an acute moral imperative to act' on growing numbers going hungry, describing the government's welfare cuts as a 'national crisis' and a 'disgrace'. The letter cited 5,500 people admitted to hospital in the UK for malnutrition, mothers skipping meals to feed their children, and many facing the choice to heat or eat. It also stated: 'Britain is the world's seventh largest economy and yet people are going hungry ... over half of the people using foodbanks have been put in that situation by cutbacks to and failures in the benefit system.' The founder of the End Hunger Fast campaign (*The Economic Voice* 2014) similarly commented that 'for David Cameron to defend what is happening in the welfare system as part of his "moral mission" when the reality is that hundreds of thousands of [Britons] have been left hungry is truly shocking.'

This sort of approach overrides arguments based on 'fairness' and comes closer to the notion of a moral absolute based on survival needs (see Shue 1996; Justfair 2014). The background to this argument is provided by a number of reports documenting poverty and suffering in the UK. The ESRC-funded Poverty and Social Exclusion Project (2013) found that even before the impact of cuts was felt, 9 per cent of households (2.3 million) could not afford to heat living areas of their home, more than half a million children (4 per cent) lived in families that could not afford to feed them properly, and more than 3.5 million adults (8 per cent) could not afford to eat properly themselves. In 2019, the IFS (Bourquin et al. 2019, Table 4.3) reported that relative poverty (at both 50 per cent and 60 per cent of median income after housing costs) had fallen from 1997, but showed a slight rise from 2013, with 15 per cent of the population in the lower band. Severe poverty (under 40 per cent of median income after housing costs) has risen more consistently, to reach 10 per cent of the population in 2017–18 – a likely underestimate, given that this group is difficult to access. The All Party Parliamentary Group (2014) has declared the state to be a generator of destitution and expressed concern about growing food poverty, while the JRF (2018) reports that 1.5 million were destitute at some point in 2017 and the WPC (2019c) has stressed the need for an official measure.

The uprating of working-age benefits was reduced for a second time in April 2014, then frozen for four years from 2016. That freeze was scheduled to end in April 2020, but no plans are in place to restore the losses entailed, and as noted earlier, cuts to HB and CTB that require payments from subsistence income have had their own impact. Meanwhile, the cost of a 'minimum basket of goods' (a standard poverty measure) was found to have risen by one third between 2008 to 2018 (Wright and Masters 2018). Commonly recognized effects of all this have been reliance on loan sharks (Local Government Association 2019), financially punitive use of bailiffs for debt collection (Credit-Connect 2019), and growing dependence on food banks, with the Trussell Trust (2019) reporting more than 823,145 three-day food parcels given out in the six months prior to September 2019 – a 23 per cent rise over the same period for 2018. The trust found the main causes of that increase to be low benefit income (36 per cent), benefit delays (18 per cent) and benefit changes (16 per cent), and it had taken to issuing kettle boxes for clients who could not afford to run their own cooker, as well as cold boxes that did not require any fuel (Butler 2014). The response to a Church of England call for renewed commitment to solidarity (Sentamu 2015) and to 'the commonality of the human journey' (29) was an emphasis on job creation and a strong economy (Domiczak 2015), but for Sentamu and others, the economy would not be enough. It took the arrival of the coronavirus to prompt a temporary rise (nearing 25 per cent) in UC and other benefits, as previously secure workers faced the sudden prospect of dependency.

The conclusion drawn by several commentaries (JRF 2014; Oxfam 2013, 2014; Bradshaw 2015; NAO 2018; WPC 2019, 2019c) has tended to support the view that 'the social safety net is failing in its basic duty to ensure that families have access to sufficient income to feed themselves adequately' (CAP/Oxfam 2013). In an echo of the moral economy of subsistence societies (Scott 1976), the implicit judgement is that the means of basic survival is an absolute right that overrides policy concerns, a view also aired in a parliamentary debate on the use of foodbanks: 'The final verdict on any government is how they treat the poorest in society during the hardest of times. The rise in need for foodbanks is a horrifying indictment' (HC Hansard, 2013, col 820). Although benefit sanctions are one factor fuelling their use, Webster (2013, 11) reports that no impact assessment had been deemed necessary for the 2012 Job Seekers Allowance Regulations that heightened sanctions, because 'they impose no cost to the private sector or civil society organisations'. There is an implicit challenge here to the divisions that underpin this kind of auditing, one that has the potential to move beyond a questioning of administrative calculation to engage in what Nussbaum (2007) terms the cultivation of compassion – which she also views as indispensable to legal rationality. Her argument is an attempt to bridge social divides through a morality of common humanity, and the civil society actors who document the suffering that flows from a punitive constriction of welfare spending are all in some way engaged in this endeavour.

Their accounts of the *experience and effects* of welfare reform feed into a debate about *purpose*. Wiggan (2012) has written of 'the subordination of social policy to the goals of economic policy', while organizations like Oxfam (2012) signal a need to 'rethink what we value as a society'. This orientation moves us away from an analysis of the 'moral economy' *internal* to the government rhetoric, toward an *external* evaluation of the morality of its aims and effects – in Booth's (1993) terms, an evaluation that restores the question of *telos* to economic thinking. Here we find an attempt to claim the language of morality for a different set of objectives, and one step in this direction involves shifting the emphasis away from the behavioural assumptions and disciplinary measures that underpin attacks on 'dependency culture'. An alternative is to look instead to securing 'fairness' through guaranteed standards in both employment and subsistence and this comes closer to a capabilities approach to rights that looks to human flourishing and dignity (Sen 2005). This might be construed as a different way of seeing and at least in part as an exercise in revalorizing the poor, thereby offsetting the negative elements of civic stratification bred by a stigmatizing conception of dependency. Such an approach would place the realization of human potential at the heart of public policy by taking fellowship as the motivational basis for social cooperation and endorsing a list of basic capabilities as the appropriate goal (see Nussbaum 2007).

Following Will Hutton (2014), such an exercise could begin with recognition that 'public services and safety nets are not inconvenient social burdens' but are a 'collectively owned means of guarding against the hazards and risks that every human might confront' – an argument since given force by the coronavirus crisis. Others have sought to challenge the 'deficit scare' as a justification for shrinking the state at the expense of the most vulnerable, and for cutting benefits while reducing taxation for the better off (Keegan 2014; De Agostini, Hills, and Sutherland 2014). There is also a reframing of dependency by looking to supports for 'too big to fail' banks (Chakrabortty 2014), to TCs that subsidize employers paying below subsistence wages, and to HBs that go to private landlords (Chu 2014), as well as by bringing corporate welfare into the picture. Farnsworth (2013) cites the Office of Fair Trading statement that available data do not 'present a clear view of the total amount of subsidy provided by the public sector to private business', which is surprising given intense concern over the measurement of 'welfare' spending of every other kind (Hood and Johnson 2014; *The Economist* 2014).

Indeed, the classification and definition of subjects and objects of policy are one means by which social relations are constituted, as reflected in both the civic stratification model and the construction of chains of equivalence. Yet the existing political rhetoric that links deficits and dependency to morality has not been extended to corporate supports. Sinfield (2013, 31) points to a presentational issue in which 'the art is being able to present yourself as a "giver to" rather than a "taker from" the state', and asks who really benefits and to what extent from state expenditures. In 2011, just before welfare reforms were launched, the outstanding cost of the bailout to banks stood at 31 per cent of GDP (*Guardian* 2011), more than four times the figure for that year's (pre-reform) spending on working-age benefits (OBR 2019, Chart 4). The moral economy question may therefore be framed as 'Whose economy?', in an attempt to reverse the arrangement described by Booth (1993) whereby the economy embeds its driving goals and values within society. In this vein, Massey and Rustin (2014, 173) argue that 'neoliberalism represents the market economy as virtually coterminous with society itself, as determining its entire system of values ... [whereas] the economy should be seen as a means to the fulfilment of broader human ends'.

The comment may be read as an implicit invitation to link the purpose of the economy to conceptions of human flourishing, and here the economy is not viewed as a technical matter beyond politics; rather, each government policy is seen as one element in a wider narrative, which is accessible to analysis in these terms. The authors argue that economic policy must therefore be understood as part of a cultural and ideological struggle whose purpose and values are actively constructed and maintained and are therefore amenable to challenge. Their position thus embraces both a political and a moral dimension in seeking to embed economic purpose within broader human purpose.

CONCLUSION

This chapter set out to explore the conceptual tools available for understanding UK welfare reforms conducted in the name of morality, and began with a review of contemporary treatments of the concept of moral economy. Two strands of argument were identified – one, that all socio-economic systems have an underpinning moral schema internal to their functioning, and the other, that some external moral evaluation of such systems should be possible. In terms of the first strand, the welfare reforms and their underpinning rationale may be seen as an attempt to embed a supporting set of moral presuppositions. For an understanding of this process I have drawn on arguments about the role of political ideology and rhetoric in decontesting key concepts (Freeden 1996) and establishing an illusion of coherence and 'fullness' (Laclau 2014); both approaches can be supplemented by Lockwood's (1996) view of the role of moral standing in civic stratification. However, such argument raises the question of how to evaluate and/or (re)contest such a system – the second strand of the moral economy approach.

We have considered the role of political rhetoric in constructing 'the way we see ourselves' but have also sought ways to approach such framing in the process of critique. In fact, the work of both Freeden and Laclau would seem to permit a multi-level approach, which need not be confined to the construction of a full-blown counter-rhetoric. Drawing on the outputs of third-sector organizations and institutional bodies, augmented by other public sources, we have seen that policy can be assessed in its own terms in the form of 'rationality', to contest claims to internal coherence; it can be assessed against an established framework of commitments, in the form of 'legality', to contest the content of core concepts; and it can be assessed against recognition of human dignity and the aim of human flourishing, in the form of 'morality'. These three approaches are of course interrelated, and though 'morality' is the closest existing argument comes to a counter-rhetoric, it may nevertheless be strongly supported by 'rationality' and 'legality', while in combination they might furnish the substance for an alternative 'moral economy' in which the realization of all human potential takes central place. This framework is further elaborated in the chapters to come, but first we extend our analysis to consider academic understandings of the relationship between social citizenship and international migration. We will see that these two areas, though often viewed in terms of opposing interests, have increasingly been brought together in both the design and the justification of policy measures.

2

Welfare, Migration, and Civic Stratification: The Shifting Terrain of Rights

DOMESTIC WELFARE AND MIGRATION

Domestic welfare and international migration are two fields that the intellectual division of labour has traditionally treated separately, insofar as each pursues a distinctive theoretical and substantive agenda. However, political and economic factors have conspired in Britain to bring their material and intellectual foci much closer together. In Cameron's (2011) conception of welfare dependency and international migration as 'two sides of the same coin', conditions and sanctions for the benefit population were linked to the aim of reducing demand for low-skilled workers – often EU citizens – whose access to benefit under free-movement guarantees had become a focus of concern. Given this linkage, policy in both areas has engaged a moral message of earned entitlement, which invites a sociological approach that examines such policies together by means of a unified frame of analysis. This chapter therefore places the moral economy of the austerity decade in the context of shifting conceptualizations of the relations between domestic welfare, migrant rights, and human rights; it then outlines the analytical potential of a civic stratification approach.

In addressing what he considered to be an overgenerous welfare system and an out-of-control immigration system, David Cameron (2011a) argued that 'migrants are filling gaps in the labour market left wide open by a welfare system that for years has paid British people not to work'. One policy response was to tighten disciplinary conditions and increase sanctions on domestic welfare claimants. Soon after, Cameron (2013) extended the charge of dependency by arguing that 'you can't control immigration if you have a welfare system that takes no account of who it's paying out to ... Ending the something for nothing culture is something that needs to apply in the immigration system as well as the welfare system.' Welfare was thus to provide the means of control for both sides of the coin.

Prior to the coronavirus crisis, welfare support for the domestic population in Britain had been subject to reductions in the value of benefit for both working and workless households;[1] this unfolded in tandem with an enhanced system of conditionality enforced by financial sanctions (JRF 2014c; Fletcher and Wright 2018). These trends have mirrored the deployment of heightened conditions, monitoring, and surveillance[2] in regulating the entry and stay of migrants. The package as a whole amounts to an erosion of social citizenship in a quest to undermine inward migration. There is evidence in Britain that migrants make only limited demands on the welfare system (Portes 2015; McInnes 2014; Kennedy 2015), that they rarely directly compete with indigenous labour (MAC 2014; Metcalf 2016), and that migration fuels rather than dampens economic growth (OBR 2015; Inman 2019a). Such evidence has not, however, dislodged a complex of policies that together requires some rethinking of how we conceptualize the relationship between migration, citizenship, and human rights.

Scholars have for some time recognized scope for a policy link between domestic welfare and migration, though much related analysis has been at the macro-level. Jessop (1999), for example, has documented the shift from a Keynesian welfare national state model toward a Schumpeterian workfare post-national regime, driven by a changing global division of labour based on innovation, flexibility, and competitiveness. In a related argument, Düvell and Jordan (2002) see the drive for a more flexible labour market, paired with increased selectivity and control over immigration, as inherently connected to the enhanced 'activation' of citizens through an increasingly disciplinary approach to welfare. A further concern with respect to welfare, as outlined by Bommes and Geddes (2000), has been a fear that the vulnerable position of some migrants within deregulated labour markets could heighten their need for welfare inclusion. To offset this possibility, Britain has erected barriers against unskilled non–European Economic Area (EEA) migrants, who are anyway denied welfare rights until permanent settlement – while entitlement to benefits for EEA migrants under the Treaty for European Union has been time limited.

The corresponding right to freedom of movement will in any case end with Brexit.

In light of all this, the present chapter examines a pattern of change that has underpinned the welfare/migration regime in austerity Britain, especially with respect to a recognition and understanding of the role of rights in shaping the contours of society. Despite a growing awareness of the link between domestic welfare and the management of migration (e.g., Bommes and Geddes 2000; Sainsbury 2012; Düvell and Jordan 2002; Shutes 2016), scholars have yet to produce a fully integrated analysis of this kind, though there is good reason to do so. In Britain, the rise of a conditional, contractarian model of social rights for the domestic population has echoed a drive for enhanced control over conditions of entry and stay for transnational migrants (in which we can include asylum-seekers). Indeed, it no longer seems adequate to assess migrant rights against a normative model of citizenship as the notional yardstick of guaranteed social inclusion without some corresponding attention to how far citizenship itself falls short of this promise. Such questions necessarily move us onto the terrain of rights, understood not simply as formal legal protections or entitlements, but as a social and political construction in a field of contestation.

THE SHIFTING TERRAIN OF RIGHTS

This approach to rights as a constructed terrain can be found in one of the earliest sociological approaches to the study of citizenship, Marshall's (1992[1950]) famous essay on citizenship and social class. Marshall's account of the sequential unfolding of three sets of rights – civil, political, and social – offers an account of the formation of British citizenship that has commonly been deemed evolutionary. However, alongside his focus on the progressive unfolding of rights we also find an account of rights as emerging from struggle, such that 'the preservation of economic inequalities has been made more difficult by the enrichment of the status of citizenship' (45). Highlighting the importance of social rights, Marshall saw this 'modern drive towards social equality' (7) as the latest phase in the evolution of citizenship, though his essay was, of course, set in the context of rights delivered by virtue of membership of a national community. The expansion of international migration and the gradual elaboration of universal human rights have led some to see his tripartite model as requiring a fourth phase of rights – the universal, or post-national (Turner 1993; Bottomore 1992).

This has pushed theorizing about rights beyond the boundaries of the nation-state, and related argument (Beck 2006) has called for a cosmopolitan outlook in both empirical and theoretical work; this in turn has launched speculation and debate about the scope and significance of an emergent cosmopolitan society supported by universalist principles. However, when Hannah Arendt (1979[1948]) adopted the now famous phrase 'the right to have rights', she was reflecting on the problematic relationship between citizenship and human rights, especially as illuminated by the position of transnational migrants and asylum-seekers. Writing around the time of the formulation of the Universal Declaration of Human Rights, but looking back to the stateless persons generated in the fallout from the First World War, she noted the following paradox: 'We became aware of the existence of a right to have rights and a right to belong to some kind of organised community only when millions of people had emerged who had lost and could not regain those rights' (Arendt 1979, 296–7). In her account, a meaningful claim to rights rested upon a recognized relationship with a body that held the duty and capacity to honour those rights, and even today rights are standardly delivered through the nation-state system.

The situation is somewhat changed since Arendt's time of writing, and there now exists a plethora of treaties and conventions that can be called into play to support the position of non-nationals. However, the question of how to understand the relationship between citizenship, migration, and rights is by no means settled (Benhabib 2004). Arendt's paradox turned on the fact that people without full membership of a national polity via citizenship had no means of claiming their 'inalienable' human rights, but subsequent writing has reversed the problematic to question how national membership can coexist with the presence of non-citizens who hold a significant array of rights. Hence the view that 'a new and more universal concept of citizenship has unfolded in the post-war era, one whose organising and legitimating principles are based on universal personhood rather than national belonging' (Soysal 1994, 1).

We thus have two distinct historical moments, both of which measure the power of universals against the guarantees of citizenship, and both of which focus on human rights as the potential driver to fill what has been termed a 'citizenship gap' (Brysk and Shafir 2004) with respect to the position of transnational migrants. This juxtaposition of citizenship and human rights can also be linked to contemporary debate on cosmopolitanism, through the argument advanced by Beck (2006) that trans-national forces are reshaping the nation-state, blurring the boundaries between migrants and citizens and shifting the locus of legitimacy from the national to the transnational level.

There is an implicit normativity both in the idea of citizenship as full inclusion and in assertions of an emergent post-nationalism, while normative argument is more explicit and overt in cosmopolitan literature. Insofar as there is a dynamic quality to associated debate, it has been expansionary. Marshall viewed the gradual unfolding of civil, political, and social rights, however imbued with struggle, as an 'urge forward towards a fuller measure of equality' (18) that becomes self-reinforcing. In post-national argument we find the claim that 'privileges once reserved for citizens of a nation are codified and expanded as personal rights', such that 'global modalities of rights reverberate through national level arrangements' (Soysal 1994, 1, 6). Similarly, Beck's treatment of cosmopolitanism, while recognizing the possibility of popular resistance, looks to a process of 'cosmopolitanisation' whereby 'trans-national identities and institutions disaggregate national bonds' as 'the nation state is broken open both from within and from without' (Beck 2006, 85).

However, neither the Marshallian model nor the cosmopolitan ideal has ever been fully realized, and we are now witnessing another reversal of the national/post-national question as attention turns to the erosion of citizenship rights, which can no longer be thought to function as a taken-for-granted source of social inclusion. While the core of Marshall's argument anticipated more recent theoretical developments that see the granting of rights as a form of recognition and reward, and even contain some potential grounds for expansion, he also observed that a 'stratified status system is creeping into citizenship' (40). Cautioning against 'any hasty attempt to reverse present and recent trends' of his time, he noted with concern that 'conflicts within our social system are becoming too sharp' (49).

His rarely mentioned apprehension foreshadowed a situation that appears as the converse of his more optimistic orientation – that is, rights function less as a guarantee of inclusion and more as a tool of governance that derives its force from an associated system of conditionality and constraint. In fact, the Marshallian conception of citizenship as full membership was approximated but never completely achieved in Britain's postwar welfare state, which has been characterized by incremental forms of conditionality (see the introduction to this book). Indeed, after the financial crisis of 2008, the Marshallian promise of guaranteed social inclusion was all but eliminated; the dominant drive of the ensuing decade of austerity was to shrink the state in the name of deficit reduction – though that shrinkage has itself been brought into question by the coronavirus crisis.

There have, then, been two challenges to Marshall's model of citizenship – one from the inside with increasing cuts, conditionality, and surveillance in domestic welfare provision, and the other from the outside, with the argument that (in Europe at least) we have witnessed the development of a post-national society (Soysal 1994, 1). In terms of actual realization, both the Marshallian model and the cosmopolitan model have fallen far short of their espoused ideals, and indeed, their future prospects are now simultaneously under threat. Citizenship rights have long since been disaggregated, with civil rights universally applied and social rights extending to long-term residents. However, the distinctive guarantees of citizenship are further undermined when the harnessing of rights as a mode of control is increasingly applied to citizens and migrants alike. The system may operate in different ways and to different effect for the two groups, which are themselves subdivided, but there are some significant overlaps, while the idea of citizenship as 'hard on the outside and soft on the inside' (Bosniak 2006, 4) has become ever more tenuous.

The reduction of welfare dependency within the domestic population, and a drive to limit transnational migration and asylum, have been at the forefront of political concerns in the UK for at least the past three decades (see Morris 1994, 2002a, 2007, 2010). Successive governments have overseen the erosion of domestic welfare in Britain, with enhanced conditionality, discipline, and control, alongside related efforts to monitor and limit the presence and rights of transnational migrants. This brings the experience of citizens and migrants closer together, though not necessarily in the manner anticipated by cosmopolitan writing (e.g., Beck 2006). Furthermore, while the two groups are often pitted against each other, the treatment of each has commonly prompted litigation, through recourse to domestic, universal, and/or EU guarantees, all now themselves under challenge. These developments have marked a significant reconfiguration of rights in Britain, and the nature of the changes entailed can best be understood in the broader context of an evolving debate about the role of rights in shaping social life.

Welfare, Migration, and Civic Stratification

This chapter argues that with the paring away of both domestic welfare and migrants' rights, the experiences of citizens and migrants have moved closer together, *via* exposure to the disciplinary dimensions of each domain and their areas of overlap. Devices of governmentality and control that operate in the administration of migrant rights through monitoring, conditionality, and surveillance have increasingly been applied to citizens. Conversely, the controls that permeate domestic welfare also extend to resident migrants and to workers from EEA countries, who (pre-Brexit) have had entitlement to social rights. This has been accompanied by tighter conditions of entry and stay for non-EEA migrants, so that the expansionary dynamic implied by the notion of an emergent post-national society is in practice now operating in reverse. As a consequence, the distinction between migrants and citizens has indeed become blurred, in that increased conditionality for working-age benefits (both for working and workless claimants) mirrors resource concerns and conditions that have been written with ever greater firmness into immigration control.

Migrant rights have commonly been measured with reference to the yardstick of full social inclusion through citizenship, with human rights called on to address the 'citizenship gap' (Brysk and Shafir 2004) entailed in the denial of a full array of rights to non-nationals. However, the partial achievement and then active erosion of citizenship guarantees has raised the possibility that universal human rights will become the normative yardstick for both groups. There could therefore be an advantage to addressing these developments within the same frame and in terms of the reconfiguration of a whole regime of rights.

CIVIC STRATIFICATION

It may be helpful at this point to look in more detail at the notion of 'civic stratification' (Lockwood 1996), a concept introduced in the previous chapter, and one that has enormous untapped potential both for addressing the emergent system of rights and for tracing the processes that are driving change. In conceptualizing the system of inequality generated by the granting or denial of rights by the state, Lockwood's model is constructed from two basic components. The presence or absence of rights refers to the structure of formal entitlement, which yields patterns of inclusion or exclusion with respect to a given set of rights. Moral or material resources refer to the informal influence of privilege or disadvantage in their delivery, yielding patterns of gain or deficit. This framework is an advance on Marshall in showing how inequality can be built into entitlement – as with the stratified conditions attached to different groups of benefit claimants – and in more fully conceptualizing how deficit can interfere with the delivery of a right. Indeed, far from guaranteeing equal standing, as Marshall hoped, rights can be implicated in its erosion, as with attacks on an alleged dependency culture and the punitive use of sanctions in relation to benefits.

Furthermore, while the principle focus of Lockwood's framework was the internal functioning of citizenship and its related rights, the model has the potential to go much further, by providing a means of analysing the management of transnational migration, as outlined in my own work (Morris 1997, 2002). The formal dimension is apparent in the varying legal statuses that a transnational migrant might occupy; this fashions a system of differential access to rights. The informal dimension again becomes apparent where a stigma attaches to claiming a right (as with allegedly 'bogus' asylum-seekers, or EU migrant workers), or where there is an informal or discriminatory impediment to access or enjoyment. Finally, Lockwood's model offers the possibility of building movement into a system of rights, most notably through his concept of civic expansion; in this argument the accrual of moral resources – perhaps with the support of civic activists – can provide the basis for a claim to improved rights. However, he neglects to consider the converse possibility of contraction, which has been apparent in austerity Britain in relation to both migrant rights and the welfare rights of citizens.

Civic Stratification and Domestic Welfare

Many of these developments take on an added significance when viewed against the dramatic scaling back of welfare for the working-age domestic population, in the name of a declared 'moral mission' to reduce welfare dependency and increase conditionality (Cameron 2012). As we have seen, this mission has been underpinned by expressions of concern for the position of 'hard-working families', 'the hard-working taxpayer' or the 'abused taxpayer', and political speeches have been peppered with references of this kind. The related policy programme promised to replace a 'culture of dependency' with a 'culture of responsibility' (DWP 2010a) and rests on a heightened, incremental system of conditionality and sanctions, which has seen a rise in the numbers of people in Britain dependent on food banks.

More than 1.6 million packages were handed out for 2018–19, an increase of 19 per cent over the previous year (Coughlan 2019).

Lockwood's (1996) original article addressed the issue of civic integration as a mediating factor in class formation – the latter a reference to the emergence of class groupings as collective agents of social change. His analysis focused in particular on welfare because, as he put it, 'the endemic contradiction between citizenship and capital had so far been managed by the fine-tuning of social rights' (535). This configuration then links to his central question – under what circumstances are conditions of inequality tolerated or rejected – thus according welfare provision its classic role of ameliorating class difference. However, he goes some way beyond this formulation to explore the ways in which the institutionalization of citizenship is both embedded in and contributes toward the structure of social inequality, and in so doing he recognizes the role played by judgements of merit and desert in establishing the legitimacy or otherwise of economic and social relations in capitalist democracy.

His analysis of civic stratification in relation to welfare thus places great weight on the deficit experienced by its recipients, by virtue of the way the system is administered, the reconstitution of recipients as second-class citizens, the demeaning requirements often attached to receipt, and being 'publicly singled out as lacking in civic virtue' (539). The capacity of welfare dependents to form a collective consciousness and pursue concerted action is in turn undermined by the particularization of their treatment within the system as failing individuals and by the 'vertical divisions' among them. This yields a fragmentation and variety that the notion of an 'underclass' of welfare dependents, or a rhetoric of 'shirkers' versus 'strivers' (Jowit 2013), is inadequate to address.

All elements of this analysis are apparent and have been exacerbated in recent welfare reforms. The deservingness or otherwise of state dependents has been a prime site of rhetorical intervention by Conservative Party politicians in the context of the austerity regime that was set in train as of 2010. In this rhetoric, calls for social justice are made not on behalf of the disadvantaged but in the name of the hard-working taxpayer, and the ensuing welfare policy has been designed to correct behavioural choices that have supposedly been 'skewed' by the welfare system. The underlying intent, however, has been to meet the needs of a 'modern flexible economy' that must be unimpeded by the functioning of the welfare system (Duncan Smith 2014).

Welfare thus becomes a tool for refashioning economic and social relations, and its stratifying features take a number of forms. We saw in the previous chapter that these have included an across-the-board freeze on levels of working-age benefits for a four-year period, as well as a cap on the weekly amount of benefit an individual household can receive, a two-child limit on receipt of child tax credits, and enhanced job search or work preparation requirements for all relevant groups. These reach beyond the traditional claimants of Job Seekers Allowance to the chronically sick or disabled deemed 'fit for work' and to lone parents whose youngest child is aged three or over. The sanctions (temporary loss of benefit) that are imposed for a failure to meet requirements have been heightened, and have been ratcheted up according to the severity or frequency of such failure (see WPC 2018). Their extension to those in receipt of in-work benefit in the form of tax credits is also under consideration.

One stratifying effect of the changes has been what amounts to heightened condemnation of the entire benefit-dependent population (with the exception of pensioners), along with an extension of this category to include the working poor. In addition, the working-age dependent population has suffered collectively from the freeze in uprating benefit levels and from the targeting of those most precariously placed in the labour market, developments that each act as multipliers of class disadvantage. However, the welfare system is itself internally stratified – not simply in terms of protecting state pensions from the impact of 'reforms', but in the subdivisions that classify groups according to both the nature of their need and the intensity of intervention deemed to be warranted. These interventions have included voluntary or compulsory participation in the various 'Work Programmes' in operation, repeated assessments of the sick and disabled to judge their capacity for work, the requirement on lone mothers to demonstrate work-readiness at an ever earlier stage in the life of their youngest child (see WPC 2018), and a cap on the total amount of benefit income a household can receive. Civic stratification is also at work in the contrasting levels of support offered in response to the coronavirus. At the time of writing, £2,500 per worker per month is on offer to businesses to shore up the positions of previously secure employees; compare this to an increase in the UC personal allowance or Working Tax Credits amounting to £1,000 per claimant per year.

A further stratifying element is apparent in the often gendered nature of the welfare reforms, which have been crafted in ways that affect women more than men, as with the heightened job search requirements for lone parents, the vast majority of whom are women. It may also occur indirectly, through the way in which benefit cuts fall, thus constituting a deficit – hence the household benefit cap has had a disproportionate effect on lone parents, who currently make up 85 per cent of those affected, the majority of whom are women (Syal 2019). Uneven impact also flows from the effect of the cuts on children – cuts that have made it more difficult for the caring parent to meet their children's needs, particularly in relation to the benefit cap, the two-child CTC limit, and the across-the-board freeze in benefit rates. Women are also disproportionate users of public services (Elson 2012), whose whittling away in the name of deficit reduction amounts to a further gendered aspect of civic stratification. Similar arguments have been made in relation to people with disabilities, who make up 8 per cent of the population but bore 29 per cent of the first round of cuts (Butterworth and Burton 2013, 33), and on black and minority ethnic (BME) groups, who are concentrated among low-income households (Women's Budget Group 2017).

Stratified Rights and Migration

Lockwood's model was based on the inequalities that emerge in the operation of citizenship, and he made only passing reference to 'guest-workers'. However, the elaboration of a system of stratified rights is further illustrated by the position of transnational migrants. It has long been recognized that there are different legal statuses that govern the terms of presence and stay on a national territory, as set out in Hammar's (1990) tripartite distinction between citizens, denizens, and aliens, to which EU citizenship has added a further dimension. In fact, the reality is much more complex than Hammar's model suggests, and increasingly so, for in the field of immigration we have seen an ever-expanding hierarchy of legal statuses, each with a different set of rights attached. Much of this differentiation in relation to rights turns on rights to work, welfare, and residence.

Welfare rights are commonly denied in the early stages of residence, and immigration checks may be built into the delivery of welfare (see Morris 1998; Sainsbury 2012). These devices are discussed in more detail in the chapters to follow, but briefly put, self-sufficiency is a key issue in applications for permanent residence. There may be preferential access to the labour market and to residence for certain categories of worker; restrictions on access to rights may be harnessed as a means of deterrence – as with asylum-seekers denied the right to work yet held to subsistence-level support; qualifying conditions may be in place for family (re)unification, such as the Minimum Income Requirement for an incoming spouse; family (re)unification rights may be withheld from certain categories of migrant; and failed asylum-seekers may face a readiness-to-leave requirement as a condition of support. Indeed, the structures of civil society are permeated with forms of regulatory oversight extending from the macro- to the micro-level, harnessing techniques and procedures of control in what Foucault (1991) has termed a process of governmentality.

Of course, within the EU the rights of EU citizenship have to date overridden some of the constraints built into the immigration system, by virtue of the terms of free movement between the member-states, but even here there has been scope for differentiation, as with phased access to labour market and welfare rights for newer member-states, and with Romanian and Bulgarian migrants viewed as posing a particular threat. There has also been a contraction of rights, and prior to the referendum on EU membership we saw various measures introduced to scale back the welfare rights of workers from other EU member-states, with statutory time limits placed on the duration of benefits for the unemployed (JSA), tighter conditions of access, and more restrictive guidance as to what constitutes worker status.

Many other aspects of migration management in Britain's decade of austerity have rested on contractions, with the terms governing non-EEA entry for employment narrowed – as with the removal of a Tier 1 visa to search for work and the capping of numbers entering under various categories of worker (Gower 2015). New thresholds have also been imposed, as with the minimum income required for permanent settlement and for family unification, the latter being set at an amount considerably above earnings from full-time employment at the minimum wage. There has been an erosion of the level of maintenance provided to asylum-seekers, and a radical restriction of support is planned for failed asylum-seekers or others trapped without a legal status. Another dimension of control has been the explicit intent to create a 'hostile environment' for undocumented migrants, with the denial of a right to rent property and the criminalization of various other activities. The latter include renting to someone without legal residence, employing someone who does not have the right to work, working without permission, driving without legal residence

– all accompanied by a huge expansion of the powers of immigration officers to search and seize property.

While civic stratification is not explicitly designed along racial or ethnic lines, it serves to problematize particular forms of migration such that race becomes salient to the way differential formal statuses operate. Stuart Hall's (1996[1978], 55) observation that 'class is the modality in which race is lived' is to this extent borne out. The distinction between desirable (highly skilled) and undesirable (low-skilled) migrants, for example, is a product of the 'dynamic, shifting and contested' processes (Yuval-Davis, Wemyss, and Cassidy 2017, 1049) that are captured by the notion of bordering and lived out in its quotidian practices. Race and ethnicity then become concretized in migrants' differential positions within the system, through their encounters with officialdom (Guenter et al. 2016) and in the 'racialization' expressed through patterns of hostility, stigmatization, and discrimination. The process is defined by Yuval-Davis, Wemyss, and Cassidy (2017, 1048) as 'discourse and practice which constructs immutable boundaries between collectivities', boundaries that then serve to naturalize hierarchical power relations. We see examples played out in the Windrush scandal and 'right to rent' discriminations (discussed in Chapter 5) and in the 'no recourse to public funds condition' that rebounds disproportionately on black and minority ethnic children and their mothers (Woolley 2019). These lived experiences of racialized bordering are what Guenter and colleagues (2016, 393) have in mind when pointing to the 'multitude of sites' where rights are granted (or denied) on bases that go beyond formal indicators of legal residence or nationality.

Position and treatment within the overall system is again compounded by gender, and here we must look at the distinctive ways in which women migrate and how this shapes their experience, and especially their access to rights. Disproportionate numbers of women migrants are domestic workers, care workers, sex workers, and incoming spouses (Kofman et al. 2000), all of which reflect women's particular association with the private sphere. Domestic workers and care workers employed in private homes may experience difficulty establishing their rights as employees; indeed, their very presence in a country can depend on their maintaining good relations with their employer. Protections for these workers have been significantly reduced in Britain, duration of stay is strictly limited, and they are debarred from progressing to permanent settlement (Gower 2016). Similarly, incoming spouses (who are disproportionately women) are in a position of dependency in the early years of their stay, as their lawful presence rests on maintenance of the marital relationship. The probationary period for this group was extended in 2012 from two years to five, a period during which they are denied access to public funds and have no right to be in the country independently of their marriage. It is also significant that those granted leave to remain on human rights grounds as parents of dependent children are disproportionately women and often lone parents (Woolley 2019). Since 2012 they have been subject to 'no recourse to public funds' unless they can meet the prohibitively demanding requirements for a lifting of this condition, guidance for which has recently been ruled unlawful (*W (by litigation friend J) v ssHD* [2020] EWHC 1299 (Admin)).

THE MORAL DIMENSION OF RIGHTS

In fact, for both domestic welfare and immigration policy we find a distinctive moral economy in operation, not in Thompson's (1971) sense of expectations driven from below, but rather as a discourse from above, one that increasingly shapes access and entitlement to rights by shrinking repertoires of desert. We have seen a set of parallel manoeuvres that harness access to rights as a means of governance and that operate by building constraints and controls into the administrative and operational regimes. Following Lockwood's model, we see that civic stratification generates differential formal entitlements, which are closely linked to differing conditions of access, as with the system of welfare requirements, and sanctions and the terms of entry and stay on national territory. It is in this sense that citizens and migrants are increasingly exposed to similar techniques of discipline and surveillance. However, both are also subject to informal impediments or discriminations that prevent the full enjoyment of rights by a particular group, and this informal dimension repays closer consideration. Its functioning is captured by the notions of gain and deficit and driven by what we might loosely term moral standing in society, as shaped by elements of wealth, influence, and prestige, and defined by Lockwood (1996, 536) as 'advantages conferred by social standing and social networks, command of information, and general knowhow, including the ability to attain one's ends through the activation of shared moral sentiment'.

Thus, while the formal dimension of civic stratification is apparent in the varying statuses of migrants, or categories of benefit claimant, as delineated earlier in this chapter, the informal dimension pertains wherever there is a prestige gain leading to preferential treatment, or conversely an indirect impediment to claiming a right that is formally held. This may take the form of a discrimination built into the practical operation of a right, or a stigma that prevents the full enjoyment of such a right. Examples of the first would be the minimum income requirement (MIR) for family reunification, which may be difficult to meet for those disadvantaged in the labour market; the disproportionate impact of the household benefit cap on single parents; and the suspicion and mistrust surrounding migrant workers, which may be reinforced by sanctions on employers of undocumented labour. An example of stigma that affects the enjoyment of a right is the use of 'asylum-seeker', or even 'illegal asylum-seeker' as a negative term, alongside a growing assumption that the majority of claims to asylum are not genuine (May 2015). A similar example in relation to domestic welfare is found where political discourse builds a close connection between benefit dependency and fraud.

Of particular interest, however, is the way in which the informal aspect of civic stratification introduces a dynamic element to the model, and in Lockwood's account particular significance attaches to the possession or accrual of moral resources in supporting expansionary claims to rights. His discussion of this possibility focuses on the 'inner logic' of citizenship, which he argues will always reach beyond its limits, engendering expectations in excess of current achievements, and the same may be argued of rights more generally. In examining this expansionary potential Lockwood looks to the role of what he terms 'civic activists' in mobilizing demand for a fuller array of rights, not least through their growing recourse to legal challenge. Indeed, we can link this possibility to Alexander's (2006) observation that the law not only has the capacity to divide and exclude, but also offers the possibility of 'civil repair'. The consolidation of universal human rights and their incorporation into domestic regimes has been one focus for such activity, especially in relation to legal recourse where human rights law is enshrined in domestic legislation, as in Britain's Human Rights Act. Furthermore, the idea of expansion is applicable not only to a whole regime of rights but also to the experience of particular groups within that regime, who may accrue improved standing or 'moral resources' – sometimes with the support of civic activists (e.g., Morris 2010) – and hence improve their formal position. One interesting effect of the COVID-19 crisis has been to make the key services supplied by 'low-skilled' migrants more visible, which may possibly enhance public perceptions of their 'moral standing'.

Much contestation has focused on the non-discrimination requirement under the ECHR and ICESCR (see Elson 2012 on gender and Butterworth and Burton 2013 on disability). However, this issue also furnishes examples of deficit, which in Lockwood's schema operates as the converse of gain. Though in his account the term applies to the experience of particular groups or individuals in accessing a right, we can further elaborate its dynamic function within a whole regime of rights. In the earlier discussion of gender, we saw that women's association with the domestic sphere can translate into a deficit with respect to their access to rights in the public sphere, and we have noted other examples in relation to the indirect effect of some control practices. The significance of moral resources, however, merits particular attention. One instance of deficit occurs when the receipt of a right itself creates what Lockwood (1996, 538) terms 'an incipient status group of a negatively privileged kind'. This he sees as likely to occur in relation to dependent statuses – as in receipt of state benefits – and here the unemployed, the disabled, and asylum-seekers furnish examples. Panic in Britain with respect to EU migrants from Romania and Bulgaria, supposedly attracted by the benefits system (Travis and Malik 2013), provides another instance – a forerunner of the concerns that contributed to the Brexit vote. Public perceptions of this group meant that they lacked 'moral leverage' in Lockwood's terms because of their assumed motivation for migration. An associated lack of esteem is also likely to be bound up with cultural or racial prejudice.

While Lockwood's schema sees a potential for civic gain to fuel expansions in a whole regime of rights, there is no corresponding discussion of deficits, arguably because his framework is set up in terms of two oppositions in neglect of a third. In combining his two axes of inequality, Lockwood develops a fourfold typology, comprising civic exclusion and civic expansion, civic gain and civic deficit, which are in fact two paired oppositions. However, the opposite of civic exclusion is civic *inclusion* (not expansion), which then leaves scope for considering a third opposition – civic expansion and civic contraction – and could refer to the shifting character of a whole regime of rights, or of a particular area within its ambit. In other words, not only do rights expand, but they can also contract. We are now drawn to consider the relationship between the formal and informal elements of civic stratification with reference to both public policy and public opinion. In particular, we must look more closely at the dynamic whereby a group may accrue moral standing in society or may suffer its erosion, and at the relationship between this process and the political climate under austerity.

THE SOCIAL AND POLITICAL DYNAMIC OF MORAL STANDING

A number of interesting insights emerge when we combine the formal and informal aspects of civic stratification and apply the resultant dynamic to an understanding of welfare provision and immigration law. Questions of desert and the elaboration of conditionality and surveillance have for some time been expanding in relation to domestic welfare, as we saw in previous chapters. Viewed alongside the elaboration of different migrant statuses, and the related alliance between rights and controls, this suggests that the entire complex of civic stratification is amenable to manipulation by the state in relation to its own policy goals. Though such manipulation may be constrained to a degree by EU law (pre-Brexit) and human rights obligations, social rights are the least justiciable of recognized universal rights, while control over access to national territory remains a fiercely protected privilege. Contractions of the kind documented earlier have the potential to rebound on the informal dimension of rights and in so doing to shape the public understanding of given categories, such that the granting of rights may confer or acknowledge public standing, while their denial may undermine it.

This then is the basis of the untapped potential in Lockwood's framework for understanding the significance and functioning of rights in society, not least the scope to combine migrants and citizens within a single frame of analysis. However, some elements require much fuller elaboration and are of particular significance for this study as a whole. I am referring here to the contraction of rights and the erosion of moral resources. Just as the accrual of moral resources can enhance a claim to rights, their absence or erosion can undermine such a claim, or confirm a group in its negative status, and this possibility has been apparent in the thrust of political discourse. Recurrent and interconnected themes are identifiable in political speeches on the welfare reforms, which can be summed up as a move from irresponsibility to austerity (Cameron 2009) as part of a moral mission to break the culture of dependency (Osborne 2012; Cameron 2012) and render fairness to the 'hardworking tax payer'. Immigration appears as a subtheme, with claims of 'millions coming here from overseas while millions of British people were left on welfare' (Cameron 2013), and hence the view that welfare and immigration are intimately related. This amounts in Lockwood's terms to an erosion of the moral standing of both migrants and of domestic welfare claimants.

Much of the dependency discourse has been empirically challenged, by arguments that unemployment accounts for a very small portion of the welfare budget (e.g., Milligan 2014; Pettinger 2016); that benefit claimants do not have higher incomes than the working population;[3] that claims of 'benefit tourism' are not supported by the data (Portes 2015; McInnes 2014); that corporate benefits exceed the annual welfare bill (Chakrabortty 2014); and so on. However, more significant than such arguments has been the drawing of moral boundaries for public consumption to offer a set of legitimizing principles for a particular vision of the socio-economic order. This phenomenon has increasingly been discussed in terms outlined in Chapter 1, which point to the primacy of the economy in shaping the 'value based architecture of the community' (Booth 1994, 663) and the related construction of a 'moral economy'. Hence the associated argument that all economies are moral economies, in that they all rest upon some underpinning claim to morality, which then shapes the public standing of particular social groups.

It is therefore of interest that overlapping political discourses have been applied to domestic welfare and to migration at a time when there have also been overlaps of experience – both groups have been affected by the erosion of welfare rights, and both are subject to an increasingly 'flexible' labour market. The political rhetoric that shapes moral standing has thus been harnessed in a drive to refashion the UK economy through a radical reduction of public spending, while eroding the public supplement to low pay, stringently disciplining the unemployed, and fomenting public concern about alleged abuses of welfare by both the domestic *and* migrant populations. In this regard, it is significant that the shrinking of the state has been dramatically curtailed by the arrival of the coronavirus, which has made the vital contribution of often 'low-skilled' migrants more visible, while also exposing both the inadequacies of the welfare safety net and flaws in the argument of 'dependency culture as previously secure workers have found themselves reliant on state support.

UNIVERSAL RIGHTS?

Lockwood views universal human rights as one possible driver behind an expansion of rights. So the question now arises of whether such rights can be called into play to arrest contraction? In the past, citizenship rights have served as the yardstick for migrant rights. So do universal human rights now become the yardstick for both? And what has been the scope for a successful challenge to contraction in these terms? The chapters that follow detail a number of legal challenges both to aspects of the welfare reforms and to contractions of migrant and asylum-seeker rights that are rooted in human rights guarantees, and as we will see these challenges have had some (albeit limited) effect. For the present chapter, we can simply note their further significance as an illustration of the changing nature of the relationship between the rights of citizens and those of non-citizens, as both groups have increasingly looked to authorities grounded beyond the nation-state for a defence of their rights.

The previous chapter noted the fragility of universalist guarantees of socio-economic rights, which only rarely function as absolutes, exceptions arising where treatment is demonstrably inhuman and degrading, thus engaging Article 3 of the ECHR.[4] There have been some moves toward making this argument in relation to the effects of financial sanctions on benefits claimants (Public Law Project 2019), especially in relation to those with limited capability for work and given the absence of any guaranteed minimum for the claimants affected. The argument has yet to be tested in the courts, though a possible action related to the death by starvation suffered when a vulnerable person's benefits were stopped may also make this case (Butler 2020). More commonly we find a complex interplay of political judgement, judicial caution, and legal disagreement in the balancing of national interests against international (universal) obligations, with decisions turning on resource constraints and 'fairness' to the taxpayer.

Legal challenges to welfare contraction have therefore required a degree of creativity in making a case, and challenges are commonly pursued as test cases brought by interested civil society organizations that actively seek out claimants whose circumstances can test a particular point of law. Legal purchase in relation to welfare austerity has often been rooted in charges of discrimination, which is prohibited under Article 14 of the ECHR (and therefore the HRA) but confined to the other rights secured by the convention, or issues falling within their general ambit. However, Article 1 Protocol 1 (A1P1), which protects the peaceful enjoyment of possessions, has been deemed to apply to social security entitlements, and it has provided a basis for three separate challenges to the benefit cap. A similar argument, combined with the right to respect for family and private life (Article 8 of the ECHR), has also been made in relation to the two-child limit for CTC.

Other challenges have engaged Article 6 of the ECHR/HRA in claims for access to justice, which has featured in challenges to welfare sanctions, to truncated rights of appeal, and to the conduct of the Work Capability Assessment (WCA). Further recourse to universal principles has looked to the UN Convention on the Rights of the Child (UNCRC), in relation to those aspects of welfare reform that have a direct or indirect impact on the well-being of children, though this has been the terrain of considerable judicial disagreement. All of these cases have drawn on universal human rights to defend citizens' claims to social rights, though most judgements show clear signs of deference to the executive. This points to the ultimately political nature of the matters at issue and to the constrained purchase of human rights claims when resource protection and parliamentary sovereignty are in play, even in the face of a breach of the guaranteed minimum that is the hallmark of Marshall's social citizenship.

The chapters that follow will also document the various ways in which migrants and asylum-seekers have sought recourse to supranational norms – *via* human rights instruments or in some cases EU law – when contesting resource-related contraction and constraint. A similar array of rights is at issue, and indeed a clear separation between citizens and migrants does not always hold. Thus, some of those affected by the benefit cap are revealed to be settled migrants (see SG and Ors v SSWP [2015] UKSC 16, para 75), while the minimum income requirement for family unification affects British citizen sponsors[5] as well as migrants with settled status. Other contractions more directly targeting migrant access to public funds have affected children who often also hold British citizenship, which places children's rights under the UNCRC again in contention. Similarly, children's rights have featured in challenges to the minimum income requirement for family unification, as has discrimination under Article 8 in relation to gender, race, and low income. These arguments are elaborated in Chapter 7.

Discrimination in relation to Article 8 has been the basis of a challenge to 'right to rent' checks aimed at barring access to accommodation by undocumented migrants but affecting other foreign-seeming prospective tenants, some of them British citizens. Under EU law, discrimination has also figured in challenges to the removal of EEA homeless migrants. Minimum standards of reception have been tested in relation to the reduction of support for asylum-seekers and have also been linked to claims of discrimination against the children of asylum-seekers. In other cases, a claim under Article 6 (access to justice) yielded success in challenging the residence test for legal aid and refusals of exceptional case funding, while in two rare cases, violations of Article 3 have been raised in relation to support for failed asylum-seekers pursuing a new claim, and in the implementation of the 'no recourse to public finds' (NRPF) condition. However, challenges have much more commonly turned on the weighing of national interests against obligations under international law, and as with domestic welfare cases, rights are then carefully balanced against questions of legitimate policy objectives and parliamentary sovereignty.

CONCLUSION

Attempts to combine domestic welfare and migration within the same analytical frame are therefore revealing in a number of ways – not least the fact that both areas display a degree of overlap, having prompted recourse to international law in relation to discrimination, children's rights, and access to justice. A combined perspective also highlights how both areas have been subject to similar devices of conditionality and control, and thereby a contraction of rights, and how the treatment of citizens has come more closely to approximate that of migrants. Neither the Marshallian/citizenship frame nor the cosmopolitan/post-national frame offers much analytical purchase on such developments, each being shaped by an expansionary orientation, and each being blinkered to the primary concerns of the other. However, the notion of civic stratification holds considerable promise for overcoming these limitations. It conceptualizes a technique of governmentality that extends to the delivery of both citizens' and migrants' rights, while also providing an incipient theory of the drivers of change, in which intervention by civic activists and the construction or erosion of moral standing both play a critical role.

While citizenship rights have traditionally provided the yardstick against which to measure claims of post-national expansion with respect to migrant rights, in conditions of contraction we find that human rights become the yardstick for both. Hence, while universal claims have to some degree driven expansion, a question now arises as to how far they can arrest contraction. The issues noted earlier have provoked a variety of human rights claims, but most are precariously balanced, allowing the courts to extend considerable leeway to the legislature and executive even as they leave the door open for continuing contestation. We also find a degree of overlap between migrants and citizens while the entire complex of domestic welfare, migrant rights, and human rights is rendered inherently unstable by contested implementation and interpretation.

In this configuration, we can also begin to see the dynamic nature of the relationship between the formal and informal dimensions of rights. In Lockwood's schema, the development of public understanding and sympathy may heighten a group's access to moral resources, which can then be deployed in the process of civic expansion. A claim to rights is thus in some sense a claim to public standing; from this, it follows that the conferral of a right can act to confirm or to bolster a group in the eyes of the public, as in the argument that rights represent a form of 'recognition' (Honneth 1995). Where a group is subject to a deterioration in their public standing or their moral resources, claims-making becomes more difficult and that group may become vulnerable to an active erosion of their rights. Similarly, a group denied rights may in consequence suffer a diminution of public standing; indeed, a dynamic of this kind arguably underpins the muted public response to welfare cuts. Furthermore, the linkage between domestic welfare and migration as 'two sides of the same coin' in political discourse has set two target populations in opposition to each other and has diminished public perceptions of the legitimacy of both, albeit it in different ways. We see one example of the fallout from this configuration in the following chapter, which addresses austerity measures as one backdrop against which the referendum on membership of the EU was played out.

3

Moralizing Welfare and Migration: A Backdrop to Brexit

A MORAL ECONOMY OF WELFARE AND MIGRATION

This chapter considers the discourse of morality and fairness in the speeches of David Cameron and traces its operationalization beyond the aggressive curtailment of welfare rights for domestic claimants toward increased restrictions on the rights of EU nationals. Combined with an attack on the 'abuse' of free movement, a claimed displacement of British workers, and a policy of deficit reduction, the effect was to place a denigrated and disadvantaged domestic population in a zero-sum relation to EU migration, though the driving rationale was unsupported by available empirical evidence. There are two strands to the following analysis: (1) an outline of the discursive content of key political speeches; and (2) the implementation of such discourse in terms of the formal and informal dimensions of civic stratification, a distinction that respectively refers to legal entitlement to rights and to the related moral standing of affected groups.

These two analytical strands combine to reveal a perverse effect of the discursive and policy package. In setting domestic welfare recipients and migrant groups in opposition, together they provide the context for a strong degree of Brexit support in the deprived areas most affected by welfare reform but not commonly subject to high levels of inward migration. The chapter's closing section uses this background to cast fuller light on a particular aspect of the referendum result, which Goodwin and Heath (2016, 331) argue was 'delivered by the left behind – social groups united by a general sense of insecurity, pessimism and marginalisation' – in what Munch (2012) has termed the 'liberal competition state'.

We saw in Chapter 1 how recent aspects of economic and welfare state change can be understood in terms of a reformulated notion of 'moral economy' (as in Booth 1994; Sayer 2007; Clarke and Newman 2012), a notion given contemporary relevance by the argument that all economies are moral economies, implying and depending upon a supporting moral frame. Attention has therefore turned to the production of moral sentiment in shaping socio-economic practice (Fassin 2009; Sayer 2007) and to the way that publicly circulated moral meanings offer a basis for generating and justifying social classification (Hitlin and Vaisey 2013). Nowhere is this more apparent than in the fields of welfare and migration, where economic and moral distinctions become difficult to separate.

Fassin (2009a, 1254) notes the 'inexorable expansion' of uses of the term moral economy and has sought to 'tighten and revitalise' the notion in exploring its contemporary relevance. He offers the following definition: 'We will consider moral economy to be the production, distribution, circulation, and use of moral sentiments, emotions, and values, norms and obligation in social space.' In Fassin's account, moral economies represent the 'mental states of collectivities', which he views as unstable and fluid realities, that are historically created, modified and destroyed. These observations bring us close to Sayers's (2007, 262) formulation in which: 'Moral economy studies the norms and sentiments that structure and influence economic practices, and how they are reinforced, compromised or overridden by economic pressures.' While Fassin foregrounds the actual production of moral sentiment, and Sayer its place within the economic system, taken together, these two scholars direct attention to the role of moral sentiment in embedding economic practice, which will not always be benign.

Where management of the welfare state is concerned, Lockwood (1996, 535) has observed that 'the leading edge of compromise is some idea of merit or desert which is closely tied up with the value put on individual achievement and self-responsibility'. This approximates his notion of moral resources, and the existence of a long-established hierarchy seems to confirm this view (see Ormston and Curtice 2015; Curtice, Phillips, and Clery 2016). A ranking in terms of public sympathy has traditionally moved from the elderly, to the sick and disabled, to the unemployed, and finally to immigrants (Van Oorschot 2008). Herein lies the scope for a 'moral economy' of welfare and migration that seeks to foster and consolidate the turn away from a solidaristic morality toward greater particularism, to embed the welfare system more firmly within a set of disciplinary requirements, and to implement ever more finely drawn boundaries of desert. We are thus directed to the question of how social norms can be the site of political interventions, and how these interventions are made apparent both in political discourse and in the design and operation of a given system of support. While Titmus's (1970, 238) hope was that the very existence of a welfare state would cultivate a social and moral sense of solidarity, there was always a possibility of movement in the opposite direction, and where cuts or controls might threaten to offend public morals, political attention can turn to the refashioning of moral sensibilities.

CONTESTED MEMBERSHIP
OF THE WELFARE COMMUNITY

This chapter therefore engages and elaborates themes from related literature on the reconfiguration of welfare, economy, and solidarity within a changing global division of labour, underpinned by a distinctive moral construction of economic and social relations. In this context, Munch (2012) characterizes the 'liberal competition state' as a turn away from collectivized social inclusion toward individualized forms, such that social provisions are subsumed under strategies of activation and deterrence. He notes that a key issue in this process is who succeeds in the symbolic struggle, and though this struggle operates at the level of political rhetoric, it can shape the way that welfare problems are perceived and tackled.

A social insurance system essentially collectivizes risk. It involves some acceptance of a sense of collective fate as well as some recognition of the equal standing of participants – hence Marshall's (1992[1950]) conception of citizenship as a confirmation of equal social worth. Mau (2003, 45–6) argues that a willingness to share depends on the 'moral persuasiveness' of welfare institutions, but he also recognizes that this is subject to a 'politics of interpretation', which can have nationally variable outcomes (Taylor-Gooby et al. 2019). The factors at play in terms of public acceptability are financial contribution, personal desert, and social belonging, which raise questions as to what is fair and who is worthy that have no ready answer, each being open to interpretation, manipulation, or persuasion. Hence

Lockwood's (1996, 536) argument that 'the ethos and practice of citizenship is at least as likely as class relations to structure group interests and thereby fields of conflict and discontent'.

Migration is clearly part of this picture, and Freeman's (1986) classic article provides a persuasive account of a dynamic whereby the welfare state requires closure because 'it establishes a principle of distributive justice that departs from the distributive principles of the free market' (52). His argument is that in establishing a guaranteed social minimum, welfare requires a moral grounding in fellow feeling, while also providing a baseline for resisting deterioration in the terms and conditions of employment. Foreign workers may offer an alternative to the domestic population as a supply of more tractable labour, but Freeman argues that this will succeed only if those workers can be excluded from access to welfare rights, or if welfare standards are more generally undermined – both of which have featured in British policy.

The points at issue are therefore migrants' terms of entry and stay in the host country, the extent of their access to the welfare system, the degree of public acceptance of their presence, the regulation and buoyancy of the labour market, and how far any related erosion of domestic guarantees can be sustained. Many of these factors fall into the realm of political choice and influence, and the way that politicians may seek to embed welfare and migration within a refashioned moral vision thus constitutes a site of contention. Unresolved questions remain concerning the unit of membership and belonging (Beitz 1983), who is included in the 'community of value' (Anderson 2013), and where any related gain or loss will fall. However, as Deckard and Heslin (2016) note, there is now a significant population whose identities transcend national borders and who exist alongside the deteriorating status of (lower-class) citizens within their home nations.

While debate has traditionally been framed in terms of the impact of migration on the welfare state (e.g., Freeman 1986), Geddes (2003) takes a reverse approach. He argues not only that resource pressures require a tightly defined community of membership with respect to welfare entitlement, but also that entitlement itself is increasingly viewed in relation to immigration control. This relationship is driven by fears of a 'pull factor', described by Mayblin (2016) as a 'political imaginary' whereby simplified understandings of complex phenomena become embedded in material practices. Thus, the assertion that welfare benefits serve as a 'magnet' (Cameron 2014a) for migrants

Moralizing Welfare and Migration 77

serves to justify policies that minimize welfare inclusion in a drive for deterrence, while at the same time enhancing possibilities for monitoring and control. A crucial element is the classification of migrants by their grounds for entry (Morris 1998; Sainsbury 2012) and hence by immigration status, and the related specification of inclusions and exclusions with respect to welfare support. Marshall's focus on social inclusion is thus reversed as welfare rules become part of a filtering system linked to the sorting of migrants by criteria of worth.

Analysis in this mode is clearly advanced by the application of Lockwood's (1996) concept of 'civic stratification' as a system for the differential granting of rights shaped by underpinning judgements of merit or dis-merit, respectively referring to formal entitlement and what might be termed informal 'moral standing'. We saw in Chapter 2 that application of the concept can be extended from the inequalities generated within citizenship to include the elaboration of migrant rights (see Morris 1997, 2002). It is deployed in the present chapter to address within one frame both how citizenship is internally stratified by the measures of discipline and control that accompany welfare claims, and how migrants are stratified by their basis of entry and the associated granting or denial of rights. In each area formal legal standing and informal judgements of merit are shown to be in play, and in this vein Anderson (2013) notes that laws on citizenship, welfare, and migration create rather than reflect differential status positions. Together, she argues, they represent a set of social, economic, and political relations that say much about how we make sense of ourselves. In Lamont and Molnar's terms (2002) they offer an instance of how symbolic boundaries, given sufficient consensual support, will soon translate into social boundaries.

Key questions for an understanding of this configuration are how legitimacy and desert are defined with respect to welfare entitlement and how far national sovereignty extends in this matter. Both issues are highlighted in Britain's moves to limit the welfare rights of EEA workers. While 'post-national' claims have been linked to the erosion of national sovereignty and the assertion of universal rights, inclusion within the welfare community is carefully constrained and can provoke resistance from the domestic population, some of whom are themselves confined to the margins of their own society. Such tensions have been apparent in Britain for some time (Düvell and Jordan 2002), acquiring particular significance in the run-up to the referendum on EU membership, since under EU law, the free movement of

78   *The Moral Economy of Welfare and Migration*

workers carries an associated entitlement to social rights. In fact, case law from the Court of Justice has supported restrictions on access to non-contributary social assistance in two important recent cases from Germany,[1] with outcomes that seem to be moving in the direction favoured by Britain (Barbulescu and Favell 2019). However, the political discourse underpinning the configuration of welfare and migration embraced by the 2010 Coalition government and its Conservative successor appears to have militated against David Cameron's Remain and reform agenda.

MAPPING THE DISCOURSE

The following analysis of political discourse over this period is based on David Cameron's party conference speeches, together with his more targeted welfare and immigration speeches. These texts are supplemented by cross-reference to speeches from the then minister for work and pensions (Iain Duncan Smith), and the then immigration minister (Damien Green) – twenty-four speeches in all. A reading of these sources is informed by Freeden's (1996, 2003) approach to mapping ideology, whereby 'social truths' depend on the translation of abstract concepts into substantive content. Ideology in this context is viewed as a recurrent pattern of beliefs and values dedicated to (re) ordering the social world and given expression through the communicative devices of political discourse. As we saw in Chapter 1, this framework directs attention to how contestable political concepts (such as morality) are given concrete substance or 'decontested' in key political statements. Associated analysis will therefore rest on the identification of 'core' concepts that are central to a given position and the way their substantive content is provided by closely related (adjacent) concepts that flesh out their meaning – as with morality, fairness, and responsibility. These in turn are amplified by more loosely linked 'peripheral' concepts, which are used to give further background support.

Examples are provided below, though in practice this process of translation does not operate exclusively at the conceptual level, but rather moves from greater to lesser degrees of abstraction. In fact, as a supplement to analysis, the resultant discourse can also point to social groups or behaviour patterns that serve as reference points for its key elements and that can be linked in terms of related mutual affinities or oppositions. This is what Laclau (2014, 68) terms the

Moralizing Welfare and Migration

logic of equivalence and difference, or the construction of 'equivalential chains'. We will see later how such chains are made up of mutually associated concepts and behaviours and can be used to show how a discourse has the potential to unite or divide social groups according to their standing in relation to the key issues in play.

For the present chapter, a thematic analysis of all the above-noted speeches by Cameron was conducted to identify recurrent themes, along with their core concepts, substantive (adjacent) content, and more loosely associated (peripheral) content. Analysis in this mode is an interpretive rather than a mechanical exercise, and as in Freeden's account it requires a hierarchical approach that begins by identifying dominant concepts and then traces their substantive content through threads of meaning and association. 'Fairness' stands out as a recurrent theme: it appears in a large majority of Cameron's speeches, often allied with 'morality' and closely associated with responsibility. Thus, texts must also be read for proxy concepts or phrases that act together with or substitute for dominant concepts and serve to frame more detailed references to specific policy issues. As we see below, addressing 'the moral hazard of welfare', tackling the 'something for nothing culture', linking 'what you pay in to what you get out', and ending 'abuse' of free movement all stand for 'fairness'. Readings must therefore identify not just a recurrent vocabulary but also recurrent meanings, which then permit a line to be drawn from abstract principles, to substantive content, to promised policy change. A further step may look toward target audiences and implicit oppositions, which often are clearly signalled in political speeches – as with 'hard-working British taxpayers' (Cameron 2014c) or, more vaguely, 'putting British people first' (Cameron 2014, 2014a).

Analysing the Discourse

The following discourse analysis proceeds chronologically, citing indicative statements that reveal an emergent pattern of meaning in Cameron's key speeches. Thus, his pre-election 'Age of Austerity' speech (Cameron 2009) announced a reshaping of Britain on the basis of responsibility, followed by a stated desire to 'change the way we think about ourselves and our role in society' (Cameron 2010). These objectives were linked in 2010 and 2011 to an expanded notion of fairness, which was aimed not just at who gets help but at 'who gives that help through their taxes' (Cameron 2010), such that 'real fairness

... is about the link between what you put in and what you get out' (Cameron 2011). By the 2012 Conservative Party Conference, Cameron had announced the related programme of welfare reform as a 'moral mission'. In Freeden's terms, morality emerges as a core concept, closely associated with the adjacent concept of fairness, contrasted with personal irresponsibility and social profligacy and peripherally linked to an overriding drive for deficit reduction and a pledge to address the 'something for nothing culture' (Cameron 2012a; Duncan-Smith 2013). The lines of equivalence and difference are thus drawn to associate unfairness with profligacy, dependency, and welfare recipients (both in-work and out-of-work), as set against austerity, responsibility, and hard-working taxpayers.

However, the same set of speeches contains a further opposition – one that offers in some respects to redeem the welfare recipient – and that is the opposition between migrants and the British people. By the time of Cameron's 2011 conference speech, immigration had been made an explicit part of the welfare picture, and the economy inherited from New Labour was argued to have left 'a welfare system that trapped millions in dependency [and] an immigration system that brought in migrant workers to do the jobs that those on welfare were being paid not to do' (Cameron 2011; see also 2013). So breaking the 'cycle of dependency' meant 'sorting out welfare and immigration', which in turn meant capping net migration. The theme was repeated in other speeches, such that 'welfare and immigration are two sides of the same coin ... We will never control immigration properly until we tackle welfare dependency' (Cameron 2011a; see also Duncan-Smith as reported by Gabbatt 2011).

The language deployed in relation to welfare reappears, but 'fairness' is turned to address the position of 'British born people stuck on welfare' (Cameron 2011a); British people affected by illegal migration (Cameron 2011a); communities under pressure regarding schools, housing,[2] and health care (Cameron 2011b; Cameron 2013); and immigration that damages the labour market and pushes down wages (Cameron 2015). We also learn of a 'hard-working British public' concerned about migrant exploitation of services and benefits (DWP 2013a). In these scenarios, the 'fairness' challenge to migrants is about making sure 'you put into Britain, you don't just take out', while the 'fairness' challenge for policy is again about protecting the British taxpayer (Cameron 2013, 2013a, 2014c).

Moralizing Welfare and Migration

An early focus (Cameron 2011a; Green 2010) was on capping non-EEA migration and 'closing a loophole that allows illegals to claim benefits'.[3] However, attention soon turned to free movement guarantees under EU law, and softening statements about the benefits of migration were counterbalanced by 'fairness' as the need to end the 'something for nothing culture' among migrants. Making the case for Remain therefore entailed a refusal to 'go on endlessly paying' (Cameron 2013), assertions that no one could come and expect benefits on arrival (Cameron 2013b, 2014c), a promise to limit the stay of jobless EU migrants, and a commitment to address the 'abuse of free movement' (Cameron 2014c, 2015a) and 'rogue' EU benefit claims (DWP 2013a). This was combined with the aim of restricting access to in-work supplements (TCS), the argument being that this would 'reduce the incentive for lower paid, low skilled EU workers to come here in the first place' (Cameron 2014c).

One interesting aspect of this linkage between migration and welfare is that it places domestic welfare recipients in an ambiguous position: having been condemned by the 'responsibility and fairness' agenda, they can now perceive *themselves* as subject to unfair treatment. In the name of deficit reduction, they are exposed to heightened conditionality, capped benefits, and frozen rates, variously applying to both out-of-work and in-work benefits.[4] This welfare austerity is then accompanied by references to immediate and 'indefinite' benefit payments for EU nationals, the contested claim (see Graham 2015) of a 40 per cent rate of welfare dependency among recent arrivals (Cameron 2015a), and assertions that immigration has trapped British people on benefits and driven down wages. The contours of equivalence and difference may now be reconfigured. British welfare recipients can potentially align themselves with fairness and responsibility against the 'abuse' and unfairness that allegedly causes their dependency, to take up a position more closely aligned to a legitimate claim for recognition and protection.

OPERATIONALIZING THE DISCOURSE

The translation of rhetoric into policy can be viewed through the lens of civic stratification, and Lockwood sees a vital role for welfare policy both in the structuring of inequalities and in their legitimation. In terms of the preceding discourse, we can therefore ask how espoused principles of fairness and responsibility are made manifest in the details of policy change from 2010 onwards. The resultant measures are presented below in terms of their stratifying effects on formal entitlement; the informal dimension of civic stratification is more fully addressed in a later section.

Domestic Welfare

Although the translation of discourse into policy is not necessarily automatic or transparent, the discursive attack on dependency culture explicitly prepared the ground for radical reform of the welfare system, via the 2012 Welfare Reform Act and the 2016 Welfare Reform and Work Act. Related policy documents both anticipate and echo the speeches cited above, and prior to the 2010 election, the Conservative Party (2008), announced its 'responsibilities agenda', which proclaimed that 'ending Britain's welfare culture is a moral duty'. This aim was repeated in a consultation paper preparatory to the 2012 Act (DWP 2010), which foregrounded tighter conditions for unemployed claimants, while the Universal Credit system currently unfolding (DWP 2010a) is piloting the extension of conditions to people in receipt of low wage supplements.

The 2012 reforms began to take effect well in advance of the referendum, though they were to be amplified by the 2016 Welfare Reform and Work Act. By the time of the vote, frozen benefit rates and cuts to HB and Council Tax Benefits (CTBS) were in place, alongside greatly strengthened requirements for the unemployed that intensified with the duration of a claim[5] and carried incremental sanctions for failure to comply (Webster 2015). A wider pool of claimants had been drawn into conditionality and a two-child limit on CTC had been announced; meanwhile, an additional stratum of change was directed at reduced support for the low-paid, including plans to compel low earners to seek more hours or better pay. A radical restructuring was thus set in train to deliver an integrated system of working-age benefits (UC),[6] whose aims were to promote responsible behaviour, establish 'fairness' between givers and receivers, and impose tighter conditions on all claimants, both in and out of work (DWP 2010a). These policy aims were directed toward the need to accommodate the 'modern flexible economy' (Duncan Smith 2014), which has seen a marked increase in zero-hours contracts and false self-employment (Townsend and Savage 2016).

Moralizing Welfare and Migration

These developments have been viewed as a shift in the foundations of good citizenship such that responsibility for social cohesion and integration now falls on the individual (Soysal 2012), but this should not blind us to their stratifying effects. Thus, Munch (2012, 251) notes that one result of this individualized orientation has been to produce 'a lower class that feels no longer cared for in the national community', a key referent for some analyses of the Brexit vote (e.g., Goodwin and Heath 2016; but see also Dorling, Stuart, and Stubbs 2016). The welfare reforms to date[7] have disproportionately affected social groups that already occupy a vulnerable class position, exposing them to reduced subsistence income and punitive sanctions (JRF 2014b). They have had an additional stratifying effect in highlighting a negative status position of dependency, extended under UC to include receipt of low-wage supplements, while imposing a cumulative disciplinary regime on claimants through the details of policy design and implementation.

A further stratifying effect – one that proved particularly significant for the referendum result – has been geographical. Vastly uneven cuts to local authority spending between 2010 and 2015 amounted to an average fall of 23.4 per cent per person, rising to over 45 per cent among the hardest-hit authorities (Becker, Fetzer and Novy 2016; Crewe 2016). These cuts, which have directly affected some benefits, have fallen hardest on areas of pre-existing deprivation.

EEA Nationals and Benefit Entitlement

While all migrants acquire full social rights on achieving permanent residence, stratifying techniques of control have long been deployed to cover the intervening period. From 2010 onwards (Gower 2015), non-EEA migration has increasingly been managed through income and skill thresholds, as well as heightened welfare exclusions, but this left EEA nationals who were exercising freedom of movement under Directive 2004/38/EC and who had stabilized at around half of all transnational migrants in Britain. Under this directive, EEA workers and jobseekers are entitled to equal treatment in relation to benefits facilitating access to the labour market, though recent case law has allowed some constraints[8] (see Kramer 2015). The UK government actively sought to deter their presence through stratified devices of control that make the fullest use of permitted restrictions, and here we see a direct link between discourse and policy, in an elaboration of the fairness and responsibilities agenda.

Britain had already imposed transitional restrictions on labour market and benefit access for Bulgarian and Romanian (A2) workers for the maximum permitted period of seven years. But in 2013, with the A2 restrictions due to end later that year, David Cameron turned public attention to the alleged 'abuse' of free movement. Measures to limit out-of-work benefits for all EEA nationals were rushed through in regulations governing their access, effective from January 2014, and announced in press releases that quote directly from Cameron's speeches. They purported to reduce 'the magnetic pull of Britain's benefit system' (Cameron 2014a), combat 'rogue EU benefits claims' (DWP 2013a), and address the concerns of 'the hardworking British public' (Cameron 2014a) – many of whom were themselves subject to austerity measures aimed at deficit reduction.

When Cameron promised that 'no one can come to this country and expect to get out-of-work benefits immediately ... We will no longer pay these indefinitely', and declared that free movement 'cannot be completely unqualified' (Cameron 2013), he was clearly referring to EEA workers. This partly reflected a concern about the non-contributory nature of most benefits, which is a key feature of the UK system. In fact, free movement within the EU has never been entirely unconditional (see Peers 2016), but recent UK policy has strained at the boundary of what is permissible (O'Brien 2015) with a view to limiting access to benefits, deterring arrivals, and addressing the so-called 'abuse' of fee movement (Cameron 2014c). However, while the measures introduced were intended to reassure the 'British public', they equally served to highlight an alleged 'problem' that could be ameliorated but not eradicated while Britain remained in the EU.

Targeting EEA job search, key measures (Kennedy 2015b) have included a requirement of three months' prior residence for Job Seekers Allowance (JSA – unemployment benefit), and its extension to Child Benefit and Child Tax Credits. From January 2014 onwards[9] a statutory six-month limit was placed on JSA claims lodged by new EEA jobseekers and prior (retained) workers; this was later reduced to three months for jobseekers. A genuine-prospect-of-work test was to be applied to the latter group after three months, and to retained workers after six months, while failure of the test would mean a loss of the right to reside, which would rebound on the prospects for permanent residence. Minimum earnings guidance was introduced for the designation of worker status, new jobseekers were excluded from eligibility for Housing Benefit, and in March 2015 Parliament passed regulations to exclude EEA jobseekers from eligibility for UC.

These widely publicized measures (DWP 2013a, 2013b) were designed to limit migrants' access to benefits and discourage EEA migration to Britain, but in practice they focused attention on a 'problem' that scarcely existed. Thus, Favell (2014, 286) notes 'the government's inability to marshal any evidence in support of its own official position' and observes that such anti-EU argument is emotional and not empirical.

COUNTER-EVIDENCE AND MODES OF CRITIQUE

It is therefore important to consider how far the moral economy constructed by political discourse and advanced by associated policy measures addressed an actually existing problem supported by empirical evidence. The discourse and policy package outlined in this chapter rests on two (somewhat conflicting) claims: that domestic welfare dependency is in part attributable to the presence of migrant workers; and that EEA migrants are drawn to Britain by the availability of welfare benefits and are thus a drain on resources. In fact, data from official sources support neither claim, and the Office for Budget Responsibility (OBR 2013, Annex A) has noted that the main effect of a rise in net migration has been to increase labour supply, bring higher returns on capital, increase investment, and improve the debt-to-GDP ratio. There is, however, the question of where the benefits of this were being felt (TUC n.d.). The Migration Advisory Committee (MAC 2014) has recognized that a boost of £233bn to GDP had little impact on per capita income, and this raises broader questions about distribution and access to resources, especially given the level of cuts to local authority budgets. As Taylor-Gooby (2016, 728) has more generally observed: 'The blunt truth is that government policy presumes that most people will not share the increase in national prosperity.'

Patterns of fiscal cost and contribution will vary for different types of migrants and different economic conditions, so Dustmann and Frattini (2014) have disaggregated EEA and non-EEA migrants and looked at different time periods. They found that between 1995 and 2011, migrants from within the EEA had a net positive effect, and an even stronger positive effect between 2001 and 2011. Rowthorn's (2015) more cautious calculation concluded that the impact of EEA migration for 2001–11 was only marginally negative after standing costs such as defence were taken into account but otherwise remains positive. Furthermore, a variety of studies (e.g., Lemos and Portes 2008; MAC 2014; Ruhs and Vargas-Silva 2015) have found only minimal displacement of British workers; and even when attention is confined to low-skilled migrants, the chair of the government's MAC (Metcalf 2016, Section 6) concludes that '[they] have a neutral impact on UK-born employment rates, fiscal contribution, GDP per head and productivity'. The MAC (2014) also reports only slight downward pressure on wages for UK-born workers in semi-skilled and unskilled work (see also Devlin et al. 2014), calculated by Portes (2016) to amount to 1 per cent over eight years, not least because of protections offered by minimum-wage legislation – though note some concerns about enforcement (Booth 2020). Against this background, the MAC crucially registers a need to address the gap between public perceptions and reality, which they argue can lead to poor policy choices.

So if EEA migrants were not displacing British workers, were they excessively dependent on welfare benefits? In fact, the available data do not come close to supporting the political discourse. In the year before restrictions were imposed, EU migrants accounted for 4 per cent of all JSA claims and 2.1 per cent of all working-age benefit claims[10] (Keen and Turner 2016, Table 2b), while making up 4.8 per cent of the workforce (O'Connor and Packard 2016). Though tax credit receipt for EU migrants is proportionately higher than for British workers, at 14 per cent compared to 11 per cent (Keen and Turner 2016), HMRC figures show that EU arrivals over the four years up to 2016 paid £2.54bn *more* in income tax and National Insurance in 2013–14 than they received in tax credits or child benefits (Travis 2016a; see also Warrell 2014).[11] Yet urgent measures rushed through to address the 'problem' of benefit tourism inevitably fostered the impression of a resource drain, undermining the 'moral standing' of the target group, and with it support for EU membership.

The rapidity with which the changes were introduced left limited scope for campaigning against them, but the ensuing responses can again be classified according to the distinctions introduced in Chapter 1. Hence, the preceding material all points to a *rationality* critique, as noted by commentary from a variety of sources (e.g., Portes 2013; Glennie and Pennington 2013; SSAC 2014; Sumption and Altorjai 2016). Furthermore, the time limit placed on benefit entitlements triggered a 'genuine prospect of work' test, which was the focus of a *legality* challenge by the Citizens Advice Bureau and Child Poverty Action Group; the latter also produced a guide to its contestation (Williams 2015). The legal outcome was a caution from judges (KS *v* SSWP [2016] UKUT 269 AAC; MB *and Ors v SSWP* [2016] UKUT, 372 AAC para 57) that the British test goes beyond that prescribed by EU law (see Antonissen, Case C-292/89 [1997] ECR I-00745), leaving scope for further scrutiny.

Later legal intervention by Public Interest Lawyers and the AIRE Centre addressed the subsequent increase in levels of homelessness among EEA migrants, which was linked to an aggressive drive to remove them from Britain (see Cameron 2013b). This was found to be discriminatory and unlawful (*Gureckis and Ors v SSHD* [2017] EWHC 3298 (Admin)), and in displacing an approach based on support and advice, it prompted critique that extends into the realm of *morality* (see CRISIS 2017). Indeed, in addressing the removal of HB from new jobseekers, the SSAC (2014) quoted David Cameron's (Department for Communities and Local Government 2011) view of rough sleeping as an affront to civilized society. The same committee cites third-sector responses that point to a heightened risk of destitution and homelessness, mental health problems, and negative implications for victims of domestic violence. Academic commentary has meanwhile pointed to an underlying shift in the principles of social security that replaces a generalized contract of reciprocity with an individualized and contingent approach that 'instrumentalises and de-humanises' EEA migrants (O'Brien 2015, 112).

MORAL STANDING

We have now seen how civic stratification can operate through formal distinctions that govern both welfare eligibility for the domestic population and conditions of entry and stay for migrants. However, the management of public perceptions and sentiment accompanying patterns of entitlement in turn operates through informal distinctions of desert, underpinned by what we have termed moral standing in society. Indeed, in addition to the construction of formal statuses determining differential access to rights, Lockwood's (1996) schema points to the role of 'moral and material resources' in both the legitimation and the effects of civic stratification. As noted in the previous chapter, moral resources refer to 'advantages conferred by social standing and social networks' and – most crucially for the present

88   *The Moral Economy of Welfare and Migration*

argument – to 'the ability to attain one's ends through the activation of shared moral sentiments' (36).

In Lockwood's account such resources serve as a vehicle for civic expansion through claims for enhanced treatment in the delivery of rights, or mobilizations for the creation of new rights, though he neglects to consider the reverse dynamic of contraction. Attributions of blame, allegations of abuse, and a questioning of desert all negatively affect perceptions of legitimacy and thus moral standing, and we have seen this process at work in political discourse addressing both domestic welfare claims and the rights of free movement in Europe. This discourse and related policy measures then feed public perceptions that radically misjudge the scale of the 'problems' in question.[12] In fact, the discourse and policies designed to limit social rights – be it through enhanced conditionality for domestic claimants or the campaign against benefit tourism from the EU – are a more plausible source of any related 'moral panic'[13] than substantial evidence of abuse or significant resource drain. The effect has been to present EU migrants as competitors in a struggle over shrinking resources rather than as net contributors who are the latest target of a shift in the nature and purpose of welfare protection. Their legitimacy and desert are thus placed in question, and their moral standing is impaired.

Lockwood argues that institutional structures for delivering the rights that are central to social integration may also affect class formation (or class de-formation), and political discourse has not simply condemned domestic welfare claimants and EU migrants – it has set them against each other. In an increasingly 'flexible' labour market (Inman 2016, 2019; Field and Forsey 2016), we have seen enhanced welfare conditionality and sanctions for out-of-work benefits and the proposed extension of both to in-work benefits, accompanied by discursive oppositions between welfare dependents, migrants, and hard-working taxpayers, and supplemented by accusations of benefit tourism and abuse of free movement. Thus, for both domestic welfare recipients and EEA migrants an attack on moral standing by means of political rhetoric has been a prelude to increased conditionality in the delivery or denial of rights, while also fuelling resentment toward the latter group.

Government rhetoric on migration and benefits has been misleading with respect to both the level of claims and their likely duration, and several bodies have noted a lack of supporting data (MAC 2014;

Portes 2015a; House of Lords written question HL4654), and even a lack of significant labour market displacement (Devlin et al. 2014). Indeed, the European Commission in the UK (2013) has highlighted the need for a more nuanced and evidence-based public narrative on these issues, while Wadsworth (2015) observes that the key significance of immigration lies less in its empirical effects than in its impact on public perceptions. But as Munch has observed, it is the rhetoric itself that shapes how problems are perceived and tackled, and in this context, the promise of phased-in access to tax credits for new arrivals – the most relevant aspect of Cameron's EU negotiations – looked ineffectual. Given the government discourse on domestic welfare, migration, and benefit tourism, Britain's attempt to secure concessions on free movement – concessions themselves constrained by EU law – served to confirm these problems in the public eye and to further erode the moral standing of EU migrants.

Questions could be raised about the extent to which migrants and domestic welfare claimants might make common cause – non-standard workers gain from EU-level employment protection (JRF 2016), and a number of 'crossover' issues affect both groups. Both have been exposed to exploitation in a 'flexible' and poorly regulated labour market (MAC 2014; Metcalf 2016; Field and Forsey 2016; Booth 2020); both are affected by austerity measures in the operation of the welfare system; both experience increased conditionality and surveillance in accessing their rights; and both suffer from the erosion of public services associated with reductions in local authority funding (Crewe 2016). However, one key to understanding public perceptions must be the political construction of a world view based on a vision of 'limited good',[14] whereby the presence and rights of migrants detract from the resources and opportunities available to the domestic population. Thus, Dorling, Stuart, and Stubbs (2016) note the likely connection between austerity and labour market precarity, on the one hand, and a *perceived* pressure on housing, wages, and public services as attributed to immigration, on the other.

REFLECTIONS ON THE BREXIT VOTE

The results of the referendum are well-known (Becker at al. 2016). Leave succeeded on 51.9 per cent of the vote (53.4 per cent in England),[15] based on a broad coalition of three different groupings: Eurosceptics (23 per cent of the population, 75 per cent voting Leave), the older working class (16 per cent of the population, 73 per cent voting Leave), and an economically deprived anti-immigrant group (12 per cent of the population, 95 per cent voting Leave) (Swales 2016). The Leave vote was in practice multifaceted and has been attributed at least in part to nostalgia for Britain's once dominant place in the world, and to an insular retreat into backward-looking racialized narratives of Englishness (Virdee and McGeever 2017). In fact, the assertion that Brexit was 'delivered by the left behind' (Goodwin and Heath 2016) has been viewed as an overstatement – although two thirds of voters in classes D and E voted for Leave, they amounted to only 24 per cent of the total, while nearly two fifths of support came from members of classes A, B and C1 (Dorling 2016).

Nevertheless, the pattern of support for Leave among low-income and low-skilled groups living in deprived areas remains of interest, given the narrow margin of the result and also because these circumstances make for unstable sentiments, rendering people open to persuasion from differing political positions (Munch 2012, 251). The groups concerned have been characterized by feelings of anger, of apathy, and of 'not existing' (McKenzie 2017), and Dorling, Stuart, and Stubbs (2016) observe that 'a large proportion of votes to leave the EU might be understood as a visceral reaction from those who felt increasingly powerless as a result of globalisation, widening economic inequalities and a failure of successive UK government administrations to redistribute income and wealth more equitably for more than thirty years'. Thus, the geography of deindustrialization, inequality, and decline was already well established. However, for voters in the areas affected the immediate backdrop to the result was sketched out by Cameron's discourse on welfare and migration and their mutual association, albeit reinforced by more generalized assertions of the need for immigration control (Valluvan and Kalra 2019).

The referendum was held in the context of an austerity drive geared to deficit reduction, a government discourse condemning EU migrants' indefinite and immediate benefit entitlement, increased precarity of employment (Field and Forsey 2016), and a lack of wage growth at the lower levels (Allen and Elliott 2016). While the most direct link in the discourse was made between unemployment and migration, British workers facing insecurity, cuts to tax credits, and attacks on dependency would also have been susceptible to an argument that foregrounded 'fairness' but left them precariously placed. Aggregate summaries of the vote and analysis at local authority level all paint the same picture: low income was a key predictor of a vote for Leave (Goodwin and Heath 2016), together with a sense of worsening personal circumstances relative to others (Swales 2016), especially evident at a time of benefit cuts and freezes. At highly disaggregated ward level,[16] deprivation correlated strongly with support for Leave, which was also characterized by high unemployment, low income, and a traditional reliance on manufacturing (Becker, Fetzer, and Novy 2016; Beatty and Fothergill 2016).

Becker and colleagues (2016) stress the multi-causal nature of the result, arguing that explanatory power will come only from understanding on a variety of dimensions, and this is apparent in a delicate balance between value-based and resource-based factors in proffered accounts. While documenting and endorsing the socio-economic correlations noted above, Goodwin and Heath (2016) point to a pre-existing value conflict that underpinned earlier growth in support for the UK Independence Party. In this scenario, political and media elites are argued to espouse support for social liberalism, multiculturalism and EU membership, with 'left-behind' social groups united by a more nativist response to perceived threats of rapid social and cultural change. Goodwin and Heath (2016, 31) then suggest that as a result these groups have 'long felt excluded from the mainstream consensus and used the referendum to voice their distinctive views'.

Becker and colleagues (2016) note the explanatory power of 'political' factors[17] but also point to the uneven burden of fiscal consolidation in arguing that support for Leave was at least in part related to distributional issues. Indeed, a mapping of the vote confirms that cuts to welfare and to local authority funding, each strongly associated with entrenched deprivation (Beatty and Fothergill 2016; Becker et al. 2016), correlated closely with Leave support. By 2015, the areas worst hit by benefit cuts were losing four times as much per year per working-age adult as the least affected; these were typically older industrial areas and deprived seaside towns (Beatty and Fothergill 2016) – precisely the terrain of high levels of support for Leave. Becker and colleagues (2016) also point to local authority spending cuts (which affected some benefits), and found that authorities experiencing higher levels of cuts were more likely to favour Leave, in part because the geographical pattern of loss coincided with pre-existing deprivations.

Becker and colleagues therefore observe that voters may have mistakenly weighed the costs of EU membership against the sizable extent of recent cuts to benefits and domestic welfare spending, and turned away – a response endorsed by resigned cabinet minister Iain Duncan Smith (2016). However, the propensity to vote Leave has also been seen as a generational divide, with the young being more likely to support Remain, and this might seem to cut across arguments pointing to an austerity effect. But Dorling, Stuart, and Stubbs (2016) have noted a disproportionate middle-class presence among voters in the 18–24 age group, with classes A, B, and C1 accounting for 72 per cent. They therefore suggest that inequalities of wealth and opportunity could have shaped the pattern of turnout, such that the younger voters most affected by widening inequality expressed their discontent by a lower propensity to vote at all.

Fiscal consolidation and entrenched disadvantage thus provide the context for what Goodwin and Heath term a values conflict. Together, these factors help make sense of one superficially surprising aspect of the referendum result. Swales (2016) found concern about immigration levels to be the biggest single factor distinguishing Leave and Remain supporters, though in fact areas with the highest level of migration expressed least concern and tended to favour Remain, while the strongest Leave areas were generally those with the smallest migrant populations (Travis 2016). Goodwin and Heath (2016), however, note that it was the *rate* of change that affected people's vote, with a rapid rate being associated with Leave, even when overall levels of migrant presence were low. This specifically applied to the previous decade's inflow of East European migrants – a group who were more geographically dispersed than previous arrivals (Wadsworth 2015). Becker and colleagues (2016) note a likely interaction effect when an increased flow of lower-skilled migrants into a disadvantaged local population coincides with exposure to welfare reform and spending cuts. Similarly, McKenzie's (2017, 276) ethnographic study of mining towns in decline points to a fear of outsiders that is connected to a sense of abandonment, financial struggle, and political remoteness.

This would seem to offer a recipe for strong Leave support, but we should also look to the political environment in which these effects operated.[18] Attention to this background can amplify aggregate analysis of the voting patterns of those termed 'left behind' to provide a more dynamic understanding of their position. In fact, the circumstances favouring support for Leave were significantly enhanced by the policies and discourse promoted by David Cameron from 2010 onwards, such that his aim to 'change the way we think about ourselves' militated against his Remain agenda. We have already noted the Cameron government's condemnation of dependency in the domestic population (for both in-work and out-of-work benefits), heightened cuts and conditionality in their benefits, a claimed association between welfare dependency and migration, and unfounded assertions about benefit tourism and the abuse of free movement. In sum, a section of the domestic population whose 'moral resources' were weak and whose moral standing had been systematically impugned saw their welfare rights eroded and their living standards fall, and were classically offered a target to blame – albeit one that flew in the face of empirical evidence.

The 'Just About Managing'

When Theresa May became prime minister, she seemed to speak directly to the concerns of the 'left behind', announcing a mission to make Britain 'a country that works for everyone' (May 2016) and promising to deliver a society with 'fairness and solidarity at its heart' (May 2017). She appealed in particular to people 'working around the clock' and only 'just about managing' (JAMs), but a close reading of her early speeches shows more consistency with the Cameron discourse than first appears. Her 'Shared Society' speech (May 2017) acknowledged a need to support the vulnerable, but its focus was her promise 'to help those who have been ignored by the government for too long because they don't fall into the income bracket that makes them qualify for welfare support'. Thus, while there was no overt attack on dependency culture, the old dividing lines remained in place – as did most of the benefit cuts and freezes.

In fact, cuts still unfolding at the time particularly affected supplements for the low-paid and for families with children (Sodha 2016), raising questions about who exactly were the JAMs. Even so, fairness continued to be a rallying cry for those 'out of work or on lower wages because of low-skilled migration' (May 2016a), and so too was the 'injustice' experienced by those 'who see others prospering while [they] are not' and whose 'very identity' was under threat (May 2017). 'Brexit means Brexit' (May 2016a) promised them a reclamation of sovereign independence, a rejection of compromise measures, and a resumption of control over immigration. In the general election of December 2019, the promises of 'levelling up' underprivileged areas and 'getting Brexit done' performed the same function in delivering a Conservative victory.

94

However, with a punitive benefits system, stagnant wages, and a falling pound, not to mention the impending loss of EU funds, many seem set to be disappointed, especially in the Brexit voting areas of economic disadvantage (Partington 2017; 2017a).

CONCLUSION

This chapter began by viewing government speeches for the period 2010–16 as the expression of a moralizing discourse rooted in conceptions of fairness, responsibility, and protection for the hard-working taxpayer. The moral economy it embraced laid the groundwork for an erosion of social rights through increased conditionality and deteriorating living standards; meanwhile, its extension from welfare to migration placed domestic welfare recipients in an ambiguous position. Condemned for their own dependency, they nevertheless were presented as unfairly subject to the impacts of migration. Although available empirical evidence is far from supporting the discursive claims and policy changes that came to focus on the position of EU migrants, it is argued here that the Brexit vote is at least in part the outcome of a zero-sum vision that set domestic welfare recipients (in and out of work) and EU migrants in opposition.

The Brexit story, though unique, illustrates several points of general interest, not least in offering a particular case study of what has been termed the liberal competition state, and the shifting contours of welfare, economy and solidarity within a changing global division of labour. The preceding account has documented the reconfiguration of welfare in a country in retreat from the Marshallian ideal of social inclusion while increasingly reluctant to embrace the construction of a post-national Europe. In so doing it has documented a turn away from collectivized protection toward individualized activation and deterrence that has targeted domestic welfare dependency as well as freedom of movement within the EU.

The argument illustrates the significance of what Munch (2012) terms the symbolic struggle in relation to welfare, economy, and migration, showing the importance of political rhetoric in constructing affinities and divisions both *within* the domestic population, and *between* those most heavily affected by austerity and incoming migrants. This account has also argued that an understanding of the dynamics in play could be further advanced by the concept of civic stratification. That concept is used here to extend a purely discursive approach both by tracing the formal translation from discourse to policy and by outlining the subsequent informal impact on the moral standing of its targets. The absence of evidence to support key elements of the Conservatives' policy is significant, in that it illustrates the role of discourse in creating the *appearance* of a problem to be solved – in this case the welfare/migration nexus. Aspects of the Brexit vote have sometimes been understood as a values conflict between the 'left behind' and a more distant liberal elite (Goodwin and Heath 2016), but we should not neglect the way such conflict was actively fuelled by a discourse and policy intended to shore up *support* for Remain. The outcome of the referendum in areas of economic deprivation thus amounted to a perverse effect of so forcefully pitting free movement in Europe against the interests of domestic welfare recipients, all in a bid to reform but remain within the EU.

Though it addresses a peculiarly British phenomenon, the analysis offered here presents some points that could prove of wider significance. It illustrates the political volatility that can develop when internal inequality, falling living standards, identity, and sovereignty are in play, and when immigration is perceived or presented as a crisis issue. A popular call for national policies that speak to these concerns potentially undermines the scope for cohesion at EU level, and the whole combination is ripe for exploitation by appeal to a national group or groups who feel that their interests are not well represented. The account above points to the ease with which political discourse can override empirical data, the significance of political rhetoric in shaping how problems are perceived and tackled (see Munch 2012), and the ready availability of migrants as a focal point for discontent. The role of political rhetoric in boundary drawing and the resultant emergence of contestable margins in policy design and implementation is taken up in the next chapter.

4

Reconfiguring Rights: Boundaries, Behaviours, and Contestable Margins

The present chapter extends the civic stratification analysis to incorporate the treatment of non-EEA nationals, as well as Britain's response to the refugee crisis of 2015 that preceded the 2016 referendum on EU membership. It moves on from the focus on discourse in the previous chapter to map the contours of rights in their concrete designations across the three fields of domestic welfare, migration, and asylum, and to analyse the associations between welfare, conditionality, and control in each area. Though Shutes (2016) does not explicitly engage the concept of civic stratification, she does offer an additional refinement that builds on the work of Clasen and Clegg (2007) to show how *categories* of inclusion and exclusion, *circumstances* of eligibility, and requirements of *conduct* differentially affect entitlement for various groups of both citizens and migrants. The present chapter goes a step further by directing attention to the boundary-drawing at play in the stratified system of entitlement, its underpinning rationale, and the problematic outcomes it has produced.

Retaining a focus on social rights, we now advance the argument so far to show that the more complex the classifications in play, and the more severe their boundary implications, the more likely they are to generate contestable margins. This chapter therefore examines the key boundary issues that emerge across the entire welfare–migration–asylum regime; a concluding section will reflect on what is revealed by viewing welfare, migration, and asylum within the same conceptual frame. However, before embarking on such analysis, we should look to two additional theorists, whose work can complement and amplify a civic stratification approach.

BATTLEFIELDS OF CHANGE

The changes that have characterized austerity Britain offer a distinctive instance of what Munch (2012) has termed the 'liberal competition state', a model of inclusion based on the 'cult of the individual' and entailing a shift 'from collective national welfare to individualised trans-national and national inclusion' (1). In this model, Munch points to the extension of opportunity beyond the nation and to a potential breakdown of 'insider/outsider morality', noting that such transnational economic integration is closely associated with the rise of global society under the auspices of human rights and related requirements of responsible statehood. However, Munch also recognizes that formalized rights of freedom and equality are prioritized over substantive social rights, such that the opening of society and economy to the outside generates fiercer competition for scarce goods on the inside (Munch 2012, 4).

To capture the unfolding welfare dynamic, he identifies four 'battlefields' that combine in the production of change – the economic, solidaristic, symbolic (rhetorical), and institutional – which respectively address changes in the global division of labour, the underpinning structures of welfare solidarity, rhetorical struggles over legitimizing continuity or change, and institutional adjustments that may eventually refashion core principles. He argues that these battlefields interact in a process fraught with contestation that can lead to varied outcomes and hence requires empirical investigation.

An important feature of Munch's model is that political rhetoric can shape how problems are perceived and tackled and thus becomes manifest in the nature and shape of institutional change. His argument echoes the concerns of Mary Douglas (1986), who more than thirty years ago addressed the question of 'how institutions think' and identified institutionalized systems of classification as central to this function. So institutions think – or, better stated, carry meaning – through the distinctions that underpin their administrative procedures, shaping the contours of society and potentially also popular conceptions of social divisions in the process. One instance of this complex can be found in the central role assumed by welfare systems in the management of global economic change, both through enhanced 'activation' of citizens and through selective entry and entitlement for migrants (Düvell and Jordan 2002; Shutes 2016), described in the previous chapter as a distinctive moral economy.

Recognition of the control dimension of social rights is by no means new (see Bommes and Geddes 2000; Sainsbury 2012; Dwyer 2014; Shutes 2016), but Munch's framework draws attention to how political rhetoric is translated into the details of policy and practice, thus contributing to our understanding of the nature and process of welfare state change. Douglas sees such translation as raising epistemological issues concerning both the generation of a social system of knowledge and the hold that institutions have on processes of classification and recognition. Each of these insights has implications for our understanding and analysis of a system of civic stratification, respectively pointing to its supporting political rhetoric and to its role in shaping differential positions of entitlement and desert through a related process of boundary-drawing.

In similar vein, Hitlin and Vasey (2013) have written of a 'new sociology of morality' that approaches social divisions and policy initiatives in terms of symbolic boundaries and cognitive schema, while Anderson (2013) has addressed such issues in relation to both welfare and migration by reference to the idea of a 'community of value'. She argues that in creating rather than reflecting differential status positions, laws on citizenship and migration have both a juridical and normative dimension, such that the community of value is defined from the outside by the non-citizen and from the inside by the failed citizen (Anderson 2013, 4). Viewing these categories through the same lens can therefore expose the emergence of a unified normative system in which the organization of welfare and the labour market plays a key role. In austerity Britain the accompanying disciplinary dimension of policy and its behavioural assumptions operate through a system of classification based on a political rhetoric of fairness and responsibility set against a culture of dependency and a defence of the hard-working taxpayer.

According to Douglas, social judgements come ready prepared by our own institutions so and require detailed scrutiny of the categories or labels they produce to 'stabilize the flux of social life' (100). In this process, she argues, institutions create the very distinctions (or boundaries) which they then apply, based on some naturalizing principle that can 'confer the spark of legitimacy' (48). In Munch's model this is achieved when rhetoric establishes a coherent and closed system across several fields, and hence what he terms a distinctive 'paradigm', but such a development will also require a degree of 'fit' within a broader institutional matrix that stretches beyond the national level.

In times of radical change, such compatibility is by no means assured, and attention must therefore turn *both* to how far publicly circulated moral meanings offer a basis for generating and justifying the social classifications shaping civic stratification, *and* to the contestations they generate within their institutional setting; hence the 'institutional battlefield' of Munch's model.

Welfare deservingness theory (van Oorschot et al. 2017) argues that public support for welfare provision is contingent on five criteria – the so-called 'CARIN-criteria' – to justify what constitutes a fair distribution of social resources. These criteria are identified as control, attitude, reciprocity, identity, and need, though it is also recognized (Laenen, Rossetti, and Van Oorschot 2019) that the concrete meaning of these essentially abstract indicators is not fully apparent. They respectively refer to the amount of control and therefore responsibility that claimants have over their situation, their attitude in terms of willingness to assume responsibility, their general contribution toward the system, their position in relation to 'belongingness', and their level of material need. However, perceptions of each of these criteria and their hierarchical ordering are open to change, manipulation, and negotiation. We see in the examples to follow that all are implicated in the battle over who gets what from the welfare state.

This chapter thus focuses on Munch's fourth 'battlefield' of change – the institutional, as manifest in Britain's reconfigured system of social rights – and the formal contestation it has provoked. The 'institutional' context here refers both to welfare provision itself[1] – as it extends across the fields of domestic entitlement, migration, and asylum – and to official avenues of formal contestation, variously including parliamentary review, policy consultation, and judicial scrutiny. The chapter has three main sections that respectively consider key developments in the fields of domestic welfare, migration, and asylum. Applying the conceptual insights set out earlier to each measure, it identifies the following: the emergent pattern of stratified rights; its justificatory rationale; the boundaries at issue; and the contentious nature of the distinctions in play. It outlines the problematic nature of the distinctions that operate within the 'institutional battlefield' and provides a summary discussion of contestable margins for each of the three policy fields. In each field we find a justificatory rhetoric of 'fairness', an attack on welfare dependency, and related assumptions of abuse, all deployed in an elaborate exercise of boundary-drawing geared to the erosion of social rights. These features then contribute to the construction of an emergent welfare paradigm in which we find recurrent problems that cut across different policy areas.

RECONFIGURING DOMESTIC WELFARE – BOUNDARIES AND BEHAVIOURS

In the decade of austerity, a rhetoric of 'fairness' to the hard-working taxpayer has reconfigured conceptions of solidarity and refashioned the function and design of the welfare system. The underpinning rationale is captured by this statement: 'if you refuse to work we will not let you live off the hard work of others' (Cameron 2010); as well as by claims that a robust set of sanctions will end the 'something for nothing culture' (Duncan Smith 2013, 2014a). In Douglas's terms, the supporting epistemology sees dependency as a behavioural choice that is rooted in a cultural predisposition and amenable to individualized, disciplinary correction (see Adler 2016). The boundaries thereby generated are part of an intensified system of civic stratification built around the compulsion to work, imposed by heightened degrees of conditionality and enforced by cuts and financial sanctions. Informed by Munch's approach, we see a connecting chain that runs from rhetoric through solidarity to policy and programme design so as to shape a stratified structure of desert that has cast its net ever wider, generating boundary problems and contestable margins that then feature in the institutional battlefield.

Out of Work and In-Work Conditionality

In Lockwood's (1996, 539) model, welfare dependency constructs a group 'lacking in civic virtue', while that group itself is stratified by various degrees of desert. The enhanced scope and severity of conditions and sanctions then amount to a further elaboration. The highest level of conditionality – by *conduct* – has targeted the unemployed, requiring proof of work-seeking before registration and enforced by a 'claimant commitment' that has intensified job-search requirements. Fearful claimants already commit to conditions they know they cannot fulfil, but requirements under UC have risen to thirty-five hours of job search a week (WPC 2015, 26), and are accompanied by a detailed monitoring of claimants' efforts. The boundaries at issue are manifest through financial sanctions for failure to comply, and the intensified regime introduced by the 2012 Welfare Reform Act (see

DWP 2013) operated at three levels of severity, depending on type and frequency of offence, with sanctions lasting from a minimum of four weeks to a maximum of three years (compared to a prior range of one to twenty-six weeks). A further substratum has also operated through the Work Programme, which Webster (2016) has described as a sanctions-generating machine.[2] In the face of mounting criticism, the three-year sanction was abolished as of October 2019 (Butler 2019a), but the elevated requirements and conditions remain in place, though they were stalled when the coronavirus brought a temporary end to face-to-face reporting requirements.

The boundary-drawing embedded in this stratified system has been subjected to critical scrutiny over an extended period. The most troubling early finding (Oakley 2014) for a scheme seeking behavioural change was the high proportion of sanctioned claimants who lacked any clear understanding of why a sanction had been applied. Within the institutional battlefield, official reviews (AO 2016; PAC 2017; WPC 2015; JCHR 2011) have variously noted a lack of evidence to show that sanctions work, the need for a clearer distinction between active abuse and significant effort, and the scope for as many as eight different categories among those affected. All of this highlights the problematic nature of the boundaries at issue. The same reviews express concern about inconsistent and poor-quality decision-making and the impact of sanctions on debt, rent arrears, homelessness, and destitution. They have criticized the paucity of formal monitoring of outcomes (WPC 2015, 22), highlighted the inadequacy of official data (NAO 2016), and cited evidence that some people have been driven out of the system without work (Loopstra et al. 2015), such that the justifying rationale begins to crumble.

Yet a new stratum of civic stratification has been planned under UC, and conditionality is being trialled for extension[3] via the construal of low-wage supplements as a form of 'entrenched dependency' (DWP 2010), which could extend the sanctions regime to low-paid workers. The boundaries of desert would thus be redrawn, and in Douglas's terms, this epistemological shift reveals an ambiguity in the early promise to 'make work pay' (DWP 2010; 2010a), as supplements to the wage are eroded (CPAG 2017). The proposed threshold for freedom from conditionality and a requirement to seek additional earnings is to be set at thirty-five hours per week at the national minimum wage, and the underlying rationale implies abuse in addressing a 'perverse incentive' for claimants to restrict their hours and pay (WPC 2016).

Support for the low paid was therefore drawn into conceptions of dependency culture and became a target for cuts in the 2015 summer budget. As a result, cuts to in-work benefit via a reduced income threshold, together with frozen rates, an increased withdrawal rate against earnings, and reductions in the disregarded 'work allowance' meant an average yearly loss of £960 for couples with children and £2,380 for single parents (CPAG 2017). These cuts met opposition in the House of Lords, where they were described as 'morally indefensible' (Sparrow 2015), and drew a caution from the WPC (2015) that they contradicted the objective of making work pay. Effectively shrinking the category of desert, these cuts were averted for tax credits (TCS) but were initially to remain in place for the rollout of UC. Though restoring the cuts would in theory increase incentives to work, conditionality and sanctions were instead set to perform this function. Thus the shifting meaning of 'make work pay' had seemingly come to rest on individual accountability and heightened conditionality enforceable by sanctions.

Against this rationale, the WPC (2016) cited evidence that the problem was structural, not motivational; and several organizations found a disproportionate impact on the disabled and on families with children (CPAG 2017; Schmuecker 2017). In the face of such argument, the 2018 budget announced a restoration of work allowances (effectively increasing income by £630 per year) for those with dependent children or limited capacity for work, though not for the fully fit and childless. Other cuts were set to remain in place, until the coronavirus crisis of March 2020 prompted an increase of £1,000 a year (for one year) in the personal allowance for UC and Working Tax Credit, but not for other legacy benefits. This compares but poorly to the subsidy of £2,500 per worker per month available to businesses to help them retain their workers through the crisis, thus introducing a further element of stratification.

Distinctions of desert have also extended to family size in that assumptions about behavioural choice and a rhetoric of 'fairness' underpin the restriction of Child Tax Credits (CTCS) to two children per family. Paid both to low-paid and workless families, CTC has been limited to ensure that recipients 'face the same financial choices about having children as those supporting themselves solely through work' (Summer Budget 2015 HC 264 105–16, para 1.145). The limit has been criticized (Kennedy, Bate, and Keen 2017) as punishing children for the situation of a parent, and complex exemptions have been necessary for non-consensual births, multiple births, and children adopted from care. The limitation on exemptions for kinship (non-parental) care has been ruled unlawful, but a broader challenge to the overall policy was dismissed (*sc and Ors v sswp* [2018] EWHC 864 (Admin)). Recourse to the Court of Appeal also failed (*sc and Ors* [2019] EWCA Civ 615), though the court noted a conflict between 'the value attached to a child's own interests and the value attached to parental choice and responsibility' (para. 156). The Supreme Court judgement from a hearing in October 2020 is awaited.

In sum, domestic welfare has sought to incentivize work through forms of conditionality built on behavioural and motivational assumptions, while also deploying cuts and sanctions in a disciplinary system that has extended the scope of civic stratification. This has generated boundary problems concerning the attribution of personal responsibility, the erosion of guaranteed minimums, a disproportionate impact on the vulnerable, and negative effects for children. Despite related concerns raised by institutional scrutiny, the UC system is piloting a more far-reaching conditionality and sanctions regime to take in supplements to low pay (Webster 2017), and is scheduled to report in the course of 2022. Such a move would redraw the boundaries of desert while also supplying compliant labour for a 'flexible' labour market (see Dean 2012).

Capability and Caring

Stratified conditions of entitlement have also focused on Employment and Support Allowance (ESA) for the long-term sick and disabled, based on a pre-existing distinction between the Support Group, which is free from conditions, and the Work Related Activity Group (WRAG), which has limited capability for work. Placed at a lower level of conditionality than the unemployed, the latter are not compelled to seek employment, though they are subject to 'work readiness' requirements, with sanctions for non-compliance. This classification, however, rests on a controversial Work Capability Assessment (WCA).[4] Furthermore, until 2017, the WRAG received a supplement to JSA rates of £29.05 per week, though in 2012 sanctions for this group were increased from 50 per cent of that supplement to 100 per cent of the basic allowance from inception (Graham 2013; Kennedy, Murphy, and Wilson 2016). In 2017 the supplement itself was abolished, thus intensifying the impact of a sanction; the move was claimed to address 'the financial incentive that could otherwise discourage claimants from taking steps back to work', a claim described by one MP as an 'ill-founded fantasy' (Murphy and Keen 2016).

Problematic boundaries and formal contestation have again been in evidence. The WRAG cut was resisted in the House of Lords (Murphy and Keen 2016) on the grounds that there was no evidence of a disincentive-to-work effect, that it would impede efforts to find work, and that it would have perverse health effects. The rebellion was averted by attaching a 'financial privilege' to the bill; even so, the crude boundary on which the cut was based has been questioned (Murphy and Keen 2016; Griffiths and Patterson 2014), and the WCA has been discredited for poor decision-making, a high success rate on appeal (Parkin 2015),[5] and rising costs (NAO 2016a). The classification process has itself been challenged: the Court of Appeal (*MM and DM v SSHD* [2013] EWCA Civ 1565) found under the 2010 Equality Act that assessments had unlawfully discriminated against people with mental health problems, and the Upper Tribunal (*CJ and SG v SSWP* [2017] UKUT 0324) ruled that a one-month time limit on the right to appeal was unlawful, and particularly affected claimants with mental health problems or learning disabilities.

Single parents, another group traditionally subject to lighter conditionality, have been exposed to a shifting boundary that can now require work-seeking when the youngest child is age three (reduced from five in 2017), thus shrinking the category of carer (Dwyer 2014). This shrinkage has limited the scope for challenge to the benefit cap – the stratifying device introduced in 2013 that sets a limit on the total benefit a household can receive[6] – again with the aim of restoring 'fairness' to the taxpayer (DWP 2015a) and justified as improving work incentives, itself a contested claim (Ball 2013). There are exemptions for claimants in receipt of WTCS (or engaged in 16-plus hours' work under UC) or disability-related benefits, but not for the WRAG. Despite ongoing criticism (WPC 2019c), the cap encompasses single parents who are not required to work.

The carer/worker distinction proved problematic for the non-exemption of households with full-time carers in receipt of carer's allowance. This was successfully challenged in the High Court (*Hurley and Ors v SSWP* [2015] EWHC 3382) for discriminating against disabled people, and the judge found the term 'workless' as applied to such households to be offensive (para. 28). The constraints of caring responsibilities are also salient for single parents and were addressed in the court intervention by CPAG (*SG and Ors v SSWP* [2015] UKSC 16) discussed in Chapter 1. The charge of gender discrimination failed, though some judges expressed concern about non-compliance with the UNCRC; even so, the case is instructive in pointing to the different boundary issues in play. The comparison with families on an average wage discounted the benefits available to such families (CB, CTC, and HB), but even this rationale was breached when the cap was lowered in 2017. The cap has a disproportionate effect on lone parents, which partly explains why even under the reduced cap only 18 per cent of those affected were required to be actively seeking work (WPC 2019a). Finally, since some payments included in the cap are intended to support children, reductions of total benefit income are not an appropriate means of establishing a work incentive for their parents. When a further challenge targeted the reduced cap on behalf of lone parents (regardless of gender) with a child under two, it initially succeeded on discrimination regarding the right to family and private life (Article 8, ECHR). However, a ruling from the Supreme Court (*DA and Ors v SSWP* [2019] UKSC 21) found by a majority of five to two that the measure was not manifestly without reasonable foundation.

Thus, while the disabled and single parents occupy a position of lower conditionality within the system of civic stratification, this protection has been eroded by enhanced conditions of conduct for the WRAG and by the lowered age of the youngest child for work-seeking requirements. Underpinned by sanctions for both groups and exacerbated by the benefit cap, this has meant an attendant shift in conceptions of desert, and meanwhile the boundaries in play have generated scope for challenge in relation to the treatment of mental ill-health and the carer/worker divide. Evidence of improved employment outcomes remains weak (WPC 2015; Kennedy, Murphy, and Wilson 2016).

Contestable Margins

Drawing on Munch, Lockwood, and Douglas, we see that within the institutional battlefield the principles of stratified conditionality have been pre-set by the epistemological assumptions underpinning welfare policy. Challenge has been at the margins of boundary-drawing within this constraint and has variously turned on inconsistent and unreliable decision-making, the ambiguity of 'make work pay', and questionable distinctions between fit/unfit, carer/worker, and adult/child.

Institutional scrutiny has addressed these aspects of ideological over-reach, ostensibly based on enforcement to work but placing inappropriate pressure on those with mental ill-health, while also drawing the unfit, carers, and children into their ambit. Most contestation has been procedural in form, as with official reviews of the sanctions regime, but more far-reaching challenge occurs when internationally grounded guarantees can be engaged. Key examples are discrimination in relation to mental health or the well-being of children, and in this regard, the Equality Act and/or the ECHR have had the most purchase. A questioning of the construal of dependency in relation to 'make work pay' stands as an exception in addressing justificatory principles and has had some effect, but the more general problems of declining living standards, the collapse of minimum guarantees, punitive destitution, and the compulsion to take insecure work in a 'flexible' labour market have for the most part gone uncorrected. The denigrating implications of policy for the moral standing of claimants on occasion come to light, but without a broader epistemological battle about the meaning and content of a moral vision for welfare, the edifice remains largely intact.

CIVIC STRATIFICATION AND MIGRATION – THRESHOLDS, LIMITS, AND EXCLUSIONS

The logic just documented has also been applied to the management of migration, and the transnational extension of opportunity that features in Munch's model is tightly delimited in the British case. Again, we see stratified rights deployed as a means of social control, a supporting rationale citing behaviours and abuse, and shrinking boundaries of entitlement justified by 'fairness' to the taxpayer (Cameron 2013, 2014a). Outside of permanent settlement, conditions of *category* for non-EEA migrants have long specified 'no recourse to public funds' (NRPF), and this normally precludes access for five years, sometimes for ten (Kennedy 2015). However, migrant stratification starts before this, with distinctions of both *category* and *circumstance* intended to forestall recourse to benefits through a filtering system on entry, in which familiar key principles apply.

Thresholds of Inclusion and Exclusion

In April 2011, annual limits were imposed on certain visa categories and new maximum lengths of stay were introduced for some workers.

Other changes included closure of the low-skilled visa category, the right to entry for job search for highly skilled migrants, and a faster route to permanency for individuals of high net worth (Gower 2015). Skilled worker visas were restricted to graduate level at a salary threshold of £20,800 for 'new entrants' but £30,000 for experienced workers. A minimum salary of £35,000 was introduced for permanent settlement,[7] and this created some boundary problems regarding shortage occupations (Politowski and Gower 2016), with many nurses and teachers earning below this threshold – and note that reliance on migrant health workers and 'low skilled' carers has been dramatically demonstrated by the impact of COVID-19. In fact, the salary threshold for settlement was quietly lowered to £25,600 from December 2020 (Busby 2020).

Income thresholds are a form of conditionality by *circumstance*, in that they limit access for those who might become a charge on the state. The 2012 immigration rules made this explicit in relation to an increase in the minimum income requirement (MIR) to £18,600 for non-EEA partner visas (with further additions for children). The MIR reflects the amount required for maintenance 'without becoming a burden on the taxpayer', and recognition of resources in addition to the applicants' income was initially very narrow. Part of a broader objective to 'bring a sense of fairness back to the immigration system' (*MM v SSHD* [2013] EWHC 1900), the MIR echoes the rationale of welfare reform, and the probationary period excluding partners from public funds was extended in 2012 from two years to five. Despite this extension, the MIR as set was one that 40 to 45 per cent of UK workers would fail (Gower 2014, 11), though the Migration Advisory Committee (MAC), in recommending possible thresholds, stated that they were based solely on economic considerations and not 'wider legal, social or moral issues' (Gower 2014, 4). Nonetheless, the minister responsible stated that 'family life must not be established in the UK at the taxpayer's expense and family migrants must be able to integrate' (see Yeo 2014). The boundary was therefore drawn with reference to purely economic criteria and the underlying rationale is reflected in the Home Office (2012) Impact Assessment.

Following Douglas, we find an underpinning epistemology that sees contribution and integration in financial terms and that stratifies access to the national territory and the right to family life[8] by income, despite recognition that this has a disproportionate impact on members of low-paid minorities, and on women (*MM and Ors v SSHD* [2013] EWHC para 113–4). These boundaries have been contested within the institutional battlefield, but government justification in terms of policy objectives was upheld by three judgements (from the High Court, the Court of Appeal, and the Supreme Court). None of these ruled that the MIR could be struck down, though the High Court noted a disproportionate impact on British citizens and refugees (*MM and Ors v SSHD* [2013] EWHC paras. 13, 16). Crucially, however, the rules were deemed unlawful in that they failed to address the best interests of the child (para. 92), and the court saw an argument for considering the prospective earnings of an incoming spouse and verifiable third-party support in such cases (paras. 95–8). The revised rules (Desira 2017) now allow consideration of other sources of income under a ten-year route to settlement when 'exceptional circumstances' are in play, which raises further boundary questions.

The MIR thus stratifies access to family (re)unification for both British citizens and settled non-EEA migrants on the basis of income, and justified by 'fairness'. It raises boundary problems in relation to the consideration of additional resources, acknowledged discriminatory effects on minorities and women, and putative distinctions between citizens and refugees, and voluntary migrants. The contested rule eventually met a barrier in relation to domestic and international guarantees on the best interests of children. As with the benefit cap, the government and courts again had to grapple with an aspect of civic stratification whereby a child may suffer due to the circumstances of the parent.

Migrants and Welfare Rights

Migrant access to benefits has been more directly stratified through the pledge to address 'the magnetic pull of Britain's benefits system' on migration (Cameron 2014a), for which MAC (2014) has argued there is little evidence. Since non-EEA migrants do not have access to benefits until they achieve permanent residence, attention has focused on EEA migrants, and here we find stratified entitlement based on behavioural assumptions of abuse, designed to make Britain 'a less attractive place for EU migrants who want to come here and try to live off the state' (Dominiczak 2013). Free movement regulations under EU law grant three months' automatic residence as well as equal treatment for *workers* with respect to Social Security (Directive 2004/38/EC), though Brexit will mean longer-term changes. Meanwhile, Britain has stretched to the maximum permitted constraints on EEA workers benefit rights.

The changes were reviewed in Chapter 3, but briefly put, stratifying measures since 2014 (Kennedy 2015b) have limited new jobseekers to three months' JSA and removed eligibility for HB, CB, and CTCS, while EEA workers who become unemployed are limited to six months' JSA and thereafter could lose their worker status.[9] The minimum earnings threshold that was introduced to guide the definition of 'worker' has affected potential access to other benefits and is especially likely to penalize single parents (O'Brien 2015). However, the boundaries at issue have been undermined by official sources that show EEA nationals do not disproportionately claim benefits (Keen and Turner 2016). Nevertheless, the Upper Tribunal (*MB and Ors v SSWP* [2016] UKUT, 372 AAC para 57) noted a risk of exceeding EU case law, such that British guidance may 'all too easily result in raising the bar above the level ... found to be required' for a real prospect within a reasonable period. So here we see institutional challenge at the margins but without a full assault on the whittling away of jobseeker rights.

O'Brien (2015, 130) has described the whole package of change as 'back-door treaty tinkering, at odds with the aims and spirit of EU integration', though as we have observed this is itself a shifting field (see Barbulescu and Favell 2019). The UK restrictions represented a step back from the 'opening up of society to the outside' (Munch 2012) and drew boundaries that constrained any emergent post-national regime under EU law, while effecting a creeping withdrawal from minimum guarantees. We saw stratifying moves towards a conception of social security as an individualized rather than mutual form of insurance (O'Brien 2015), and an increasingly restrictive definition of worker status. The boundary-drawing entailed amounted to an extreme instance of conditionality, bordering on exclusion, and eroding the generalized reciprocity that welfare systems ideally offer, while benefiting from the availability of labour.

A further extension of civic stratification arises from an ECJ judgement (*Zambrano v ONEM* C-34/09) that created a right to work and reside for a non-EEA parent (a Zambrano carer), as required to give meaning to the status of minor-age citizens of a member-state in their national home. This ruling triggered the possibility of a benefit claim, but in November 2012 Zambrano carers were recognized in UK domestic law with the purpose of excluding them from income-based benefits. This boundary of exclusion was challenged but upheld in *Sanneh and Ors v SSWP* [2015] EWCA Civ 49 and *HC v SSWP* [2017] UKSC 73 by virtue of support available under S17 of the 1989

Children Act, provided at minimal levels by local authorities (LAS), and described as a skeletal right for a group constructed as tolerated aliens (O'Brien 2016). The DWP (2012) impact assessment cites a familiar rationale – fairness to the taxpayer, a reduced incentive to come and live off the state, and the allocation of public funds to those having the greatest connection with the UK. It is also argued that the restriction ensures that non-EEA migrants wishing to have children must first secure sufficient funds (Sanneh, para. 96); further justification (para. 97) states that the message is directed not just at Zambrano carers but at a wider audience, and in this sense it has a broader rhetorical function.

The ruling not only affects the responsible parent but also permits a lesser stratum of entitlement for some British children, who are thereby held below mainstream subsistence levels. This boundary discriminates against Zambrano children in relation to other UK nationals, and though formally contested has been deemed justifiable in policy terms. We should also note that as of 2012, non-EEA parents granted leave to remain on human rights grounds have been debarred from recourse to public funds unless exacting exceptional circumstances pertain (Woolley 2019). Official guidance on when the condition should be lifted, or not imposed, has now been ruled unlawful (*W (by litigation friend J) v SSHD* [2020] EWHC 1299 (Admin)). A key issue here was whether the claimant must already be suffering destitution, or could simply show that this was imminent. In concluding the latter, the judge identified a failure in the guidance to identify the legal duty to provide support where necessary to avoid inhuman and degrading treatment (para. 71).

Contestable Margins

In sum, we again see stratified rights, boundary problems, and formal contestation, but also a holding back from challenge to underpinning assumptions. In the case of the MIR, the institutional battle has been played out in the courts, with only marginal success, and outside of limiting factors the Supreme Court endorses a cost/benefit approach to family life. This allows a conception of welfare that draws stratified lines of exclusion against overseas partners of both British citizens and non-EEA residents, justified by conceptions of fairness and responsibility. The UKSC judgement raises few questions as to whose interests immigration policy should serve; contrast this with the family unification rights of those exercising free movement under EU law, to which an MIR does not apply. The restrictions on EEA benefit claims represented a further elaboration of conditionality as well as an excessive form of individualization that could bode ill for future domestic welfare provision (O'Brien 2015) while also eroding equal treatment guarantees – now to be disbanded under Brexit. The Zambrano ruling echoes issues familiar from challenges to the benefit cap, though children are not placed at the centre of the case, since benefits are paid on their behalf to their carers. In this respect, the boundary in play does not accord children themselves equal treatment, and again punishes a child for the circumstances of their parent(s), an issue that recurs in relation to the NRPF condition. Each of these examples has prompted recourse to international standards in the scrutiny of state actions, but as highlighted in Munch's model, institutional challenge has had only marginal success, repeatedly meeting the force of national constraint over access to public funds and sovereign control.

STRATIFYING ASYLUM – DESERT, DETERRENCE, AND DESTITUTION

Asylum seekers are a group seemingly outside of conditionality. They are exercising an absolute right to seek asylum and are not required (or indeed permitted) to work before at best a twelve-month wait. Yet they have been more than ever subject to stratified boundaries, resource constraints, and contested exclusions aimed at behavioural change, as Britain has met the refugee crisis in Europe with a strategy of isolationism, resettlement as opposed to spontaneous arrival (May 2015), and safe return reviews for recognized refugees (Home Office 2017).

Good and Bad Asylum-Seekers

Public reaction to the drowning of three-year-old Alan Kurdi (Smith 2015) prompted an expansion of the Syrian Vulnerable Persons Resettlement scheme and an additional commitment to resettle 3,000 children and families from the region, initially under Humanitarian Protection but from March 2017 with full recognition on arrival. Furthermore, a reluctant amendment (the Dubs amendment) to the 2016 Immigration Act committed the government – though dogged by fears of a 'pull factor' (McGuiness 2017, 16) – to take an unspecified number of unaccompanied minors from within Europe. That number was limited in 2017 to 480 (Elgot 2017), and while a small number of minors were also resettled under accelerated Dublin principles, that scheme has now closed. Indeed, the incoming Conservative government of 2019 has removed a commitment to facilitate family unification for unaccompanied minor-age asylum-seekers in Europe from the EU withdrawal act (Walker 2020).

A stratified distinction has emerged between those selected for resettlement and those claiming asylum on arrival 'after abusing the system' (May 2015). It is argued that the latter 'false' claims deprive those in genuine need, and the supporting rationale again rests on a discourse of abuse; thus, boundaries of desert are drawn between the more vulnerable candidates for resettlement (amenable to control) and 'the wealthiest, luckiest and strongest', who make spontaneous (uncontrolled) claims.[10] A distinction based on worth is thus established by mode of arrival, and here is an epistemology that in Douglas's terms creates its own reality. Visa regimes and carrier sanctions make entry by legal means all but impossible, rendering most asylum-seekers 'abusers' – a distinction undermined by poor decision-making and success on appeal (APPG 2017, 8). Boundary-drawing by mode of arrival filters through to a stratified reception system, which has been the focus of critical comment by the APPG, which reports that resettled refugees are better supported when accessing mainstream benefits and the labour market, while 'spontaneous' arrivals suffer a deficit in both areas.

The Asylum Support System

Stratified standards of maintenance have provoked a further boundary issue, one that has been manifest in judicial deliberation over levels of support for asylum-seekers (*Refugee Action v SSHD* [2014] EWHC 1033). In 1999 the asylum support rate was set at 70 per cent of Income Support (IS), and it increased in line with this until 2008, when the link was broken (para. 17). In 2011 the rate was frozen at 51 per cent of IS for single adults but 81 per cent for children, and in 2014 was subjected to legal challenge by Refugee Action. The Home Office (HO) defended the need to demonstrate 'fairness' to the taxpayer (para. 26), claiming erroneously that rates had risen 11.5 per cent over the preceding five years. Noting this error, the judge ruled that there had been a failure to gather sufficient information for a rational judgement. However, the HO recalculation justified the existing rate, defended by the view that an increase could encourage spurious asylum claims, thus 'clogging up the system' and impeding support for those with a genuine fear of persecution (Grice 2015).

The previous year, a parliamentary inquiry (2013) had addressed the same boundary issues, arguing that levels should not fall below 70 per cent of IS, and noting that current levels of support for children did not meet their essential living needs. Indeed, higher rates had earlier been endorsed by the HO as protecting the best interests of the child (see *Refugee Action v SSHD*, para 27). However, adjustments in 2015 further reduced support by standardizing weekly rates at £36.95 per person, thus ending preferential support for children and single parents (Home Office 2015b). A follow-up challenge (*Ghulam and Ors v SSHD* [2016] EWHC 2639) failed, with no permission to appeal.

As with the benefit cap, there were boundary concerns about eroding children's entitlement on the basis of parental status, which might well breach child welfare guarantees. However, the judge (paras. 241–2) held that what was required was merely the provision of a minimum dignified standard of living and that a difference between asylum support and IS rates was justified by the legitimate purpose of discouraging economic migration and protecting limited resources against spending in excess of obligations.

Failed Asylum-Seekers and Undocumented Migrants

Measures in the 2016 Immigration Act are designed to further stratify support for failed asylum-seekers. By the end of 2020, however, these had yet to be fully implemented. Nevertheless, the thinking behind them displays behavioural assumptions concerning the motivations of claimants, a rationale of deterrence, and contested boundary-drawing, and the justifications offered are revealing. In the system established under the 1999 Asylum and Immigration Act, failed asylum-seekers with children continue in receipt of S95 support. This is set to be curtailed, and provision for childless failed asylum-seekers and other categories of migrant under s4 of the 1999 Act are to be withdrawn. The rationale is that failed asylum-seekers are illegal migrants and should no longer receive preferential treatment, which 'sends entirely the wrong message' and 'undermines public confidence' (Home Office 2015, 3). A government factsheet on the measures (Home Office 2016b) states that 'people who do not need our help and who refuse to return home are here illegally', while those who can and should leave cannot expect to be supported by the taxpayer in making themselves 'intentionally destitute' by refusal to depart (Home Office 2015, 8; 2016, 11). There is particular emphasis (Home Office 2015a, 11; 2016, 10) that neither the lifting of the reservation on the UNCRC (s55 of the 2009 Borders, Citizenship and Immigration Act) nor local authority obligations require that a family be supported where it decides to remain unlawfully. So destitution emerges as the lowest rung on the civic stratification ladder.

However, under measures in the 2016 Act, the scope of s95 support for asylum-seekers is to be expanded to those with further submissions on protection grounds or a judicial review (JR) outstanding (Gower, Pyper, and Wilson 2015, s6), and a new s95A will support failed asylum-seekers who are destitute and who can show a *genuine obstacle* to leaving. This requirement is difficult to meet, and the onus of proof will shift from the HO to the claimant, with no right of appeal (Home Office 2016). Accusations that the outcome could be destitution and the creation of a new client group for local authority support (Harvey and Harper 2017) led to a late amendment diverting recourse to s17 through a scheme governed by HO regulations under 10A schedule 3 of the 2002 Nationality Immigration and Asylum Act (Home Office 2016). Incorporating conditionality by conduct, this applies to *families* who are ineligible for s95A but who are cooperating with departure, or who have an ongoing non-asylum application or appeal, or where necessary for the welfare of a child. It also encompasses migrant families excluded from mainstream support (e.g., Zambrano carers), while 10B will cater for 'adult' migrant care leavers with an outstanding non-asylum application or appeal, or whose appeal rights have been exhausted but who are judged to require support. Other care leavers without status will be denied the local authority route to care-leaving provision, which is intended for those 'with a long-term future in the UK' (Home Office 2016).

These stratifying measures are attempts to draw a clearer line between asylum-seekers and failed asylum-seekers, while blurring the boundary between the latter and those unlawfully present and seeking to delimit the scope for their support. HO consultation on these measures has been the principle site of institutional contestation, and one response queried whether it would be acceptable to the HO for refused asylum families to be left destitute and visibly homeless on the streets (Local Government Association et al. 2015), arguing that central and local government cannot simply be absolved of their duty of care to vulnerable children. Local authorities remain obliged under s 17 to assess any child in their area who may be in need, and in recognition of this, local authority support will be allowed while eligibility for HO support is being determined. In fact, the final version of the legislation leaves local authorities' human rights duties intact as a residual safeguard (Harvey and Harper 2017, 383).

The consultation process generated further criticism, with the Children's Commissioner (2015) arguing that the changes rely on behavioural assumptions that the government's own impact assessment recognizes are hard to evidence (Home Office 2016a). This would mean putting children at risk in spurious expectation of change from their parents and was thought to conflict with both the UNCRC and s 55 of 2009 Act. The lack of appeal is also contentious, since refusals involve boundary judgements not just about destitution but also about fitness to travel, reasonable steps to leave, and barriers to leaving – all of which are viewed as 'straightforward matters of fact' by the Home Office (2015a, 8).[11]

Restrictions on care-leaving raise a boundary problem regarding stratified support for minors, as well as when state responsibility should come to an end. This has provoked argument that the restrictions undermine protections in the Children Act for children leaving care and could contravene the UNCRC. This has been viewed as inconsistent with the aim that care-leavers should enter life with same life chances as others (Refugee Children's Consortium 2015). The Home Office position, however, is that care-leaver support is not an appropriate vehicle for maintenance pending the departure of 'adult migrants' who have no lawful basis to remain (Home Office 2016). An amendment at third reading made an exception to cover victims of trafficking (NRPF 2016), but the overall outcome will be a stratified system of care-leaving aimed at correcting perceptions that Britain provides generous long-term support for all who arrive as children (Home Office 2016).

Contestable Margins

Asylum policy is characterized by a system of isolationism and exclusion that distinguishes between resettled and spontaneous arrivals, who then experience a two-tier system of reception. For the latter group, a stratified and shrinking system of support reveals a behavioural orientation with the stated aims of discouraging arrivals, promoting a culture of compliance, encouraging voluntary return, and correcting perceptions that are assumed to attract minor-age asylum-seekers to Britain. In line with Munch's comments on responsible statehood, formal contestation has drawn upon a range of international instruments (e.g., the UNCRC, the ECHR, the Charter of Fundamental Rights) as well as domestic law giving expression to international standards,[12] but to little practical effect. In fact, beyond recognition of an objective minimum standard, legal judgements stress that it is not for the courts to determine the level of asylum support (*Ghulam and Ors v SSHD*, paras. 36–7; *Refugee Action v SSHD*, para 3). Boundary problems have turned on the appropriate relationship between minimum standards endorsed in domestic welfare and those required to ensure dignified standards for asylum-seekers. A similar exercise has weighed the degree of support required for unaccompanied minors who enter adulthood with appeal rights exhausted against domestic guarantees for minors leaving care. While institutional contestation has produced some modification at the margins, unsubstantiated assumptions of abuse pervade all measures and immigration control appears to assume priority over relief from destitution and the protection of children.

CONCLUSION:
THE EMERGENT WELFARE PARADIGM

The conditional and disciplinary drive pervading welfare provision in austerity Britain is not of course new, but throughout the austerity decade that began with the Coalition government of 2010, it has been sufficiently extended to amount to what Munch would term an emergent paradigm. He applies this notion when a consistent vocabulary of ideas, concepts, and remedies spills over from one policy area to another, reconfiguring core principles of welfare and inclusion in the process. In the British case, an attack on the 'something for nothing culture', driven by a unifying rhetoric of 'fairness', and set against assumptions of abuse, extends from domestic welfare to migration and asylum to fashion a contraction of social rights across all three fields. Analysis of the related policy measures in the present chapter has further elaborated the civic stratification approach, paying particular attention to the boundary-drawing entailed in this increasingly restrictive dynamic, as informed by Munch's attention to justificatory rhetoric and Douglas's reflections on how institutions 'think'. The argument is also advanced by Munch's battlefield approach, which focuses on the likelihood of struggle around attempts to reconfigure basic tenets of welfare policy. Bringing together these theoretical insights, this chapter has traced the stratifying devices in play for each field, the justificatory rhetoric supporting their deployment, their underpinning assumptions, and the boundary problems and contestable margins that have emerged within the 'institutional battlefield'.

Viewing domestic entitlement, migration, and asylum within the same frame, we can highlight the strategies and rationales apparent across all three fields. Each of the measures discussed deploys civic stratification to structure entitlement by shrinking categories of desert and increasing conditionality. This is then justified by notions of dependency as a behavioural choice, with associated accusations of abuse – variously amenable to discipline, deterrence, or exclusion. In the terms of Munch's model (Munch 2012, 6), we find a welfare approach based on individual achievement and responsibility, in tandem with a rhetorical shift in solidarity that prioritizes protection of the hard-working taxpayer while eroding minimum guarantees. But beyond this picture, as Munch's model foresees, key changes have been subject to institutional contestation via parliamentary review, policy consultation, and judicial scrutiny, drawing on conceptions of responsible statehood and international human rights. Each of the measures discussed rests on problematic boundary-drawing that has in most cases led to formal questioning and challenge within the institutional battlefield, though, notwithstanding some notable successes, this has yielded only marginal adjustment.

However, a focus on the institutional battlefield has also meant that in viewing the three fields together, we are able to identify not only common strategies and rhetoric but also recurrent boundary problems and points of challenge. Against almost every measure there have been charges of inadequate evidence, inconsistent and/or poor decision-making, the creation of destitution in the name of control, discriminatory effects on vulnerable groups, and/or negative impacts on children. Charges of discrimination and a failure to prioritize the welfare of children have had the most purchase in contesting problematic boundary-drawing and challenging its impact at the margins, in part because related protections are underpinned by international guarantees. Given these protections and other institutional sources of contestation, the supporting rationale is never quite securely established. However, much of the institutional battle has been fought on procedural issues that amend aspects of design and implementation but leave the broader rationale and objectives largely intact. Indeed, a number of legal judgements have exercised restraint in ruling on more fundamental challenges to government policy, and 'rational aims' linked to 'legitimate objectives' provide an official last line of defence. A more far-reaching assault on the problems documented here would therefore need to move beyond the confines of the institutional battlefield and look to the rhetorical battlefield on which the justificatory rationale is generated and sustained.

5

Moral Economy from Above and Below: Contesting Contraction of Migrant Rights

MORAL 'ECONOMY' OR 'MORAL' ECONOMY?

The present chapter outlines a moral economy approach as applied to the management of non-EEA migration and asylum. Viewed 'from above', we can identify its underlying objectives and rationale, as well as the principles of conditionality that govern the presence and stay of non-EEA migrants and asylum-seekers. However, expanding on the contestable margins identified in the previous chapter, we also find that policies have been challenged and contested 'from below' by civic activists in terms of their rationality, legality, and morality. We therefore take a closer look at the contestable margins generated by three central aspects of migration policy – family life, welfare and asylum, and support for those without status – alongside the forms of challenge they have provoked. We also consider these developments in the context of an emergent system of total control.

As we have seen, the notion of moral economy has caught the attention of contemporary social scientists and gone through various adaptations in the process, but of particular interest for the present chapter is Fassin's (2005) appropriation of the term to analyse the tension between discourses of compassion and those of repression in the governance of immigration and asylum. We have noted his definition of moral economy as the 'use of emotions and values, and norms and obligations in social space' (Fassin 2009, 18), and Fassin has applied this term to the normative principles through which immigration and asylum are construed and acted upon in policy and practice. He pays particular attention to the 'spaces of exception' that open up in the opposition between humanism and politics and sees the moral economy of our times as stemming from a unique combination of the politics of order and the politics of suffering (Fassin 2005).

In this context, he applies the idea of moral economy to humanitarian concessions that operate at the extreme margins of exclusion to address the vulnerabilities that are often generated by the system itself. However, Fassin also argues more broadly for a need to grasp the '*moral* heart' of immigration and asylum policy (366), asking what values and hierarchies of values are mobilized in a state's management of migration flows and the attendant 'war of words' (378). Fassin (2012) thus calls attention to how moral sentiments have become an essential force in contemporary discourse and argues for an approach that can 'seize morals at the point where they are articulated with politics' (12).

His understanding of moral economy, however, pulls in two directions, potentially referring both to the value frame and classificatory devices that permeate the entire system of migration and asylum management, as well as to humanistic exceptions where 'the tragedy of the modern condition can no longer be eluded' (Fassin 2012, 252). This incipient distinction is apparent in his 'Moral Economies Revisited' (2009a), which ponders the opposite of Thompson's 'moral economy of the poor' to observe that if it *has* an opposite, it would be the moral economy of the masters. In revisiting the concept, he foregrounds the process of shaping moral sentiments and broadens the remit of thinking on moral economy in a manner that chimes with arguments from Booth (1994) and others (Sayer 2007; Clarke and Newman 2012), to the effect that all economies are moral economies, in that all are supported by an underpinning value frame.

However, Fassin (2009, 18) goes further to note a shift of emphasis in recent debate, away from a traditional 'moral *economy*' approach and toward an alternative '*moral* economy', thus suggesting that economic primacy may be countered by moral principles. A focus on the production or evocation of moral sentiments can then support Fassin's (2009) further claim that moral economies are unstable and fluid realities, traversed by tensions and contradictions. This raises the possibility that such tensions will variously open up the field to claims, contestations, or full-blown moral challenges, and invites a further set of questions for migration situated outside the terms of the EU free movement regime. If the system itself constitutes what might be termed a moral economy from above, we can consider both

Moral Economy from Above and Below

how far challenges engage an alternative moral vocabulary and whether the tensions and contradictions themselves open up avenues for claims and contestations that may take other forms.

CONDITIONALITY AND RIGHTS

While humanitarian exceptions can be seen as marking the limit of tolerable suffering and may well engage an explicit moral imperative, Chauvin and Garces-Mascarenas (2012) argue that the moral economy pervading an entire system can in practice permit other modes of incorporation. They note that though Fassin applies the term moral economy where a morality of compassion is overtly at stake, conditions and requirements throughout the system may amount to a moral economy geared rather to deservingness. Their focus is on undocumented migrants, who can avail themselves of formal circuits of incorporation by furnishing proofs of presence, good conduct, and fiscal contribution, thus conforming to an overarching value frame and emerging moral economy of desert. However, Chauvin and Garces-Mascarenas also find a degree of inconsistency whereby opportunities can arise from contradictions that are located within the law, as well as from tensions that run through policy, law, and practice. Their observations thus point to a more far-reaching moral economy that displays a nascent rationality through rules and conditions that permeate the whole system, but in a regime that itself may not be fully coherent. Such tension then raises broader questions as to how claims-making and contestations come about at systemic level, what forms they take, and how far they produce change in the system itself.

These questions are advanced by Landolt and Goldring's (2015) approach to the role of conditionality in 'assembling' non-citizen status; that approach defines assemblage as a dynamic multi-scalar process constituted by social actors, power relations, discursive frames, regulatory systems, and bureaucratized administration. Without explicitly engaging the idea of a moral economy, they note that the assemblage of policies, regulations, and procedures governing non-citizen presence may be embedded within a *moral framework* of desert that operates through a system of conditionality with respect to terms of presence and access to rights. They also call for a systemic approach to analysing the production of multiple, connected, and changing categories of legal status and hence recognize that the operation of the system itself may yield contradictions and inconsistencies such

The Moral Economy of Welfare and Migration

that boundaries between statuses can be contested, breached, negotiated, or otherwise altered over time.

Landolt and Goldring focus on the uneven experiences of individual migrants as they negotiate such a system and on the 'systemic contingencies' (856) that often determine outcomes – imperfect knowledge, informal circulation of strategies, the variable use of discretion, and so on. However, they hope that an understanding of such noncitizen assemblage and the role of conditionality can inform more strategic intervention, noting that civil society action has sometimes run counter to restrictive trends. Such an endeavour must therefore look to the scope for varied forms of contestation beyond individual experience that may themselves be viewed as an assemblage of strategies, techniques, and devices engaged by civic activists, but may then provide the grounds for a more systemic conception of an alternative moral stance.

These arguments call to mind Lockwood's (1996) notion of civic stratification, defined as a system of inequality that shapes access to and enjoyment of the rights of citizenship and that also extends to the elaboration of migrant statuses outside of citizenship (Morris 2003). The role of formal statuses in governing entry to a territory and differential access to rights is now well recognized; less attention has been paid to the informal dimension of Lockwood's model, especially the role of moral resources in conferring advantages through 'the activation of shared moral sentiments' (36). Individuals or groups within the system can experience an expansion or contraction of rights according to constructions of their moral standing – as expressed in policy rationales and in battles over desert that may be won or lost by civic activists. Lockwood notes that such activists make up a small minority of the general population but that their significance should not be underestimated; indeed, a ready connection can be made to advocacy groups operating within the immigration and asylum field.

An emergent agenda thus directs attention to the functioning of a moral economy 'from above' – its dominant value frame, policy content, and forms of conditionality and control. More crucially for the present chapter, existing literature also points to tensions, inconsistencies, and contradiction within law and policy that highlight the scope for intervention 'from below' by civic activists. We might therefore expect contestation to variously address the design of policy, the plausibility of its underlying assumptions, its coherence and consistency within an existing legal framework, and the question of how and where morality bites – all having implications for the moral standing of target groups.

We saw in Chapter 1 that various writers look to organizations located within civil society for creativity and challenge on pressing policy issues. The present chapter examines this potential through an analysis of critical responses to the contraction of rights in relation to non-EEA migration and asylum. This exercise is based on a reading of items such as newsletters, campaign documents, legal actions, and contributions to formal consultations by advocacy/activist groups that challenge key features of the emergent policy regime. The resultant critical commentary is not confined to the ideological level: in addition to broad issues of principle, it covers policy content and implementation, as well as legal contestability, to yield a continuum that runs from policy and practice, through law, to moral principles. Such contestation engages the tensions and contradictions within the system in forms of argument that may be classified according to terms introduced in Chapter 1: the internal coherence or *rationality* of policy aims, their consistency with pre-established obligations and hence their *legality*, and the nature of their legitimating values and hence their *morality*. All are at issue in the construction of an alternative orientation and point to an ongoing process of challenge that illuminates Fassin's unstable and fluid realities.

AUSTERITY, MIGRATION, AND CONTESTATION

Alongside a proclaimed 'moral mission' of welfare reform (Cameron 2012), and against a background drive for deficit reduction, migration was presented as both a source of domestic welfare dependency and as itself an additional drain on welfare resources. Despite official and other sources undermining these claims (MAC 2014; Keen and Turner 2016), the aim to reduce net immigration to tens of thousands featured in the Conservative manifestos of 2015 and 2017 and was formally abandoned only in 2019. This target, which entailed a reduction of more than 50 per cent, both recognized and reinforced public concern over immigration at a time when 77 per cent of the population believed existing levels to be too high (NatCen 2013). One prominent policy response was the fuller elaboration of a system of conditionality and control in which welfare provisions were to play a key role (Gower 2015), such that devices to minimize welfare inclusion would also enhance opportunities for selection, monitoring, and deterrence.

Within this process, rules of inclusion and exclusion governed by conditions of access and entitlement combine to shape both formal legal status and informal moral standing, and various writers (Rodger 2003; Forkert 2017) have noted the role such rules play in the management of public feeling. Though the discourse has been most overtly directed at EEA migrants (O'Brien 2015), ensuing policy has had ramifications for third-country nationals and asylum-seekers, and those ramifications are the focus of the present chapter.

Key devices with respect to non-EEA migrants have included income thresholds for entry and settlement. Only the latter confers full welfare entitlement but is contigent upon five years' prior residence and, from 2011, a qualifying yearly income of £35,000.[1] Alongside such restrictions there has been official recognition of the importance of migration as a positive factor in economic growth and debt reduction (e.g., OBR 2013. Annex A), and parameters governing entry and stay may change as EEA labour becomes less available. However, other measures have raised rights-related issues that reach beyond economic calculations. As we saw in the previous chapter, these include heightened income requirements for family unification, harsh cuts in levels of asylum support, and a planned tightening of access to maintenance for failed asylum-seekers and other migrants without status.

Such measures have been introduced in tandem with an erosion of appeal rights for asylum support and immigration decisions (see Luqmani, Thompson, and Partners 2014), a prohibitively demanding definition of 'exceptional circumstances', extended use of the 'no recourse to public funds' (NRPF) condition, and reduced availability of legal aid. These changes operate in the broader context of a 'hostile environment' (see Kirkup and Winnett 2012) designed to make survival for undocumented migrants ever more difficult. The outcome is a stratified system of control that places limits and conditions on entry, erodes entitlement for those present, makes challenge more difficult the more marginal one's position, impugns the moral standing of migrants by assumptions of resource drain and/or abuse, and reduces the scope for compassion within the system.

The moral economy from above is therefore one of contribution, conditionality, deterrence, and control. However, a total system requires a perfect mesh between ideological claims, legal framework, and policy design and execution. Cracks in the system then open up room for contestation in a manner that highlights the tensions and contradictions noted by Fassin and others. Such challenge is documented below for the policy areas identified – family life, asylum maintenance, support for those without status, and the emergent system of total control. These areas have attracted strong engagement from civic activists, and this provides interesting terrain for analysis within a moral economy frame. Successes have been small in scale, but they have not been negligible.

Though reference will be made to some of the legal cases cited in the previous chapter, the focus here is not on the legal argument *per se*, but on the role of activists' intervention in formulating challenges, furnishing evidence, and contesting the principles in play. Indeed, legal judgements are an underexploited source for the social scientist, and cases that challenge policy measures and their implementation all contain clear statements of the government's justificatory argument. In addition, they provide a platform for the counter-evidence and competing value frame advanced on behalf of the contesting party, such that campaigning activity and legal test-case activity are often mutually supporting activities.

FAMILY LIFE

Family Reunification

As detailed in Chapter 4, changes to the immigration rules effective from July 2012 (Gower 2014) increased the minimum income requirement (MIR) of £18,600 for resident applicants (sponsors) seeking to bring an overseas partner, with additions for children. This level, which is more than three times higher than that of the previous regime,[2] is justified by reference to taxpayer protection. Critique by advocacy groups undermines the *rationality* of these rules in terms of their own objectives (e.g., JCWI 2012; Liberty 2013); it also informed a critical review by the All Party Parliamentary Group (APPG 2013). This review questioned the inflexibility of the rules, which, for example, excluded additional income sources such as well-evidenced third-party support or the prospective earnings of an incoming partner, to result in a 'tick-box' approach valuing form over substance. JCWI (2012) sees the resultant impediments to family unification as contradicting official endorsements of the family as the bedrock of society (JCWI 2012), especially since a large majority of the sponsors affected are British citizens, who could thereby become exiled from their own country (Middlesex University/JCWI 2015). It is also argued that the rules in practice *increase* dependency on benefits, by restricting the working hours of a sponsor parent due to child care responsibilities that an incoming partner could relieve, thus impeding their own integration.

A challenge to the *legality* of the rules culminated in a Supreme Court judgement (MM *and Ors* [2017] UKSC 10) in which the Children's Commissioner and JCWI acted as formal interveners. Though the discriminations entailed were deemed proportionate to policy aims, the claim that the rules failed to reflect obligations under the Convention on the Rights of the Child and s 55 of the 2009 Borders Citizenship and Immigration Act was more telling. The latter requires government policy to safeguard and promote the welfare of children in discharging its immigration functions, and the Supreme Court found the rules to be unlawful in that they failed to give effect to these duties (para. 92). The ruling was given added force by a broader *morality* critique from the interveners.

One aim of this critique was to humanize debate by asking 'how far the MIR promotes and protects family life, for individual human flourishing and society as a whole' (JCWI 2012, 7). Given that the minimum requirement was set with reference to economic factors, to the explicit exclusion of social and moral questions (Gower 2014, 4), the APPG expressed concern about the unnecessary and unfair separation of families, and consequent negative effects for children – often British citizens. Research conducted for the Children's Commissioner (Middlesex University/JCWI 2015) graphically documents the resultant distress: 15,000 children were affected between 2012 and 2015, and some experienced near rupture of the parental relationship. However, while the Supreme Court upheld the s 55 challenge, it also signalled the moral limitations of the law; hence, 'the fact that a rule causes hardship to many, including some who are in no way to blame … does not mean that it is incompatible with Convention rights' (para. 81).[3]

In fact, the government response to the Supreme Court ruling (Desira 2017) concedes some aspects of the rationality, legality, and morality critiques. Where there *could* be 'unjustifiably harsh consequences', some flexibility is now allowed, and alternative sources of income can now be considered in meeting the MIR, yielding a ten-year (rather than five-year) route to settlement, albeit with four costly renewal fees over this period. A further exception outside the rules – though 'very rare indeed' (NRPF 2018) – *must* be granted where a refusal *would* result in 'unjustifiably harsh consequences'. However, guidance makes clear in both cases that unjustifiably harsh consequences will not generally follow where a couple 'chose to commence their family life together whilst living in separate countries' (Desira 2017). Responsibility and desert are hence brought to bear, and the scope for a positive decision on compassionate grounds is narrow in the extreme (NRPF 2018, 95).

Zambrano Carers and NRPF Exclusions

A family-related benefit issue also arose with respect to those third-country nationals (TCNs, i.e., non-EEA migrants) whose presence is necessary to secure effective rights for a citizen child, now known as Zambrano carers (see Chapter 4). Their confinement to minimal provision under S17 of the Children Act (1989) was justified as a means to reduce 'benefit tourism' (*Sanneh and Ors v SSWP* [2015] EWCA Civ 49 para 96), but a challenge to exclusion from mainstream benefits was brought by some of the local authorities affected.

By the time the case reached the Court of Appeal and, later, the Supreme Court, the AIRE Centre (Advice on Individual Rights in Europe) had become involved as an intervener. They advanced a number of issues as to the *rationality* of the policy: that the restriction on benefits bites only after the Zambrano situation has arisen (*Sanneh and Ors v SSWP*, para. 97), commonly after a relationship breakdown, so the deterrent effect is limited; and that once support has been recognized as crucial to the caring relationship, there is no basis for denying entitlement to mainstream benefits.[4] Furthermore, Lady Hale of the Supreme Court was 'unconvinced' by official justifications (*HC v SSWP* [2017] UKSC 73, para. 51), not least that of saving money by transferring costs from one arm of government to another. However, the *legality* argument was resolved in favour of the government, with the court ruling that while the 'effective citizenship' principle (Article 20 of the Treaty on the Functioning of the European Union) required support in some form, the level of that support is governed by domestic, not EU law.

The treatment of children in the case provoked further comment that went beyond tightly framed arguments of legal purchase to enter the terrain of *morality*, most fully expressed by one of the judges. The case treated TCNs as the relevant comparator group for the denial of mainstream benefits, not other British children (para. 40). However, Lady Hale observed that this was a case not about adults' rights but about children's rights, and specifically the rights of British children to remain living in their own society (para. 39). She condemned the lack of consideration given to supporting these children; that support had fallen by default onto the local authorities, which typically provided benefits well below mainstream levels. Implicitly raising a 'fairness' issue, Lady Hale asserted that 'these are British children, born and brought up here, who have the right to remain here all their lives' and noted 'the impact on the proper development of these children of being denied a level of support equivalent to that of their peers' (para. 46).

She found the aim of strengthening immigration control to be 'irrelevant to children who are not subject to it' (para. 51), and though she concurred in strictly legal terms that the appeal must be dismissed, her comments sent a strong moral message of dissent. Similar objections can apply to the NRPF rule, where parents have been granted leave on the 'ten year route' to settlement, a focus of concern for campaigning by the Unity Project (see Woolley 2019) and Project 17. Some, though not all, of the children concerned will hold citizenship status, but such a distinction anyway raises further questions about the differential treatment of children.

The NRPF exclusion has raised particular concerns in relation to the coronavirus, in that it leaves those advised against working caught in the related lockdown but cut off from welfare support, thus creating a problem highlighted by the Mayor of London (Khan 2020) and the WPC (2020). A legal challenge to official guidance on the lifting or non-imposition of the condition succeeded on the legal duty to *avoid* inhuman and degrading treatment (Article 3, ECHR). Combining legality and morality critiques, the judge (W *(by litigation friend J) v SSHD* [2020] EWHC 1299 (Admin) para. 34) quoted from an earlier case on the denial of support for in-country asylum-seekers. This 'necessarily contemplate[d] for some a life so desolate that no civilised nation can tolerate it. So basic are the human rights at issue that it cannot be necessary to resort to the European Convention on Human Rights to take note of their violation.'

Moral Economy from Above and Below

Both the MIR conditions and the exclusion of Zambrano carers from mainstream benefits have been driven by a moral economy from above, based on assumptions of a resource drain or 'benefit tourism' that justify moves to protect public resources and lighten the taxpayer burden, though a rationality critique has placed these claims in contention. Legal constraint, while limited, derives from child welfare issues, and insofar as moral questions of familial obligation and personal distress are addressed, they have been driven by international obligations that are written into domestic law. However, concessions on the MIR under exceptional circumstances seem less the operation of compassion as against repression, but rather a further extension of conditionality over access to the qualified right to family life. Meanwhile, Zambrano children continue to be held below the maintenance levels available to other citizen children. Though the assemblage of contestation in terms of rationality, legality, and morality has had only limited practical effect, these three dimensions have nevertheless combined to challenge dominant conceptions of desert and to reframe associated questions of moral standing, while placing limits on the extent of permitted exclusion. Especially notable is the way that legality and morality arguments come together in the judgement on the NRPF guidance, to stress a duty of pre-emptive action.

ASYLUM AND WELFARE

Asylum Support

A contraction of welfare rights was also apparent in the matter of asylum support: rates were frozen in 2011 to 'demonstrate fairness to the taxpayer' (*Refugee Action v SSHD* [2014] EWHC 1033 (Admin), para. 26), and preferential rates for children were removed in 2015[5] with a view to discouraging economic migration and protecting limited resources (*Ghulam and Ors v SSHD* [2016] EWHC 2639 (Admin), para. 241).

The policy has been criticized on the grounds of *rationality*. Hence, a parliamentary inquiry (2013) informed by evidence from advocacy groups found 'no correlation between levels of support and numbers of asylum seekers in the UK'. The inquiry deemed rates too low for essential living needs and viewed the assumption that worsening conditions would induce departure to be 'dangerously flawed'. Further commentary was provided in evidence submitted to the High Court by Refugee Action (*Refugee Action v SSHD* [2014] EWHC 1033 (Admin)), which noted that the setting of asylum rates at 70 per cent of income support was justified by the fact that asylum support was a measure of last resort and intended as a short-term form of provision only (para. 17(1)). However, the decoupling of the two rates in 2008 and the subsequent freezing of asylum support in 2011 meant that the gap between the rates had grown, increasing by 6.2 per cent between 2012 and 2014. The ensuing judgement also noted (para. 10) that in 2013 more than half of those dependent on asylum support remained so for more than six months, and a quarter for more than two years. This backlog has continued to rise in recent years (McKinney 2020).

In concluding, the judge ruled that the reduction of rates from what in 2007 had been regarded as a bare minimum required justification by careful investigation in order to be viewed as rational (paras. 130, 149). The information used by the government was deemed inadequate to this task, and in particular a reduction for sixteen-to-eighteen-year-olds was found to be inconsistent with S55 of the 2009 Act *via* the duty to safeguard and promote the welfare of children (see para 156). The ruling, however, stopped short of a moral judgement; it merely required the government to recalculate, an exercise that in the event confirmed the frozen rates (Brokenshire 2014). A later challenge to the 2015 reduction in children's rates (*Ghulam and Ors v SSHD* [2016] EWHC 2639 (Admin)) argued that this discriminated against children on the basis of their parents' immigration status, in contravention of s 55 of the 2009 Act, but the charge was dismissed and the analogy rejected. It was ruled that the children in question had no confirmed right to remain and that the comparison with nationals was not relevant, given that the two categories were supported under separate statutory regimes. The judge upheld the legitimate purpose of discouraging economic migration (para. 241), observing (para. 313) that the court must not be drawn into micro-managing and that beyond achieving the minimum standard required, the setting of rates was a matter for Parliament (para. 290).

The limit of the law is apparent in the first case as an evasion of substantive judgement (by looking to a procedural solution in relation to setting the rates), and in the second case as a deferral to Parliament. Advocacy organizations have, for their part, argued the point in terms of *morality*, with Refugee Action viewing a reduction of the rates as 'inhumane' and as having 'a devastating impact on the dignity and wellbeing of thousands' (Refugee Action 2014). In addition to legal argument regarding the Public Sector Equality Duty and the EU Reception Directive, they put forward evidence of severe deprivation: 40 per cent of recipients were unable to afford food and

88 per cent had no money to buy clothes (paras. 132–3), and there was a general failure to meet children's basic needs (see also Red Cross 2015). However, the procedural victory over the government ultimately failed to address these issues; indeed, it was followed by a further reduction.

Minor-age asylum-seekers have also been a focus of public concern and civic mobilization in relation to the 'Dubs amendment' of the 2016 Immigration Act, which was designed to relocate unaccompanied asylum-seeking children from within Europe. The government's fears of creating a 'pull factor' led to tight constraints in terms of age and date of arrival,[6] though in the wake extensive campaigning the cut-off date has been lifted (Safe Passage 2018). Nevertheless, there has been widespread disappointment over the numbers accepted, which were determined by official calculations of available local authority placements, though advocacy groups questioned the rationale for the limit on the grounds that greater capacity existed. This led to an unsuccessful *legal* challenge (*Help Refugees v SSHD* [2017] EWHC 2727 (Admin)), which queried the procedure adopted for identifying places. However, the *moral* case was made more fully elsewhere (*ZAT and Ors v SSHD* [2016] EWCA Civ 810), in the form of graphic volunteer descriptions of the Calais jungle[7] as a 'living hell'.

After further legal challenge on undue delay (*TM v SSHD* [2018] UKUT 299 (IAC)), the government offered what was termed 'Calais leave' to a small number of minors with family ties in the UK who did not qualify as refugees (Grierson 2018). However, the incoming government of December 2019 removed a commitment to secure family unification rights for unaccompanied minor-age asylum-seekers in Europe from the EU withdrawal act. Third-sector organizations have pointed to available capacity with local authorities and third-sector agencies, and the reluctance to admit these minors has been termed ideological. Ministers are being urged to take a 'moral stance' and to reverse the 'moral disgrace' of the withdrawal (Townsend and Savage 2019).

Section 4 Support

Resource contestation has also arisen in relation to further submissions from failed asylum-seekers who remain present in Britain. Given child protection law, those with children have to date retained support until removal, under S95 of 1999 Act (see below for recent changes).

Provision for those without children and who could not be removed was introduced under S4 of the 1999 act, at a lower level and via a cashless 'azure card' system, to address concerns about attracting non-genuine claims (Home Affairs Committee 2013).

A parliamentary inquiry (2013) has urged the abolition of s4 and the implementation of a cash-based system, and *rationality* arguments were again advanced against assumptions of a 'pull factor' (Home Affairs Committee 2013). There was also concern about the high proportion of successful appeals against refusal, which then stood at 82 per cent (Home Affairs Committee 2013, para. 81). However, a particular problem arose from the denial of s4 support for those making further submissions that amounted to a fresh claim for asylum. Such support was only granted once their claim had been validated as 'fresh'; a practice explicitly intended to 'discourage abuse of the system'. Waiting times for a decision commonly stood at four weeks or more, and so prompted an activist intervention through the courts (*MK and AH v SSHD* [2012] EWHC 1896 (Admin) para. 123(48)). The *rationality* of the policy was called into question in that it posed a barrier to accessing asylum, in addition to creating destitution, which had knock-on effects for community cohesion. Put simply, it was leaving vulnerable people on the streets, in some cases exposed to attacks and racist abuse (para. 178).

Fairness and morality, then, provided the basis for a successful *legal* challenge to HO policy from the Migrant Law Project, with Refugee Action as intervener (*MK and AH v SSHD* [2012] EWHC 1896 (Admin)). Witness statements from a variety of organizations elaborated on the 'hugely distressing' experiences of those denied support (paras. 176–80), and the judge deemed the further submissions policy unlawful. Destitution was seen as an inevitable consequence of the waiting time for support, as creating an unacceptable risk of inhuman and degrading treatment (prohibited under Article 3 of the ECHR), and as an impediment to justice (para. 184). The argument submitted in effect brought together *morality* and *legality*, and the judge stressed that 'there are human beings behind each application' who may be extremely vulnerable (para. 183), and that the right to a consideration of their case must be upheld (para 184), thus raising an issue of fairness.

Moral Economy from Above and Below

The ongoing approach to asylum support has been based on a moral economy from above that erodes support in the name of deterrence

Moral Economy from Above and Below 133

and fairness to the taxpayer, thus harnessing deprivation as a means of control. The rationality of this policy has repeatedly been called into question, and there have been some small legal advances. However, the victory over the setting of rates was merely procedural and had no material effect, and though legal and moral obligations regarding the best interests of children have held failed asylum-seeking families within the support system, they have not prevailed against the erosion of child rates or the very limited implementation of the Dubs amendment. The s4 case on further submissions was therefore unusual in bringing morality and legality together, to succeed by invoking the basic rights of access to justice and protection from inhuman and degrading treatment. In this way, fairness and compassion prevailed against policy concerns.

FAILED ASYLUM-SEEKERS AND OTHER 'ILLEGAL' MIGRANTS

Reforming the System

Given this background, we should look again at the HO consultation on changes contained in the 2016 Immigration Act, which among other things sets out measures for 'reforming support for failed asylum seekers and other illegal migrants' (Home Office 2015a). It is surprising that four years on from an extensive consultative exercise, these measures have yet to be implemented. Even so, they are an interesting marker of the direction of travel, and the delay is perhaps indicative of the very considerable problems that have been highlighted by interested organizations.

The changes were intended both to tighten access to HO support and to curtail recourse to local authority provision under the Children Act on the grounds that 'failed asylum seekers are illegal migrants and no more deserving of support than any other migrant in the UK unlawfully' (Home Office 2015, 4). Plans therefore followed to abolish S4 support and to limit access to local authority provision for children in need and for unaccompanied care-leavers. The *rationality* of the policy has been questioned, with several organizations citing a pilot exercise in 2004, intended to enforce departure by withdrawing support, which saw only three families opting for voluntary return; indeed, thirty-two cases (almost one third of the sample) disappeared (Refugee Council and Refugee Action 2006). The proposals rest on assumptions that behavioural change will mean fewer unfounded applications and greater compliance with departure. However, advocacy groups (e.g., Still Human Still Here 2015) note that removing support will hinder the aim of managed engagement with voluntary return and that loss of basic maintenance will drive families underground (ASAP 2015a). The activist's message is one of dehumanization, desperation, and abandonment, in the face of which many will nevertheless opt for destitution rather than return home (Still Human Still Here 2015), a prospect rendered more disturbing in the context of the public health crisis posed by COVID-19. Mayblin and James (2017) see destitution itself as a mark of policy failure both of the support system and of attempts to enforce departure – and show how its costs fall heavily on third-sector support organizations.

Though it is too early for legal challenges, there is a *legality* critique that rests in part on removal of a right of appeal against refusal of support. The Refugee Council (2015) describes this loss of judicial oversight as 'preposterous' given the high proportion of decisions overturned (see ASAP 2015). Other criticisms have focused on duties to children in need, and in this regard, the Refugee Council notes a 'startling failure' to address the UNCRC as well as duties under s 55 of the 2009 Act. Several organizations have argued that a child remains in need under the terms of the Children Act even in situations where a family could return but does not do so, and have identified gaps in provision that would flow from the abolition of s 4. Affected groups include destitute non–asylum-seeking families attempting to return or with further submissions outstanding, as well as unaccompanied asylum-seeking children with further submissions or who have absconded but seek to reinstate their claims.

It is revealing that several adjustments were made to the original proposals in the face of such comment; for example, the definition of asylum was expanded to incorporate some who would previously have been s 4 cases. Also, in response to concerns following consultation (e.g., Local Government Association et al. 2015), the new s 95A will expand HO provision for *all* failed asylum-seekers (not just families), though eligibility will be more tightly linked to demonstrable efforts to leave. Finally, the late amendment to the 2016 act introducing the 10A and 10B provisions (see Chapter 4) was necessary to address the situation of families who fell outside provisions and might otherwise resort to s 17 support; however, HO oversight of this provision is significant in terms of a control agenda. While taken together the proposals do meet earlier calls to abolish s 4 and replace it with

Moral Economy from Above and Below

cash-based provision at the same level as asylum support, the latter had already fallen to much the same level as s4. The Immigration Law Practitioners Association (ILPA 2015, 10) has described the result as 'a series of tatty safety nets full of holes', in which the last resort is an appeal to the local authorities that are left to manage the resultant destitution in their communities.

A critique in terms of *morality* argues that statutory support should be available to all who are experiencing destitution (Red Cross 2015) yet the whole package of provisions rests on understanding the complexities of three different systems of support, thus putting families at risk of falling through the gaps (Harvey and Harper 2017). It is also argued that the use of destitution to enforce departure is unacceptable in a civilized society and that the new policy prioritizes immigration control over the welfare of children (Refugee Children's Consortium 2015). Advocacy groups highlight the need for an end-to-end process of support and a broader use of discretionary leave after a period in which return has not proved viable (e.g., Red Cross 2017; Refugee Council 2015). The overlapping aims of such interventions include a detailing of the human impact of destitution (Refugee Action 2017), the restoration of human dignity (Red Cross 2015), and a 'kindling of moral responsibility towards those we exclude' (Jesuit Refugee Service 2018). Some see the need for a complete cultural shift within the HO, away from a culture of disbelief and toward a more positive approach to asylum casework as saving lives (ASAP 2015a). Others (Still Human Still Here 2015; Home Affairs Committee 2013) argue that greater investment in faster and more reliable decision-making would increase the system's *moral* credibility and encourage the compliance that the HO is seeking.

Moral Economy from Above and Below

Asylum advocacy organizations forced some changes to the proposed measures, which would have further restricted support for failed asylum-seekers, by pointing to the gaps that would be created, and to a likely increased demand on local authority resources. Legal challenges may well follow when (and if) the changes unfold, especially regarding children's rights and the lack of appeal against denial of support. But perhaps the most forceful response thus far has been the argument that the changes go beyond what is morally acceptable, even given the primacy of control. Several groups have put forward

The Moral Economy of Welfare and Migration

proposals for a more compassionate approach based on human dignity. Nonetheless, the changes once in place will move inexorably toward ever harsher measures, in incremental steps toward a system of total control.

TOWARDS A TOTAL SYSTEM

The measures documented in this chapter have narrowed the terms and conditions of entry and stay for TCNs, as well as reducing asylum-seekers' support, while also operating in tandem with an erosion of access to justice. Changes introduced via the LASPO Act of 2012 take most immigration and welfare issues out of publicly funded legal aid, though JR and asylum applications remain in scope, and after intensive lobbying (e.g., ASAP 2013) so too does asylum support law as it relates to homelessness. The latter advance is to be partly reversed by the denial of a right of appeal against refusal of s95A, 10A, or 10B support, though ASAP has questioned the *rationality* of this policy, given the very poor quality of decision-making on s95 and s4.[8]

While judicial review applications can still attract legal aid, secondary legislation under LASPO was to require twelve months' lawful residence for eligibility, which had the effect of excluding (among others) failed asylum-seekers and undocumented migrants. Rerunning the moral economy of welfare contraction, this test was intended to limit legal aid to those with a strong connection to the UK (JCHR 2013, para. 1), to reduce costs, and to secure 'the best deal for the taxpayer' (*Public Law Project v Lord Chancellor* [2016] UKSC 39, para. 14), given the government view that 'we do not think that most immigration matters justify legal aid' (*Gudanaviciene v Lord Chancellor* [2014] EWCA Civ 1622, para. 150). An activist challenge to the *legality* of the test was brought by the Public Law Project and upheld by the Supreme Court. The test was deemed unlawful in that it fell outside powers granted by the legislation and excluded a group by virtue of personal circumstances or characteristics that bore no relation to the services in question (para. 34). Fairness was again at issue, and a prior ruling ([2014] EWHC 2365 (Admin) para. 77) saw the right to check whether decisions are correct as essential to upholding the rule of law as part of the grounding of a democratic society.

Nevertheless, a family (re)unification sponsor falling foul of the minimum income requirement will not have access to legal aid, failed

Moral Economy from Above and Below

asylum-seekers will have no appeal against refusal of support, and those with no further submissions but unwilling to leave will be squeezed out of basic maintenance to become undocumented. Total exclusion was then to be secured by a policy launched in 2012 'to create here in Britain a really hostile environment for illegal migration'. The underpinning moral message is that 'if you are here illegally, you shouldn't be entitled to receive the everyday benefits and services available to hard-working UK families and people who have come to this country legitimately to contribute' (Home Office 2016d). It is now a criminal offence to work without permission, to employ someone without permission to work, to drive while unlawfully present, or to rent property when there is cause to believe the tenant is unlawfully present (see Yeo 2017 for review).

The measures have been criticized on *rationality* grounds, given the absence of any means to determine their effectiveness, the failure to understand their wider impact, and their discriminatory effects (Home Affairs Committee 2018; JCWI 2015). A *legality* critique attacks the lack of a remedy for wrongful decisions, the failure to accommodate the Public Sector Equality Duty (JCWI 2015), and the promotion of actions that would be defined as harassment under the 2010 Equality Act (Yeo 2017). A legal challenge to the 'right to rent' checks succeeded in the High Court (*JCWI v SSHD* [2019] EWHC 452 (Admin)) on the grounds of discrimination against black and minority ethnic citizens who do not hold a passport, though the Court of Appeal ruled against attributing governmental responsibility. A *morality* critique goes further, condemning the measures for producing homelessness and destitution among vulnerable groups and for creating a hostile environment for all migrants (Migrants Rights Network 2014).

In fact, the hostile environment policy was undermined by public exposure when those who arrived as children in the Windrush migration to Britain[9] fell foul of residence requirements, documentation that would confirm their status having been destroyed by the HO in 2010 (McCann and Mendick 2018). Many suffered loss of work and/ or benefits, and even deportation, if unable to prove their presence in Britain before 1 January 1973, the date for removal of the right of abode from such migrants (Home Affairs Committee 2018). 'Fairness' and 'desert' were reconfigured to work in their favour (Gentleman 2018), and some elements of the hostile environment have been paused; the policy has since been renamed 'the compliant environment'. Meanwhile, however, others have been driven away from emergency medical treatment to which they were entitled, faced barriers to education, and been rendered homeless by landlord checks (for examples see Marsh 2018).

Yet the boundary marking legitimate presence is not clear-cut, and a *rationality* critique[10] shows how people can be administered into irregularity through erroneous decision-making, prohibitively high HO fees, and an absence of legal aid. The hostile environment has nonetheless sought to close the circle of incremental exclusions, and in 2012 the fourteen-year 'long presence' route to settlement was replaced by a twenty-year route followed by four *further* costly applications before settlement (Yeo 2018). Should an undocumented migrant be in a position to regularize through recourse to exceptional circumstances, issues of character or conduct, failure to comply with requirements, or owing a debt to the NHS may count against them (Home Office 2016c, para. 322). Finally, the Court of Appeal has endorsed a restrictive approach to serious health conditions (GS *(India) and Ors) v SSHD* [2015] EWCA Civ 40) and stressed that there is no ECHR obligation to provide medical treatment unavailable in the home country. A stay of removal on Article 3 grounds will therefore be granted only for deathbed cases, curtailing a key instance of compassion in Fassin's model.

Moral Economy from Above and Below

This section has moved beyond the specific confines of welfare to address related rights to justice and survival. Critical comment has highlighted the significance of the right to contest formal decisions as part of a functioning democracy (though the judgement overturning the residence test for legal aid does not restore the broader cuts).[11] Yet a rationality critique notes the tenuous nature of the boundary between documented and undocumented presence, as well as the perverse effects that can follow from attempts to impose an environment of total control. The public sympathy generated by a failure of fairness in the treatment of Windrush cases is of particular interest, highlighting both the system's fluidity and the significance of public engagement in cases of manifest injustice. Furthermore, enforced destitution and lack of access to medical care in an ongoing pandemic such as the coronavirus have health implications for the entire population that are not sustainable.

CONCLUSION – MORAL ECONOMY REVISITED

Fassin's juxtaposition of compassion and repression in immigration law and practice is compelling, but the climate in Britain under the age of austerity has pointed to an increasingly restrictive regime. The more the system becomes rule-bound by conditionality, desert, and deterrence, and shielded from legal challenge, the more compassion is squeezed out of the formal system, so that it falls to advocacy organizations to make the moral case and to advance an alternative stance from below. There is therefore some advantage to refining Fassin's approach, which seems to locate compassion within the dominant system, albeit through its capacity to open up exceptions at the margins. For a fuller understanding we can begin by examining how the moral economy from above shapes the contours of the formal system, and then consider where and how contestation arises. This adjustment permits more critical attention to the instability and fluidity Fassin identifies, which arises where tensions within the system create a space for contestation and for what he would term a '*moral economy*' from below.

This chapter has focused on the centrality of welfare issues in austerity Britain. The moral economy from above operates through an ever more rule-driven system, one whose conceptions of desert have minimized the accommodation of compassion. We have seen how this has been built into terms of entry in relation to family unification, maintenance levels for Zambrano carers, the management of asylum, and the treatment of those without status, all the while narrowing conceptions of legitimate presence. The related value frame erodes the moral standing of those subject to its operations by allegations of resource drain and/or abuse, both of which serve to justify a shrinking model of desert. However, such justification is susceptible to a rationality critique in terms of stated objectives, while legal battles emerge when policy collides with pre-existing legal obligations, and the rhetoric driving the system may be contested in terms of an alternative moral stance.

The scope for Fassin's '*moral* economy' from below therefore rests on more than a simple opposition between compassion and repression, and could be built around these three dimensions of challenge. The courts figure as the most effective avenue for achieving practical and immediate policy or procedural change, by bringing to bear the force of law and holding governments to account in terms of pre-established legal commitments (e.g., the UNCRC and Articles 3 and 8 of the ECHR). There have been some successes, though cases also reveal considerable hesitation among judges when it comes to undermining the will of Parliament. Judges may use a case as an opportunity to make a moral declaration (e.g., the asylum support and Zambrano cases), but this does not necessarily shape the content of the judgement itself except where the most fundamental rights are involved. Such rights prevailed in relation to S4 support for pending fresh claims and the challenge to NRPF guidance, while in other cases the treatment of children has marked the outer boundary of repression, albeit with only limited powers of constraint (e.g., the MIR and Zambrano cases).

Conversely, contestation based on morality (e.g. JCWI 2012; Jesuit Refugee Service 2018) may seek to engage public sympathy and provide a basis for Lockwood's 'activation of shared moral sentiments', but it may struggle to dislodge the rhetoric from above (as with the Dubs amendment). The moral argument is often strengthened by a rationality critique that undermines the practical assertions supporting dominant rhetoric, as in claims of benefit tourism by Zambrano carers, or repeated references to a 'pull factor' in relation to asylum support. Such critique can also have an impact on public perceptions, by grounding morality in concrete arguments that undermine policy in more substantive terms, making its legitimacy more readily questionable, and possibly restoring the moral standing of some marginalized groups – as with the 'Windrush migrants'.

However, unless the dominant value frame can be more conclusively dislodged and replaced, it seems that compassion will continue to be superseded by repression. Meanwhile, the erosion of publicly funded legal aid and the scaling back of appeal rights have made it increasingly difficult for individuals to challenge their treatment. Nevertheless, the three-pronged assemblage of civic activism documented in this chapter has succeeded in opening up cracks in the system of control – be they rational, legal, or moral – to maximize its inherent fluidity and instability, and to reveal its processual and mutable nature. Such critique has highlighted the contradictions and inconsistencies noted by Chauvin and Garcia-Macarenas (2012) and by Landolt and Goldring (2015), showing them to operate at a systemic level, and in some cases forcing a renegotiation of the boundaries at issue. Thus, in the absence of a perfect mesh between ideological claims, legal frames, and policy design and execution, lack of internal coherence within the system will continue to generate inconsistencies that invite and enable contestation. The role of advocacy organizations documented in the present study has been to identify and exploit these ongoing opportunities for challenge and change in a manner that questions the assumptions of a moral economy from above, to fuel the incremental advance of an alternative vision from below, through the accumulation of small successes and the articulation of a wider moral frame.

6

Activating the Welfare Subject:
The Problem of Agency

PROBLEMATIZING AGENCY

A common feature of many of the policies reviewed thus far in this book has been the aim of behavioural change, whether in relation to 'incentivizing' work among domestic welfare claimants, tightening conditions of entry and stay for family members, deterring arrival and continuing presence for labour migrants or asylum-seekers, or enforcing the departure of failed asylum-seekers and undocumented migrants. An understanding of the motivations for human action (agency) is therefore key to most of the measures we have examined, and the adequacy of such understanding has implications for the three modes of contestation that have been discussed. A policy's rationality will be flawed if it rests on inaccurate conceptions of agency on the part of target groups; questions of legality will be at issue when misplaced assumptions impede access to rights; and morality will be at issue when inappropriate conditions render claimants destitute or divided from family members. Conceptions of agency thus play a crucial role, both in the construction of sites of disciplinary control and as a focus for contestation. The main section of this chapter therefore looks at the understandings of agency revealed in the course of legal challenges to the measures that have been central to the welfare reforms. A subsequent section will extend the analysis to aspects of migration and asylum policy.

It has been widely observed (Mau 2003; Düvell and Jordan 2002; Munch 2012; Dwyer and Wright 2014; Wright 2016) that Britain, together with a number of other European countries, has been shifting away from solidaristic models of welfare toward individualized responsibility resting on 'activation' of the welfare subject. There has been an associated increase in the requirements placed on claimants, as well as an expansion of groups deemed capable of and available for work, and Wright (2012) has advanced a corresponding argument that this shift relies on an inadequate conception of agency. In this context, agency may be construed as a form of purposive rationality, in terms of both the objectives driving the welfare reform and the disciplinary devices on which they are based.

The purposive rationality manifest in claimant 'activation' has a long history and is associated by Sayer (2011) with a tendency in modernism to reduce rationality to instrumental reason. He sees the strongest expression of this tendency in mainstream economic theory (see also Shapiro 2005), where it features as the pursuit of profit maximization through a means/ends approach confined to its own internal logic. The development of the welfare state and its bureaucratic administration may be viewed as part of this configuration (Tweedy and Hunt 1994), designed to secure social integration under conditions of economic inequality. However, fiscal crisis and an associated pursuit of deficit reduction brought a heightened emphasis on the disciplinary potential of the welfare system, driven by incentives, conditionality, and sanctions.

Critique of the purposive rationality underpinning such developments has been based on its overextension, its neglect of 'practical reason' rooted in individual experience and contextual sensibility, and the exclusion of broader-based systems of value that treat people as ends in themselves rather than means to other ends (Sayer 2011, 61–2). The ensuing tensions are apparent in welfare regimes that are caught between the Marshallian ideal of full inclusion and a more disciplinary focus dedicated to the optimal extraction of labour. Wright (2012) argues that in the contemporary drift toward the latter, attendant policies carry assumptions about motivation, choice, and responsibility built on individualized conceptions of culpability and accountability that then legitimize increased conditionality and compulsion.

Driven by a quest for behavioural change, policy has been fashioned around a diminished view of agency that leaves little room for more nuanced understandings of individual subjectivity, self-reflexive thought and action, or the way that agency is differentiated by varied combinations of individual and societal factors. An appreciation of how this diminished conception operates must therefore consider not only underlying assumptions about motivation, behaviour, and feasible outcomes but also the circumstances in which agency is exercised and that variously shape the claimant's experience.

Prominent among these circumstances is the institutional setting and the specified requirements and conditions of a claim, to be understood in Wright's terms as 'context creation'. Giddens (1979, 50) has noted a failure to relate action theories to institutional transformation, such that institutions appear as a consensual backdrop against which action is engaged, without a related focus on power relations or conflict in society. In the case of welfare, the regulated interactions required by the system and their attendant differentials of power and knowledge constitute the circumstances within which welfare subjects exercise agency. This context operates in part through a process of classification that determines what can be required of which categories of claimant, as well as the claimant's ability to negotiate and possibly contest the classifying process.

More detailed regulations govern implementation, but alongside these purposive constraints lie life-world factors, captured by Emirbayer and Mische's (1998, 963) understanding of agency as 'a temporally embedded process of social engagement, informed by the past but oriented to the future'. We can therefore infer that actors carry into the present not only future-oriented projects but also a variety of relations and obligations already established. Emirbayer and Mische characterize the outcome as a web of cognitive, corporeal, and affective schema that together shape action – and this configuration is an orienting theme of the present chapter. A point of particular interest is their argument that the locus of agency lies in the range of possible responses to problematic situations. They therefore point to key moments of transformation and/or crisis and bring a political significance to bear by noting that day-to-day interactions occur within 'master frames' that are part of the broader political culture. In so doing, they not only endorse a view of structure and agency as mutually constitutive (see Giddens 1979) but also suggest that agency becomes especially apparent in unsettled times, such that pivotal moments may emerge in situations of political realignment.

Wright's (2012) approach to recent UK welfare reform offers a vehicle for taking forward this argument through an analysis of the narrowly framed conceptions of agency in operation at the policy level. She notes a tendency in welfare policy to see intention and choice as forms of calculative self-interest at the level of the individual, to the neglect of personal constraints, social context, and social bonds.

Furthermore, given that related policy measures carry moral messages about behaviour and motivations, she points to an additional dimension of agency that operates through the production of meaning at the policy level itself, again bridging the structure/agency divide. Thus, policy-makers are not to be construed as impartial rational actors, but rather as active agents who advance policy measures that are imbued with moral messages and implemented by profit-based delivery agents with their own interests at stake. Hence, Wright calls for research that captures the 'more nuanced aspects of agency', and here we might look to the crisis points generated within this system.

Distinguishing between action and agency, Reed and Weinman (2019, 10) argue that while action entails an engagement with future projects, agency implies a high probability of bringing such projects to fulfillment. Success, they suggest, is enhanced by the ability to enlist others as one's *agents*, thus constructing an 'agency chain' (14). However, in the case of welfare reform, such 'fulfillment' requires co-option of the welfare subject, whose own agency – shaped and constrained by their principles, interests, capacities, and obligations – comes into play. The discussion below therefore examines how the objectives, incentives, and sanctions driving welfare policy collide with the complexities of lived experience, as revealed below in a series of legal test cases. It shows how such challenges variously provide a forum for elaborating contested conceptions of agency, pitting the purposive rationality of instrumental reason against the lived experience of claimants, whose agency may be better understood in terms of practical reason.

INTERROGATING AGENCY

The central purpose of the discussion of cases to follow is to explore these contrasting conceptions of agency by interrogating a set of legal judgements that place agency at issue. The rationale driving welfare reform in Britain's austerity decade has been documented in earlier chapters outlining the orientation, aims, and purposes of policy, as well as the measures they have generated. This chapter instead examines a series of legal challenges to the measures identified – test cases that are widely circulated within the practitioner community – and the heart of the argument is derived from analysis of the ensuing judgements. Some have been mentioned in previous chapters, but the focus here is less on the detail of legal reasoning than on what the

146   *The Moral Economy of Welfare and Migration*

cases reveal about policy assumptions concerning agency, their practical implementation, and attendant problems for claimants.

In identifying relevant cases, one determining factor was that they should span the range of targeted reform measures listed below. In relation to these measures, each case identifies a distinct policy problem, addresses a key point of law, and stands as a referent for policy adjustment and/or future litigation. They have not therefore been 'sampled' from a general population of cases but are rather test cases whose outcome will shape the treatment of a host of similarly placed claimants. Such cases are part of a process that emerges from the actions of advocates and litigants who identify policy or practice issues ripe for legal challenge, as documented in previous chapters. For markers of this test-case status, we may note: all but one of the cases involved civil society advocacy groups in bringing the challenge to court and/or acting as interveners; most of the cases were appealed to a higher-level court (Upper Tribunal, Court of Appeal, or Supreme Court); and almost all required a significant adjustment of policy or practice. The exception to the latter point is the lone-parent benefit cap, which has nevertheless exposed continuing disagreement within the judiciary.

Given this test-case rationale, each challenge provides an opportunity to examine those aspects of agency called into play by the implementation of specific policy measures, and to explore the situated agency apparent in the claimant experience. This approach of course confines the chapter to a consideration of the individual agency at issue in each case, though this is not to deny that other forms of resistance could engage collective agency. However, that is not the focus of the present argument, and within this constraint, close interrogation of the test-case judgements uses agency as a lens through which to view the critical points at issue in policy implementation. This sets the analytical frame, and means that agency must be read into the dynamic of legal dispute. The analysis below therefore examines the purposive rationality of behavioural change against a more sociological understanding of agency that better engages the claimant experience.

POLICY RATIONALE AND THE QUESTION OF VALUE(S)

We have seen from foregoing argument that institutions may be implicated in the shaping of social norms; hence a welfare system is built around not only fiscal but also moral assumptions, which in turn play a role in steering popular opinion (Mau 2003; Rodger 2003; Munch 2012). Policy is thus, at least in part, a normative endeavour, and a disciplinary welfare regime that implies the need for coercion will generate a corresponding stigma for the welfare subject, negative perceptions of their agency, and attendant erosion of their moral standing in society. This process can be traced through the programme of welfare reform that has emerged in Britain over the last decade, and though these reforms continue trends already apparent (Harris 2008), they represent a qualitative shift in both reach and severity.

Early position papers (SJPC[1] 2006; 2007) foregrounded the need to 'get tough' on fraudulent welfare claims and propounded the view that weak expectations had made it possible to choose a life on benefits. The proposed solution was a system designed to produce 'positive behavioural effects', so among the recommendations were that unemployed claimants be actively seeking or preparing for work on a full-time basis, and that this should extend to disabled claimants and to lone parents. Such a system would be accompanied by robust application of financial sanctions for failure to comply, as well as intense enforcement through competition between providers rewarded for positive outcomes. These proposals were made concrete under the incoming Coalition government (DWP 2010, 2010a). Recurrent policy priorities are financial savings, fairness to hard-working taxpayers, increased welfare conditionality, and the incentivization of work (DWP 2010a; Kennedy 2015a), all embraced by the Welfare Reform Act (2012) and further advanced by the Welfare Reform and Work Act (2016).

The most ambitious change has been removal of the distinction between working and workless claimants through a unified system of Universal Credit[2] (DWP 2010a), though full implementation has been delayed in the face of administrative problems, claimant suffering, and poor labour market outcomes (NAO 2018). Meanwhile, however, a series of measures were established under the pre-existing system, and carried over into Universal Credit, that make policy questionable even within its own narrow behavioural terms, all having issues of agency at their heart. The specific measures to be considered are as follows:

- The 2012 Act heightened claimant conditions and financial sanctions for failure to comply; this was intended 'to provide a greater incentive for people to meet their responsibilities' (DWP

2010a, 4). Operating with three levels of severity by type and frequency of offence, and despite the abolition of the three-year sanction from October 2019 (Butler 2019a), the system remains considerably more stringent than previous regimes (see WPC 2018).

- Tighter Work Capability Assessments (WCAS) and heightened sanctions have affected Employment and Support Allowance (ESA – previously Invalidity Benefit) for those classed as having a limited capability for work (the Work Related Activity Group – WRAG), prompting concerns about faulty decisions and inappropriate conditions (Kennedy, Keen, and Mackley 2017). The abolition of a £30 weekly supplement for this group was presented as the removal of a disincentive to work (Murphy and Keen 2016), despite the fact that they are not required to seek employment.
- The age of the youngest child at which lone parents are moved onto Jobseekers Allowance and thereby full conditionality has been lowered in stages (Harris 2008; Lakhani 2009) from fourteen years in 2007 to ten in 2009, seven in 2010, five in 2012, and three in 2017 – intended 'to enable lone parents to take financial responsibility for themselves and their children' (WPC 2018, 22–3).
- The benefit cap was introduced in the 2012 Act as an absolute limit on the total amount a household can receive in benefits. It was set at £26,000 per year[3] for families regardless of size, and lowered to £23,000 in London and £20,000 elsewhere by the 2016 Act. The stated aim was to encourage responsible life choices and increase incentives to work (Kennedy et al. 2016). Note that the cap has not been adjusted upwards in light of the increased personal allowance for UC, prompted by the coronavirus crisis.
- A further measure in the 2016 Act restricted Child Tax Credit (CTC) payments per child to two children, with a potential loss of £2,780 per year,[4] such that people on means-tested benefits 'should face the same financial choices about having children as those supporting themselves solely through work' (Kennedy, Bate, and Keen 2017). Available exemptions have proved contentious.

The fertile ground for this 'activation' paradigm is apparent in Skeggs's (2014, 1) account of a dominant logic in which 'the market has become God'. She argues that monetization and commodification have reduced the person to an object of calculation and domination that constrains conceptions of both who has value and what is valued. As Skeggs makes clear, there is a gendered dimension to these issues when caring work is overlooked both as an economic contribution and as an obligation of love and duty. We also see below how limited conceptions of who and what has value can squeeze out individual hopes, ambitions and principles that do not readily conform, and how physical and mental capability become subject to a crude classification of labouring capacity.

Like Skeggs, Sayer (2011) notes the limiting influence of economistic orientations based on profit maximization, which renders an impoverished and alienated approach to understanding social life. He therefore makes a case for the incorporation of values and of 'what matters to people' into social scientific reasoning, based on people's own experiences and priorities, in a manner attuned to the conditions required for human flourishing. Such an approach, he argues, is not based on abstract moral principle, but rather takes seriously people's own personal life plans, their capacities and vulnerabilities, and their care and concern for others. It thus incorporates people's own normativity and self-understanding into an evaluation of their actions and their experience at the hands of institutions, and we might expect this form of reasoning to feature in the functioning and evaluation of a welfare system.

These arguments are explored below in relation to a series of test cases that have challenged each of the targeted measures of welfare reform listed above, with the following discussion grouped according to key policy issues. The cases reveal in different ways the impoverished conception of agency at play in the rationale and implementation of policy, as well as what happens when this is exposed to contrasting conceptions of agency rooted in claimant experience.

CONDITIONALITY AND SANCTIONS

Context Creation

One early case (*Reilly and Wilson v Secretary of State for Work and Pensions (SSWP)* [2012] EWHC 2292) was detailed in Chapter 1 and concerned two claimants sanctioned under programmes within the Employment Skills and Enterprise Scheme. The design and implementation of these programmes imposed work-related require-ments on claimants as a means of imbuing behavioural change in an instance of what Wright (2012) would term 'context creation'. The challenge raises questions about informed participation, claimant knowledge and understanding, and hence the capacity to act, while also showing how the schemes override claimants' own self-assessment of their position and their hopes for the future.

The 2011 regulations governing the programmes were challenged on four grounds: (1) failure to provide a full description of the schemes; (2) absence of a published policy supplying these details; (3) failure to provide written notice of the consequences of non-participation; and (4) forced or compulsory labour. The case succeeded on the third ground in the High Court, and the first and third grounds in the Court of Appeal (*Reilly and Wilson v SSWP* [2013] EWCA Civ 66). The Supreme Court (*Reilly and Wilson v SSWP* [2013] UKSC 68) confirmed the latter ruling, noting that the person affected by a policy must be in a position to challenge a decision by 'informed and meaningful representations' (UKSC para. 65) and also to make 'an informed decision about taking part' (UKSC para. 67). Crucially, Reilly had received no written notice and had been wrongly instructed that participation in the sector-based work academy was compulsory; moreover, neither claimant had received 'adequate accurate information about the schemes in relation to themselves' (UKSC para. 76) before being told that their participation was required. Translated into sociological language, the failure to adequately inform amounted to an impediment to agency, and underscores the power of 'undisputed practices' (Giddens 1979, 89) in shaping the claimant experience.

However, it is also apparent from detail in the High Court (EWHC) judgement (para. 186) that in resisting the schemes both claimants displayed considerable reflexive agency, as well as a commitment to work. Wilson had objections in principle to working for free and viewed the requirements as 'pointless work that has not been arranged by looking at my own needs' (para. 112) that actually hampered his job search. Reilly hoped for a career in the museum sector, where she was working voluntarily in order to acquire sufficient experience. As the EWHC judge remarked, the scheme had 'impeded her voluntary efforts to maintain and advance her primary career ambition ... and did not offer any worthwhile experience on an alternative career path', while for Wilson 'there [was] no suggestion that he would not take suitable employment if he could find it' (para. 126).

The experience of both claimants raises questions about knowledge, understanding, choice, and reflexivity and goes some way toward undermining the rationale of both programmes and the related sanctions regime. A scheme dedicated to behavioural change had insufficiently informed claimants, frustrated their reflexive agency, impeded their employment ambitions, and impugned their moral standing. However, a fuller elaboration of requirements could well have perverse effects, facilitating a form of 'calculative agency' by increasing the administrative capacity for monitoring and enforcement (Adkins 2017).

Claimant Context

The sanctions regime has attracted more general criticism for its high success rate on appeal (Oakley 2014; CPAG 2018), poor appreciation of claimant circumstances, and inadequate application of 'easements' – adjustments that take mitigating factors into account. A case in the Upper Tribunal (UT) (*RR v SSWP (UC)* [2017] UKUT 459 (AAC)) focused less on the rules themselves than on their application and interpretation. The ensuing judgement illustrates a range of related factors bearing on conceptions of agency.

RR was a Universal Credit claimant given two twenty-eight-day sanctions for failure to comply with her Claimant Commitment – a requirement for all applicants. The UT judge observed (para. 5) that this document began with the 'positively Stakhanovite statement' that 'I'll do everything I can to get paid work', including obeying instructions from the Work Programme provider and fulfilling the obligations contained in her Claimant Commitment. The latter requires thirty-five hours per week spent seeking and preparing for work, as well as daily access to a Universal Jobsearch account, with a caution that failure to comply 'without good reason' would mean loss of £10.40 per day for up to three years.

Having claimed Universal Credit for one year, RR complained about a newly allocated work coach and received an apology from the Job Centre. However, this work coach had imposed two sanctions for failure to engage in thirty-five hours per week job search, and after an unsuccessful internal review (Mandatory Reconsideration) the claimant appealed, again without success, to the First Tier Tribunal (FtT). She explained that she had logged onto the Universal Jobsearch system as required but neglected to update her record due to the distractions of a family crisis she was reluctant to disclose to the new work coach. She felt this omission should have been noticed as 'an oddity', given her past record of compliance. On further appeal, the Upper Tribunal (UT) found that the FtT judge had erred in treating the thirty-five-hour job search requirement as immutable. Deductions could be allowed for temporary circumstances, including a domestic emergency, and the latter could reasonably embrace the claimant's divorce hearing due some months later, with its attendant stresses (para. 31). The UT therefore found for the claimant.

This history highlights the complexity of individual agency in such cases. While the regulations do in fact allow scope for dealing with temporarily disruptive events, their application and interpretation rested on the unsatisfactory work coach and an error on the part of the FtT judge. The moral standing of the claimant was again at issue in relation to motivation and good faith in meeting the conditions of her claim. More significantly, the history raises the question of reasonable expectation when individual agency is impaired by a domestic crisis and thus closely tied to relations with others – an instance of Wright's interconnected agency.

CAPABILITY AND CARING

Classifying Embodied Agency

Human agency is also necessarily embodied, and this recognition has particular significance for ESA claimants, in relation both to the classifying process and to the significance of its outcomes. The requirements imposed on claimants are determined by a threefold classification – full conditionality, work-related activity (the WRAG), and no conditionality (the Support Group) – resting on judgements of capacity and therefore agency. However, the WCA itself raises questions about capacity and agency in terms of the ability to navigate assessment, especially for those experiencing a mental health condition. Ruling on an earlier UT judgement, the Court of Appeal (*MM and DM v SSWP* [2013] EWCA Civ 1565) found that mental health patients had been placed at a substantial disadvantage and that the SSWP was in breach of a duty under the Equality Act 2010 to make reasonable adjustments in order to secure as full as possible entry into everyday life (and hence full agency).

Both the *outcome* in terms of benefit entitlement and the *experience* of the assessment itself were held to be implicated (paras. 73–7). Decisions about capacity to work had been undermined by the failure to secure full understanding and engagement from those undergoing assessment; this was compounded by assessors' lack of expertise and by an intimidating determination process, which could generate false or inadequate judgements (para. 31).

Critical commentaries (Kennedy, Keen, and Mackley 2017; Murphy and Keen 2016) have noted that the WCA is too simplistic; also, that it overstates capacity, deals badly with fluctuating conditions, and is difficult for claimants to navigate – especially since 50 per cent of them have mental and/or behavioural disorders. However, many feel unable to contemplate an appeal (Rethink Mental Illness 2017), and in 2013 a prior requirement of in-house Mandatory Reconsideration raised an additional barrier, prompting further challenge. A Mandatory Reconsideration request was required within one month of a decision, or under 'special circumstances' up to thirteen months afterwards. Refusal of an extension in effect established the DWP as gatekeeper to the independent appeal process, thus raising questions of fairness, access to justice, and the power to decide, all of which rebound on agency.

A decision in the case of two refused ESA claimants (*CJ and SG v SSWP* [2017] UKUT 0324 (AAC)) reasserted appeal rights for *all* DWP benefits, since the judge saw a high risk that merited claimants would miss the time limit and thus lose benefits to which they were entitled. Noting that 'many claimants will be vulnerable for reasons including issues relating to their mental health or learning disabilities' (para 83), the judge stressed 'the ordinary need to have regard to context in the application of any legal rule' (para. 61) and to 'the realities relating to persons claiming benefits' (para. 86).

This judgement in effect underscores the importance of contextual agency, but despite concerns about the assessment process, those appealing a negative decision for the WRAG are treated as jobseekers with attendant requirements until the decision is overturned. Hence, a questionable assessment of capability exposes claimants to the behavioural requirements of full conditionality, with financial penalties, bodily suffering, and impugned moral standing should they fall short. Reported effects include a worsening of conditions, anxiety, financial hardship, and individual trauma, all of which further

The Moral Economy of Welfare and Migration

undermine agency and work prospects (Kennedy, Murphy, and Wilson 2016).

Embodiment and Interconnected Agency

Misdirected 'incentives' to work and related questions of agency have also arisen from the benefit cap, which allows exemptions for households in receipt of *some* disability benefits – Attendance Allowance, Disability Living Allowance, and Support Group ESA. A case arose concerning the *non-exemption* for recipients of Carers Allowance – a benefit for people providing thirty-five hours of care per week, whether or not in co-residence. Some co-resident carers fall under the household exemption for Disability Living Allowance, but the official definition of a household is restricted to partners and dependent children and so does not cover non-spousal or non-resident adult carers. The case at issue (*Hurley and Ors v SSWP* [2015] EWHC 3382 (Admin)) challenged a failure to fully accommodate constraints arising from intimate obligations of care for others, again highlighting the interconnected rather than purely autonomous nature of agency.

The purpose of the cap, as outlined by the relevant minister, was 'all about influencing behaviour' (para. 18), and a DWP official explained that it was 'designed to achieve long term behavioural effects by changing attitudes to welfare and work'. Carers subject to the cap should therefore face the same choices as others – to take up work or adjust their budget (para. 25). However, the claimants at issue were involved in complex relations of mutual support that constrained their options. One was a lone parent of four children who was also caring for her grandmother and had been evicted as a result of the cap; the other was a grandson who suffered from mental health problems and dyslexia but was providing non-residential support for his grandmother. In both instances, the 'choices' available to the carers – taking up employment and/or moving to cheaper accommodation[5] – would disrupt a pattern of care and mutual support at considerable cost to the state (para. 35).

The non-exemption of carers' allowance from the cap was thus deemed indirect discrimination against disabled people. In delivering this decision the judge urged reconsideration of the policy, given 'the hardship it can and does produce and the lack of real benefit to the State' (para. 75). More significantly, the claimants' agency was shown to be rooted in a pattern of mutual support that official definitions

Activating the Welfare Subject 155

of a 'household' and ill-informed conceptions of autonomous behavioural motivation had failed to recognize or accommodate.

LONE PARENTS AND THE BENEFIT CAP

Identity, Agency, and Intersubjectivity

The benefit cap has also raised problems for lone parents that demonstrate other aspects of the interconnected nature of agency, as well as its relation to identity and intersubjectivity. One such case (*JS and Ors v SSWP* [2013] EWHC 3350) followed the initial implementation of the cap at £26,000. The stated aims of the measure were to reduce welfare spending, shift welfare culture by incentivizing work, and ensure fairness to working taxpayers (para. 1); however, among the benefits included in the calculation are those paid on behalf of children. A challenge was brought on behalf of three single parents and their youngest children (all younger than four), based on various forms of discrimination under the ECHR. However, the case came to turn on gender discrimination, together with the unreasonableness of the measure in common law. It was argued that a large majority of those affected were female lone parents, that under the 2012 act lone parents with a child under five were not required to work (para. 99), and that working households were anyway better off before the introduction of the cap (para. 89).

Agency entered the picture through the argument that 'it is quite unrealistic to believe that these claimants can work' (para. 82), in view both of the difficulties of childcare arrangements and of the lack of available jobs. Furthermore, the alternative response of moving to cheaper accommodation was problematic in relation to children's educational stability, available support networks, and for two of the claimants, their strong cultural/religious ties. The interconnected nature of these constraints was heightened by the fact that two of the women were fleeing domestic violence and thus had limited housing options – all pointing to the fact that mothers of young children are not independent agents in a position to respond to simple financial incentivization.

The same arguments were rehearsed on appeal (*SG and Ors v SSWP* [2014] EWCA Civ 156), but the Secretary of State justified the policy as advancing change in the welfare culture (para. 44), arguing that 'if child-related benefits had been excluded from the cap its

156 *The Moral Economy of Welfare and Migration*

discriminatory effect on women generally would have been reduced or eliminated altogether. But the scheme would have been seriously emasculated' (para. 56). The appeal failed – in effect, lone parents were to be incentivized by removing needs-based benefits from their children – but the identification of women's interests with those of their children, and the impact on their agency, became central on appeal to the UKSC (*SG and Ors v SSWP* [2015] UKSC 16).

A majority of the judges (three of five) argued that treatment of the child does not depend on the sex of the parent and thus had no bearing on the claim of gender discrimination. However, a dissenting minority of two supported the appeal, and as Lady Hale argued, the government must do more than simply justify the cap – it must also explain why it had adopted a scheme that had disproportionately adverse effects on women (para. 188). While disability-related exemptions meant the cap does not apply to those least able to work, the same logic had not been extended to lone parents with a child under five (para. 200). They too were not required to work, but they also lost benefits otherwise available to cover their own and their children's needs (para. 209). Lord Kerr went further than this, questioning whether the interests of lone mothers can be separated from those of their children: 'A mother's personality, the essence of her parenthood, is defined not simply by her gender but by her role and responsibility as carer of her children' (para. 264). The compulsion to work and the removal of benefit both placed this responsibility at issue.

The view that the cap is discriminatory therefore engages women's agency through the argument that their employment options are constrained by their caring responsibilities, that a reduction in the benefit paid on behalf of children is being used to incentivize lone mothers into work, and that in the absence of employment these women depend on state benefits to fulfill a caring role that is part of their identity. Their agency is thus construed as a feature of the inter-subjective relationship with their child(ren), and the benefit cap is at odds with this recognition, which is endorsed in other aspects of welfare policy.

Differing Degrees of Agency

The majority UKSC judgement dismissed the appeal, seeing the disparity of impact between men and women as having an objective and reasonable justification (para. 96). A further case (*DA and Ors v SSWP*

[2017] EWHC 1446 (Admin)) looked to the particular position of lone parents (regardless of gender) with a child under two, in another instance of interconnected agency. By this time the cap had been lowered and lone parents with a child aged three or over had been made subject to full conditionality. The point at issue was 'the difficulty and sometimes impossibility of lone parents with a child under two of being able to work' (para. 16), which was recognized in their exemption from work-seeking requirements. As the judge acknowledged, the parents concerned 'are not workshy but find it, because of the care difficulties, impossible to comply with the work requirement ... (hence) real misery is being caused to no good purpose' (para. 43).

The argument thus turned on their restricted agency. The claimants were not lone parents by choice (para. 30), and incentivizing them to work 'had no real traction in circumstances where there was no realistic prospect of working' (para. 86). However, in the subsequent appeal (DA and Ors v SSWP [2018] EWCA Civ 504), evidence had to show the parental situation to be 'materially different' from that of other claimants (para. 92), and the majority opinion relied on a debatable interpretation of relevant statistics (para. 109): 16 per cent of lone parents with a child under two who had been capped had moved into employment, and this was deemed insufficiently different from the 30 per cent of those with a child under five who had done so. The former group did not therefore constitute a distinctive 'other status' warranting different treatment.

Against this view, a dissenting judge looked to expert commentary and general knowledge of the greater problems and costs involved in childcare for very young children (para. 156), especially given a shortage of suitable jobs and the uncertainty involved in flexible working and zero-hours contracts (paras. 170–1). However, the EWHC decision was overruled – in effect, constraints on the agency of lone parents with a child under two were not deemed sufficiently different from those faced by other lone parents to amount to a case of discrimination. That decision was upheld by five to two in the Supreme Court (DA and Ors v SSWP [2019] UKSC 21).

'CHOICE' AND THE TWO-CHILD LIMIT

This final case was a challenge to the two-child limit on CTC, applicable to new claims as of February 2019. CTC is a means-tested benefit for households both in and out of work, a guaranteed minimum now removed by a measure that claims to enhance the life chances of children through responsible decision-making by parents. The stated aims revolve around agency in terms of parental decisions about family size, but despite exemptions, the two child limit does not fully accommodate unforeseen circumstances.

Exemptions covered by the regulations include multiple births, adoption where a child would otherwise be in care, non-parental care, and non-consensual conception (rape). All were to apply *only* to the third child, and hence, the only routes to CTC for a third child would be multiple birth or rape – the latter stigmatizing the child concerned. A further requirement that in such cases the mother not be living with the perpetrator in practice removes support at a critical time and undermines the woman's capacity to leave (CPAG 2016). A case was brought on behalf of four adults (*SC and Ors v SSWP* [2018] EWHC 864 (Admin)), each with a third or subsequent child for whom CTC was not payable – variously resulting from abuse, a failure of the birth control pill, medication as an impediment to birth control, and care of a grandson.

The policy aim foregrounds reflexive agency in urging parents to 'think carefully about whether they can afford to support additional children' (para. 30). However, the challenge points to a flawed notion of 'choice' in that 'conception and birth cannot be neatly categorised as voluntary or involuntary' (para. 47). Though gendered constraints are again apparent, there was no clearly defined group on which to hang a discrimination charge, and the aims of the policy were deemed legitimate and lawful (para. 148). This left only one outstanding feature of the challenge – the exception for cases of non-parental care, which may be construed as another instance of interconnected agency. The judge found that confining this exception to children born *before* non-parental care was engaged was irrational in that it discouraged a family from assuming a responsibility that would otherwise fall to the local authority.

Despite having little further legal purchase, the case reveals the flawed assumptions behind the policy and its failure to engage with life as it is lived by many of those affected. Indeed, the House of Lords secondary legislation scrutiny (2017) found that official response to criticism amounted to little more than stock phrases, doubted that the measure could ever be made to work, and felt it risked punishing families for circumstances beyond their control (see Kennedy, Keen, and Mackley 2017, 4.31).

Though questions may be raised about how representative these cases are, something can be said of their general applicability. The *Reilly and Wilson* case determined the treatment of an estimated 3,789 to 4,305 related appeals (DWP 2018); the judgement in *RR v SSWP* was explicitly issued as guidance for other such cases (para. 2); carers' allowance has now been exempted from the benefit cap; the WCA has been found to disadvantage mental health patients, who make up half of its clientele (Kennedy, Keen, and Mackley 2017, 3); the right of appeal for *all* DWP benefits has been reaffirmed; and the two-child limit has been amended to exempt non-parental care. While lone parents have not been similarly successful, they do account for 85 per cent of households subject to the benefit cap (Syal 2019), and their treatment has provoked considerable disagreement within the judiciary and in Parliament (see Work and Pensions Committee 2019).

PURPOSIVE RATIONALITY AND PRACTICAL REASON

Each of the above cases addresses a particular feature of Britain's recent welfare reform, and each is bound up with policy objectives aimed at behavioural change. They all open up questions concerning conceptions of agency that both invite and inform sociological thinking on this topic. The policies address agency through financial incentives, behavioural requirements, and associated sanctions, but with scant recognition of the context in which agency is exercised, and with little accommodation of more complex features of capacity and interconnectivity.

It was noted earlier that the measures documented can be construed as a form of purposive rationality with respect to both the objective of behavioural change and the means adopted to achieve this. However, it has also been argued that they are based on a pared-down understanding of agency that leaves out of account what Sayer terms practical reason, as revealed by a more situated appreciation of the claimant's context. Each of the cases explored exemplifies a different aspect of the tension between these contrasting understandings of agency. Each also demonstrates the narrow institutional framing of *who* has value and *what* is valued, whether in relation to individual hopes and plans, accommodation of varied and variable capabilities, patterns of care and concern for others, or the whole complex fabric of claimants' lives.

Incentives, caps, and coercion thus reflect the institutional conception of agency as it arises in the welfare context. This, Giddens would argue, amounts to more than a consensual backdrop; it also conveys a distinctive moral message fashioned by active policy agents, initiating what Reed and Weinman would term an 'agency chain'. However, given that the central objective of these policies is behavioural change, an understanding of how they are experienced by claimants is crucial to their efficacy and their legitimacy, in terms of both the regulatory framework in operation and its mesh with the complexities of daily life. Each of the measures sketched out in the present chapter thus constitutes a pivotal moment in the unfolding of a distinctive welfare culture, as the 'master frames' noted by Emirbayer and Mische (1998) encounter the constraints of lived experience.

Interrogation of the legal challenges that identify and isolate these moments has served here to demonstrate complexities of agency that go far beyond the policy rationale. The cases considered engage context creation in terms of, respectively, governing regulations and requirements; complexities of claimant circumstance that require nuanced interpretation; capacity and agency in the classification of claimants, their ability to negotiate the system, and the determination of (in)appropriate requirements; embodied agency and interconnected agency in relation to varied obligations of care; intersubjectivity that binds together the interests of mother and child; and the illusion of choice in circumstances that may defy individual control. All have been consigned to a distant second place in a drive for optimal extraction of labouring capacity and defence of the hard-working taxpayer.

However, the sociological interest of the cases goes further than an abstract opposition between conceptions of agency based respectively on purposive rationality and practical reason. Critical commentary on the impact of welfare reform has noted the disproportionate impact on women and on people with disabilities (Butterworth and Burton 2013), and several of the cases discussed here show why. They reveal the ways that agency may be internally differentiated by limitations rooted in gendered responsibilities and by failures to accommodate variable degrees of physical and mental capacity. They also show that these constraints could be ameliorated by appropriate policy intervention. There is therefore a strong argument not only for translating abstract conceptions of agency into embodied and situated human existence, but also for viewing agency in the context of institutional enabling or constraint.

The cases considered all expose anomalies in the formulation and implementation of policy, and most yielded successes that have forced procedural or policy refinements, but the broader framework of reform remains largely intact. Amending the flaws of policy design and implementation revealed by the cases considered cannot of course supplant the wider moral assumptions and social steering that the welfare reforms embrace, though they go some way toward undermining them. A more fundamental challenge would need to displace the moral messages and underpinning objectives that lie behind measures advanced by the welfare reform. Yet viewed through a sociological lens, the cases reveal ill-formed policy assumptions, limited understanding of claimants' circumstances, and questionable attributions of individual responsibility that rebound on the moral standing of claimants, while also furnishing real-life instances of the complexity of human agency. Before closing the chapter, however, it is worth considering how much purchase such argument has beyond the specifics of the welfare reform as detailed above.

AN EXTENDED PARADIGM

In fact, these arguments could equally well apply to much of the policy formulation relating to the control of immigration and asylum. As noted in Chapter 4, Munch (2012) has argued that a policy paradigm exists when a consistent vocabulary of ideas, concepts, and remedies spills over from one area to another. The policy initiatives detailed in earlier chapters furnish some examples, and while the crucial role for conceptions of agency has not been exposed to legal scrutiny to quite the same degree, we can draw not only on legal judgements but also on wider sources of commentary and critique.

Chapter 3 has shown how a dominant theme of immigration policy in the run-up to the referendum on EU membership was based on clear assumptions about motives, with a commitment to deal with the 'abuse' of free movement (Cameron 2014c; 2015a) and 'rogue' EU benefit claims (DWP 2013a). However, we also noted official figures showing that EU migrants do not make disproportionate claims on benefits (see Keen and Turner 2016); indeed, the government's own independent Migration Advisory Committee (MAC 2014) found no evidence that benefits act as a draw to migration. Yet ensuing policy was based on the assumption that the availability of benefits was driving migration, and despite the lack of supporting evidence, a package of measures was introduced to address 'the magnetic pull' of Britain's benefits system (Cameron 2014b). The intention was 'to discourage people ... from migrating here without a firm offer of employment' (Kennedy 2015b, 14) and thus contribute to a broader aim of bringing overall net migration down to the tens of thousands (Prince 2010) – though note that the changes were introduced at a time when economic migrants from the EEA had an employment rate of 86.5 per cent (Cooper et al. 2014). There has indeed been a fall in EEA migration since the changes were introduced (Partington 2019b), but this has provoked alarm among employers, including the NHS, and is more plausibly explained by the inimical and uncertain environment that has developed in the wake of the referendum on EU membership.

Assumptions of abuse also underpinned a Home Office drive in 2010 to remove homeless EEA nationals (McGuinness 2017a), and in 2017 there were close to five thousand expulsions (Kentish 2017) under regulations to address an 'abuse of the right to reside'. A case brought by the Public Interest Law Unit (PIL) with the AIRE Centre intervening (*Gureckis and Ors v SSHD* [2017] EWHC 3298 (Admin)) turned on agency via the question of whether rough sleeping could be construed as an abuse of rights. The judge in the case did not consider that rough sleeping could ever amount to a means of artificially fulfilling the conditions of presence (para. 100) and found there was no intention to illegitimately secure an advantage. The notion that significant numbers of EEA migrants were strategically sleeping rough is inherently implausible, and in fact, the targeting of EEA rough sleepers for removal was ruled to be discriminatory (para. 113). However, strangely absent from the legal deliberation is any discussion of the background context for agency and intent on the part of rough sleepers. Here the context of action has been shaped by the benefit changes, especially the withdrawal of HB from EEA jobseekers (see SSAC 2014), and there are reports that EEA migrants – who may have been working – had been incorrectly refused UC (Butler and Rankin 2019). They could also be negatively affected by 'right to rent' requirements (O'Carroll 2019), the likely effects of an increasingly casualized labour market, and the very high cost of housing in London – where rough sleeping is particularly concentrated (*Gureckis and Ors v SSHD*, para. 107). CRISIS (2017) extended the argument by urging a less coercive approach to agency that focused on the wishes and best interests of the individual, following a model of support and advice.

The exclusion of Zambrano carers from mainstream benefits was similarly based on motivational assumptions, and we have seen that the stated rationale for the policy was a reduction of 'benefit tourism' (*Sanneh v sswp* [2015] EWCA Civ 49 para. 96). Among the claims made for the measure were that it would remove the incentive for people coming to Britain to claim benefits, and that it would press TCNs wishing to have children here to ensure that they first had sufficient resources. Critical comment has argued that the restriction on benefits bites only after the Zambrano situation has arisen (*Sanneh and Ors v sswp*, para 97) – often flowing from a relationship breakdown – and that the deterrent effect is therefore limited. O'Brien (2016) has pointed out that the children concerned are British citizens and not the result of a TCN acting alone, so as with the two-child CTC limit, justification is based on simplistic assumptions about the dynamics of family life. A similar argument can be made about the minimum income requirement for family unification, and especially the allowable exception for 'unjustifiably harsh consequences', as formal guidance makes it clear this will not generally follow where a couple 'chose to commence their family life together whilst living in separate countries' (Desira 2017).

More overt linkages between agency, motivation, and welfare provision can be seen in the evolving treatment of asylum-seekers, as for example in the debate over the denial of a right to work for the first twelve months, and thereafter in shortage occupations only, even though this would reduce welfare costs. Despite support from the House of Lords for a more open approach, an amendment to the 2015 Immigration Bill was rejected on the grounds of 'sending the wrong message'. Advocacy groups argue that this view lacks evidence to back it up, and can anyway be countered by positive effects on integration, public perceptions, and the economy more generally (Gower 2019, 8). Indeed, research more generally (Crawley and Hagen-Zanker 2018) shows that decision-making about where to apply for asylum involves a complex mix of factors, which include not only prospects for work but also family circumstances, existing support networks, and prospects for family unification, besides being often based on imperfect knowledge. Yet fear of a 'pull factor' is an ever-present influence on policy-making, described by Mayblin (2016) as a 'political imaginary' that endures despite a large body of conflicting evidence.

We find a similar set of arguments in relation to welfare support for asylum-seekers and failed asylum-seekers, the latter now framed in policy consultation (Home Office 2015) and government 'factsheets' (Home Office 2016b) as 'illegal migrants'. Chapter 5 has shown how asylum support policy has for some years been driven by deterrence, aimed at those who 'seek to come to or remain in the UK in an attempt to benefit from the support arrangements we have put in place' (Home Office 2015, 3). A freezing of support in 2011 was based on the assumption that higher rates of support attract non-genuine claims, despite the absence of evidence to show any such correlation (Parliamentary Inquiry 2013), while a similar logic underpins provisions in the 2016 Immigration Act to restrict support for failed asylum-seekers. This was on the questionable assumption that worsening conditions would drive people to leave, despite a conflicting conclusion from earlier HO research, which found that removing support simply drove people underground (Refugee Council and Refugee Action 2006).

The limited conception of agency in play in a recent revival of this policy is apparent in the statement that 'there is no obligation ... to accommodate illegal migrants who *intentionally make themselves destitute* by refusing to leave the UK when it is clear they are able to' (Home Office 2016, 10–11). Measures included in the 2016 Act will impose tighter requirements to show a 'genuine obstacle' to departure and shift the onus of proof to claimants who are ill-placed to secure the relevant evidence. Furthermore, support groups have argued that many failed asylum-seekers have real fears about returning to their country of origin and see remaining in the UK in an undocumented capacity as the only option for protecting their children (e.g., Coram Legal Children's Centre 2015) – another instance of interconnected agency.

Finally, anti-trafficking policy has long wrestled with agency-related problems in attempting to address a continuum that extends from exploitative labour relations partly enabled by restrictive immigration regimes, to captive coercion for activities including (for example) sexual slavery and cannabis cultivation (Broad and Turnbull 2019). A more specific issue arose in relation to the social support that is provided for those identified as potential victims of trafficking through the National Referral Mechanism (NRM). Until July 2019, financial support was limited to a period of forty-five days, during which a conclusive decision was made; that support was then ended unless a rare extension was granted (amounting to only 11 per cent of cases).

Agency was at issue in two ways – expert practitioners had found recovery and rehabilitation from the mental and physical traumas involved (i.e., a restoration of full agency) to require a much longer period; meanwhile, the Minister for Crime, Safeguarding and Vulnerability argued that 'if all victims of modern slavery were granted automatic discretionary leave, we expect the NRM would increase by people seeking access to benefits' (Murphy 2018, 7). In fact, a policy to reduce the level of financial support from £65 a week to £37.75 in 2018 was halted only after legal challenge (*K and AM v SSHD* [2018] EWHC 2951), but a further challenge (*NN and LP v SSHD* [2019] EWHC 1003) has now secured Home Office agreement to remove the 'cliff edge' cessation of support and instead build a needs-based system – as yet to be developed (Anti-Slavery 2019).

The examples above variously illustrate policy assumptions of bad faith and abuse in relation to freedom of movement under EU law, an overly simplistic understanding of the dynamics of family life in relation to Zambrano care and transnational unions, a limited understanding of the constraints that shape the decisions of asylum-seekers and failed asylum-seekers, and an inadequate grasp of the complexities of recovery from trauma for victims of trafficking. As with the welfare reform, in each instance we find a limited conception of agency at play in policy formulation, the absence or neglect of evidence that could raise doubts about its efficacy, a poor appreciation of the complexity and interconnected nature of people's lives and motivations, and a failure to consider the wider context in which agency is exercised or curtailed.

CONCLUSION

Against a background drive to reconfigure the welfare system, the legal cases discussed in this chapter have pointed in different ways to the inadequate conceptions of agency that operate in the design and/ or implementation of policy. They provide concrete examples of the questionable nature of policy assumptions within an actively constructed agenda that seeks to impose behavioural change to the neglect of situational, relational, and embodied context. Yet these assumptions are crucial to the moral message of welfare reform, in that agency carries with it an associated conferment of responsibility and thus has an impact on moral standing as underpinned by reasonable expectation. Agency, however, emerges as the fulcrum for the crises produced when political master frames clash with the reality of claimant experience, and hence has provided a focal point for contestation.

Similar arguments have purchase in relation to migration and asylum, and we have seen policies repeatedly designed around the assumption that benefits are a 'pull factor', despite a lack of supporting evidence, as in the case of EEA migrants. Similarly, assumptions relating to benefit tourism misrepresent the Zambrano situation, which only arises after presence in Britain has been established. Decision-making on the part of asylum-seekers has been shown to rely on a complex of factors, often with only partial knowledge of conditions in the destination country, and the number of asylum applications shows no correlation with support rates. Destitution has not proved an effective means of enforcing the departure of failed asylum-seekers and undocumented migrants, while the fixed-term period of maintenance for victims of trafficking has been argued to impede recovery and the restoration of full agency.

The instances detailed in the present chapter thus show how a more refined understanding of agency can serve as a valuable tool for analysing the design and implementation of policy measures, the crisis points they generate, and their legitimacy in terms of the lived experience of those affected. Ill-designed objectives of behavioural change have been shown to apply across a range of policy fields and are a key feature of the moral economy that underpins the entire welfare–migration–asylum complex. The implications for the moral standing of its subjects can arise either through holding them responsible for their circumstances under conditions of severely constrained agency, or through assumptions about fraud or abuse that are unsupported by evidence. The related dynamic therefore constitutes one area of common ground in the treatment of domestic welfare claimants, migrants, and asylum-seekers. The following chapter undertakes a more widely framed overview of such 'crossover' aspects of policy, tracing what can be termed the 'topology' of Britain's welfare–migration–asylum complex.

7

The Topology of Welfare–Migration–Asylum: Britain's Outsiders Inside

BREACHING THE CITIZEN/NON-CITIZEN BINARY

We have seen how a coming age of austerity, announced by David Cameron in 2009 (Cameron 2009), was embedded in the 2012 Welfare Reform Act and the 2016 Welfare Reform and Work Act. At the same time, the Immigration Acts of 2014 and 2016 heightened controls over the entry and stay of migrants and asylum-seekers and radically reduced their access to services and support. In 2013, Sarah Teather[1] declared that 'the immigration proposals feel as if they are hewn from the same rock as welfare' (Aitkenhead 2013), raising interesting questions about the nature and effects of this overlap. The present chapter considers the welfare–migration–asylum complex from this perspective. It seeks to identify commonalities of approach, technique, and effect, which can usefully be viewed through the concept of topology (Mezzadra and Neilson 2012) to reveal much about the way we are governed not just as citizens but as a total population.

As we saw in Chapter 2, citizenship has traditionally been seen as the yardstick of full inclusion, captured by Marshall's (1992 [1950]) model of membership as the full array of civil, political, and social rights, the latter securing a right to 'share to the full in the social heritage and to live the life of a civilised being' (8). The model has been criticized for its neglect of the exclusions entailed, and Arendt (1979[1948], 299) famously characterized the absence of citizenship as the 'abstract nakedness of being nothing but human' for those lacking membership of a community willing and able to deliver basic (universal) rights. Agamben (1998) mirrors these sentiments in his deployment of the concept of 'bare life' as experienced in 'the camp', an (extra)legal space of abandonment that serves as society's constitutive outside. So he argues that Western politics has constituted itself through an exclusion, in which bare life features as both a subject and object of political order and thus as part of the *polis* by virtue of being defined outside the structure of law. He also argues, somewhat obscurely, that the camp emerges as the 'hidden paradigm' of modernity – one whose 'metamorphoses and disguises' we must learn to recognize (123). This is something we return to later in the chapter.

Empirical referents for 'bare life' can be difficult to identify, and in fact Agamben (1998, 131) argues that once politicized by declarations of rights, the insider/outsider threshold must be constantly redrawn. Certainly, since Arendt's time of writing the binary opposition between citizens and non-citizens has been challenged in a number of ways, not least by conceptions of a postnational society (Soysal 1994) in which residence supersedes citizenship, albeit in uneasy coexistence with indeterminate locations outside of secure (settled) status. Indeed, subsequent work has increasingly focused on the complex array of stratified distinctions that fall between the extremes of total exclusion and the notionally full membership of citizenship (Morris 2002). Thus, Sigona (2015) points to multifaceted mediations and mobilizations that penetrate even 'camp' life to yield hierarchies or degrees of inclusion, while undocumented status has been seen not as an absolute marker but as a condition that may be overridden by accumulated emblems of desert, as well as modes of informal participation that fall short of security (Chauvin and Garces-Mascarenas 2012). Conversely, understandings of exclusion now reach beyond notions of the camp as a discrete and separate location to address the expansion of internal borders that permeate the fabric of society (Morris 1998; Yuval-Davis, Wemyss, and Cassidy 2019).

Scholarly focus has therefore shifted away from the image of exclusion as a physical and extra-legal space toward the uses of law to stratify and divide, while also allowing the possibility of selection and incorporation. Fassin (2009) has had a particular interest in how bodily frailty can offer a route to security, but he also opens up wider questions about how life is shaped by the political choices implicit in the 'moral economy' of contemporary societies. He uses this term to capture the assumptions and requirements underpinning political decisions: a power over who should live what sort of life and for how long – the power 'to let live and reject into death' according to the worthiness of individual lives (52).

The emerging picture shows how a notionally bounded society is riven with practices that make it increasingly porous (Van Houtum and Van Naerssen 2002), and in which classification plays a crucial role, so that the notion of bare life is displaced by a sensibility to the making and breaking of social categories (Huysmans 2008). Thus, Fassin (2010) looks to the extension of 'bare life' into 'qualified life' through the hierarchical sorting of individual subjects within a bounded territory. The thrust of related argument has been to complicate dualistic notions of inclusion and exclusion and to focus on differentiations that can occur within the same legal and political space (Koenoenen 2018). Indeed, while Agamben does not elaborate on what he terms the 'metamorphoses and disguises' of 'the camp', he does observe that 'the camp is now securely lodged within the city's interior' (176). Thus, we find that bare life is not confined to a discrete physical space of exclusion, but rather infiltrates the fabric of mainstream society through the incorporation of destitution into devices of discipline and control.

Just as the legal/illegal binary is rendered more complex in this process, so too is the insider/outsider divide. Indeed, many of the above insights concerning selectivity and conditionality, along with their related effects have also applied to citizenship, not only through selection for inclusion but, conversely, through an erosion of the guarantees that accompany membership. Questions of desert have long been a feature of the British welfare system, yielding the hierarchical divisions within citizenship captured by Lockwood's (1996) concept of civic stratification, though these distinctions have since received less detailed attention than migrant hierarchies. There is, however, growing recognition of a congruence, and a central endeavour of the present study has been to develop an orientation that combines citizens and migrants within the same intellectual field.

The outcome amounts to a mode of governance whereby the granting and denial of rights becomes implicated in a system of control. Its overlapping techniques and effects are documented below and include the creation of a hostile environment for both migrants and welfare claimants, administrative error and failures of justice, stratified entitlement and its discriminatory impacts, negative treatment of children to influence parental behaviour, and the creation of destitution as a disciplinary measure whereby bare life infiltrates the administrative architecture of society.

TRACING COMMONALITIES

Düvell and Jordan (2002) have noted that official recognition of a need for skilled workers can coincide with high unemployment to yield selective recruitment of migrant labour alongside intensified 'activation' of citizens via the welfare system. Anderson (2013) goes further, arguing that while citizens and migrants have been mutually defining, their interrelation is not adequately addressed as a binary opposition. In fact, the 'illegal' migrant and the 'benefit scrounger' are intimately connected in that both fall outside the 'community of value', with each failing in various ways to meet the requirements for inclusion.

The idea was graphically captured in Bauman's (2003) treatment of 'wasted lives', which views society as operating through a series of filters whereby the state generates vulnerability while absolving itself of responsibility. Redundant citizens are thus excluded from within, while migrants and asylum-seekers are subject to partial or selective inclusion from without, and hence Landolt and Goldring (2015) look for variation within the categories of both citizen and non-citizen. Differential inclusion with respect to conduct and desert then serves as a key mechanism in elaborating boundaries that are never fixed or impermeable but rather constitute a system of 'chutes and ladders' for citizens and non-citizens alike.

Notions of hierarchy, selection, and filtering thus abound, and Mezzadra and Neilson (2012) introduce a further elaboration through the notion of 'topology'. In its original (geometrical) sense, topology is concerned with properties of space that are preserved without rupture under continuous deformations such as stretching, twisting, and bending. Mezzadra and Neilson apply this idea to the 'different kinds of folding and filtering that challenge the rigidity of the distinction between inclusion and exclusion' (60). Though principally concerned with the experience of migrants, they recognize at various points that insights derived from a topological approach have huge implications for citizenship. In fact, this approach brings a valuable additional dimension to exploring the increasingly complex relations within and between citizen and non-citizen status, and the proliferation of subject positions occupied by those who are neither fully insiders nor fully outsiders.

For Mezzadra and Neilson, a topological approach accommodates fluidity and differential inclusion alongside new regimes of control,

The Topology of Welfare–Migration–Asylum   171

and in noting the implications for citizenship, the authors have in mind the breaching of external borders and expanding forms of access to membership. However, they could go further, to address the processes at work in a simultaneous loss of standing for some citizens. Without relinquishing recognition of hierarchy, and with it the forms of privilege that still attach to citizenship status, the idea of folding and filtering encourages attention to the recurrent rationales and techniques that apply to migrants and citizens alike, and the similarities of experience they engender.

Running through the stratified system of rights we find vulnerable groups exposed to similar problems and constraints as the rhetorical and administrative devices driving an increasingly disciplinary system translate into concrete experiences. These experiences point to ever more refined classifications and boundary distinctions; they also reveal more far-reaching aspects of the way we are governed as a total population, in relation to both the cross-cutting devices of control and their more extreme effects.

THE SYSTEM, ITS RHETORIC, AND ITS RATIONALE

In Britain, a composite discourse has shaped policy in the fields of welfare, migration, and asylum. Beginning in 2010, a series of political speeches launched the programme of welfare reform as a 'moral mission' (Cameron 2012), promoting a conception of 'fairness' aimed not just at who gets help but also at 'who gives that help through their taxes' (Cameron 2010). Immigration controls were built in through plans to limit the entry of migrant workers who 'do the jobs that those on welfare were being paid not to do' (Cameron 2011; see also 2013), prevent migrant 'exploitation of services and benefits' (Cameron 2014a), and address 'abuse' of the asylum system (May 2015).

An array of devices with significant overlaps across all fields has been harnessed to these ends, and while hierarchical distinctions remain in terms of citizenship and immigration status, the minimal guarantee of social inclusion that is the hallmark of Marshall's citizenship has been diminished if not abandoned. Across the fields of welfare, migration, and asylum we find an appropriation of access to rights as a mode of control that operates through cuts and conditionality aimed at behavioural change. We have seen how, in a 'moral crusade' (Simmons 2010) based on incentivizing work, the domestic welfare system under austerity has worn away working-age benefits through reductions and freezes (McInnes 2018); financial sanctions for failure to meet heightened conditions; a (shrinking) cap on the total amount of benefit a household can receive; a two-child limit for child tax credits (CTCs); and reduced support for those with limited capability for work (Kennedy, Keen, and Mackley 2017). Furthermore, Universal Credit (UC), which combines in-work and out-of-work benefits in one system, has built in a five-week waiting period and replaced hardship payments with loans and is piloting the extension of conditionality to the working poor.

Welfare issues have also been central to immigration control. In advance of Brexit, EEA migrants saw reduced access to Housing Benefit (HB) and time-limited duration for unemployment support (Kennedy 2015b). Non-EEA carers of citizen children (Zambrano carers) are allowed to work but if workless are barred from mainstream benefits and eligible only for lesser local authority provision (*Sanneh and Ors v SSWP* [2015] EWCA Civ 49; *HC v SSWP* [2017] UKSC 73, para. 51). Other non-EEA migrants face heightened minimum income requirements (MIRs) for entry both as workers and as family members (Gower 2015), and since 2012, leave to remain for human rights reasons, or on the basis of a twenty-year presence, has imposed a ten-year route to settlement (Yeo 2018), with permission to work but 'no recourse to public funds' (NRPF). Asylum support rates (already below mainstream welfare) were frozen between 2011 and 2015, and preferential rates for children were removed in 2015 (Gower 2015a). Failed asylum-seekers, care leavers without status, and undocumented migrants are only to be supported if they can show they are taking reasonable steps to leave (Harvey and Harper 2017, 356–7).

This then is the resource-related structure or 'topology' of the welfare–immigration–asylum regime, in a system resting on erosions of entitlement and forms of conditionality intended to incentivize or deter particular behaviours. Although the system displays a hierarchy of positions and entitlements, conceptions of layering, folding, and filtering can serve to capture its recurrent rationales, objectives, devices, and techniques, as well as their often overlapping effects across a variety of groups. In what follows, these overlaps are traced along various dimensions of the resultant configuration, from the construction of a hostile environment, to administrative

The Topology of Welfare–Migration–Asylum

error, recurrent discriminations, the treatment of children, and the harnessing of destitution as a mode of control. This chapter therefore goes beyond the mapping exercise undertaken in Chapter 4 to focus on the resultant effects and experiences for targeted groups.

CREATING A HOSTILE ENVIRONMENT

We saw in Chapter 5 that a prominent feature of the emergent immigration regime has been the declared intent to create a 'really hostile environment' for irregular migrants (Kirkup and Winnett 2012). This deterrent approach, which goes far beyond the target group, culminates in measures designed to make life prohibitively difficult for undocumented migrants (a term that includes failed asylum-seekers). The guiding rationale is that those unlawfully present should not be able to access 'the everyday benefits and services' that are routinely available to others (Home Office 2016d). A notable development has been the creation of new criminal offences to prevent undocumented migrants' access to work, housing, health care, bank accounts, and driver's licences, and to enhance the (error-prone) capacity for checks on status by employers, landlords, banks, and the NHS (Yeo 2018b). This extension of powers was 'based on a conviction that they were right in principle, rather than on any evidence they were working' (Independent Chief Inspector of Borders and Immigration, cited in Yeo 2016). As with the reform of domestic welfare, one purpose of the initiative has been to construct a moral message for public consumption.

In fact, the hostile environment has been remarked on more for its flaws than for its effectiveness. The most telling outcomes have been the 'Windrush scandal' of lost jobs and denial of benefits and health care for Commonwealth migrants with a legitimate right of abode (NAO 2018; PAC 2019), and the courts' recognition that landlord checks on the 'right to rent' have a discriminatory impact on black and minority ethnic (BME) citizens – though they have been deemed justifiable by the EWCA (*JCWI v SSHD* [2020] EWCA Civ 542). Commentators have also highlighted the dangers of driving vulnerable people away from all contact with authority and support (e.g., Corporate Watch 2017) – one reported effect of embedding Home Office officials in local authorities (Busby 2019). The hostile environment also extends to official neglect, and the NAO (2018) has criticized the Home Office's lack of a duty of care in this context.

Though the parallel is not exact in terms of explicit intent, public comment has begun to draw comparisons between the fall-out from the hostile environment and the functioning of welfare reform (see, for example, Moore 2018; Ryan 2019; Goodrick 2019), most notably with regard to the system's target-driven culture,[2] its privatization of administration and control (see, for example, House of Commons 2017), and its use of destitution as a policy tool.[3] A task force was established in 2010 to address 'unacceptably high' levels of benefit fraud, error, and debt (DWP 2015), and there is an online 'Benefit Thieves Reporting Form', though 86 per cent of reports from the public have been found to be baseless (Cowburn 2018). Meanwhile, it is argued that intensifying demands have created a climate of fear that risks driving people away from support, puts them off claiming (WPC 2019b; 2019c), detracts from their efforts to find work (JRF 2014c; CPAG 2018), and screens everyone for potential wrongdoing in a system of total surveillance (Alston 2018). Particular concern has been expressed about conditionality and sanctions for the long-term sick and disabled (WPC 2018); the lack of an evidence base (DWP 2018); failure to monitor outcomes, especially the increased exits from benefits for unknown destinations (WPC 2015); and the DWP's lack of interest in or understanding about the impact of its policies (WPC 2019b, 2019c).

There are further concerns surrounding the functioning of UC: a reported 44 per cent of recipients have fallen behind on bills and on rent or are experiencing financial difficulty (PAC 2018). One result has been the growth of private landlords refusing to let to 'DSS' tenants (Evans 2019) in an echo of the 'right to rent' checks on migrants. The PAC found that UC has created unacceptable levels of hardship for many and operates with a fortress mentality, within a system that is failing claimants. The WPC (2019c, 4) points to a pressing need to improve how the DWP gathers and responds to front-line evidence. It reported (2019, 12) that not a single statistic was available on whether claimants were receiving payments on time – indeed, one third of claims never reached payment stage and there was no follow-up system in place (Alston 2018, 9).

So it appears that the notion of a hostile environment, with its dysfunctional effects, applies well beyond the treatment of irregular migrants; it now permeates much of the functioning of what we can term the topology of the welfare–migration–asylum complex. Its features and effects are examined more fully in what follows, in

The Topology of Welfare–Migration–Asylum

relation to administrative error, cross-cutting discriminatory effects, the treatment of children, and the creation of destitution.

ADMINISTRATIVE ERROR AND ACCESS TO JUSTICE

The more complex a system of control becomes, the more error-prone it will be, and the implementation of both welfare and migration/ asylum policy reveals multiple instances of poor decision making (evidenced by success on appeal), as well as raising questions of access to justice. All of this points to a form of ideological overreach in terms of ambitions for control that are not matched by the capacity, and sometimes the legality, of the attendant administrative systems.

Welfare problems are apparent both in the 'legacy' system that preceded UC and in the roll-out of UC itself. These relate both to claimants' capacity to negotiate the system and to poor decision-making on the part of officials. Since its inception in 2012 the sanctions regime has been criticized for poor communication to claimants, a failure to monitor its impact, and poor-quality decision-making (Oakley 2014; NAO 2016; PAC 2017). There is a high degree of error in the Work Capability Assessment, evidenced by the fact that more than 50 per cent of appeals against fit-for-work decisions have succeeded (Kennedy, Keen, and Mackley 2017). There have been successful challenges to the assessment process (*MM and DM v SSWP* [2013] EWCA Civ 1565) and the time limit for appeal (*CJ and SG v SSWP* [2017] UKUT 0324 (AAC)), both of which were held to disadvantage mental health patients. Retrospective validation of faulty regulations was ruled to be a denial of access to justice for a large number of pending sanctions appeals under the Work Programme (*Reilly and Hewstone v SSWP* [2014] EWHC 2182 (Admin)). Since 2012, in-house Mandatory Reconsideration has partly displaced external review, while of those challenges that do advance to appeal, 81 per cent succeed (CPAG 2018).

As the UC system unfolds, wider questions have been raised (PAC 2018) about a systematic culture of denial and defensiveness on the part of the DWP, a failure to monitor the treatment of vulnerable people, variations in sanction rates across the country, and an over-reliance on work coach discretion. There have been reports of a system riddled with errors that causes 'chaos and misery' for claimants (Butler 2019), including wrongful refusal of EEA workers (Butler and Rankin 2019), loss of income on transition from the prior (legacy) system

(Butler 2019b), and an incapacity to deal with anything but the simplest claims (*Johnson and Ors v SSWP* [2019] EWHC 23 (Admin)). Philip Alston, the UN Special Rapporteur on extreme poverty, notes the paucity of alternatives to online application, even though only 47 per cent of those on low income use broadband at home, 21 per cent of the population do not have basic digital skills, and only one third have been able to verify their ID online (Alston 2018).

The picture of administrative error, high success rates on appeal, and problems for users is repeated in relation to immigration and asylum issues. Half of all immigration appeals now succeed (McKinney 2019), while immigration status is a key determinant of benefit entitlement. Within the asylum system there have been reports of poor decision-making, as well as incompetence and bullying within a target-driven culture (Hill 2019). The success rate on appeals is around one third (Sturge 2019). Access to support for asylum-seekers and failed asylum-seekers also has a history of poor decision-making: success for 'destitution' appeals has fluctuated between 60 per cent and 82 per cent since 2011 (ASAP 2015) – usually as a consequence of the HO's failure to apply the correct test and/or to consider submitted evidence. Despite this, changes to provision for failed asylum-seekers in the 2016 act (yet to be implemented) will remove the right of appeal, viewing obstacles to return as 'simple matters of fact' (HO 2016).

Further problems flow from the 2012 regulations that have replaced Discretionary Leave (which allowed access to public funds) with a ten-year route to settlement and NRPF. This leave is commonly granted to parents of children with seven years' presence or citizenship, and while it is possible to apply for removal of the condition in cases of destitution, there are many barriers to success. In fact, in a case supported by the Project 17, the instructions to caseworkers on when such a condition should *not* be imposed have been deemed inadequate in relation to Article 3 of the ECHR (*W (by litigation friend J) v SSHD* [2020] EWHC 1299 (Admin).[4] Other groups have faced similar problems, with excessively demanding requirements of proof of destitution for sanctioned claimants seeking hardship payments (Webster 2019a), as well as for asylum-seekers and failed asylum-seekers applying for basic maintenance (ASAP 2015). Each of these groups must furnish exacting and sometimes humiliating evidence of their lack of funds and support, and additional difficulties arise from the absence of legal aid.

The Topology of Welfare–Migration–Asylum

More fundamental administrative failings have been revealed in the implementation of the hostile environment. PAC (2019) notes the HO's failure to monitor the impact of a policy that requires documentary evidence, despite its own systemic failure to keep accurate records, and effects that can rebound on *all* migrants and minority citizens. The committee has condemned a failure to keep accurate records, a complacent and neglectful approach to system failings, inadequate impact assessment, and life-changing decisions made from faulty data. There have also been official warnings that the settlement scheme for EEA nationals risks a repeat of the Windrush scandal (Home Affairs Committee 2019), which resulted from the HO's destruction of documents that would have confirmed the legitimate status of those affected.

In summary, common to the governance of welfare and migration/asylum we find administrative error and inefficiency, poor record-keeping and decision-making, lack of response to awareness of error, inadequate use of discretion, and instances amounting to the formal or effective denial of access to justice. Many of these problems have been compounded by cuts to legal aid under the LASPO Act of 2012, which removed most welfare and immigration cases from its scope. The poor evidence base underlying these changes was itself deemed a neglect of due diligence (Amnesty International 2016).

RECURRENT DISCRIMINATION AND CROSSOVER EFFECTS

Fairness has been a prominent theme of political discourse in relation to both welfare and migration, pitting each against the other and setting both in opposition to the hard-working taxpayer. Claims to fairness have been problematized in various ways (see Chapters 1 and 3), but one distinctive feature of the whole welfare–migration–asylum complex is the recurrent evidence of discrimination revealed by test-case challenges. Examples have been detailed in previous chapters, but of particular note for the present argument is a repeated pattern of inequity that has 'crossover' effects for the entire welfare–migration–asylum complex. Thus, each area displays the use of stratified devices of entitlement and control, each has produced demonstrable discriminations, and each has effects that cut across the citizen/non-citizen divide.

When the benefit cap was first launched, the Joint Committee on Human Rights (JCHR 2011) cautioned that 80 per cent of capped households had three or more children and that 30 per cent contained an ethnic minority member, though minorities account for only 20 per cent of benefit claims. The cap's unequal impact on women, lone parents, large families, and minority ethnic groups has since been argued in court (*JS and Ors v SSWP* [2013] EWHC 3350), but the discrimination entailed has been deemed justifiable in terms of policy objectives. Of those households currently affected, 72 per cent are lone-parent and 64 per cent have a child under five (DWP 2020). The two-child limit for receipt of CTC has had a similarly skewed effect on large, low-income families and hence on BME groups (*SC and Ors v SSWP* [2018] EWHC 864 (Admin) para. 37), but again, its legitimate aims have been upheld, albeit with the exemptions noted in Chapter 4.

Both measures have a significant impact on second- or third-generation migrants, and while new migrants are excluded from mainstream benefits until they have achieved permanent residence, it is notable that two claimants challenging the cap (see *SG and Ors v SSWP* [2015] UKSC 16) respectively arrived in Britain from Algeria and Belgium. In fact, the cap affects both settled migrants and refugees. An illustrative case (*Nzolameso v City of Westminster* [2015] UKSC 22) involved a refugee lone mother of five who was unable to meet her Westminster social housing rent as a result of the cap. She refused alternative accommodation outside the area, and here the 'fairness' issue concerned lack of transparency in the local authority's decision-making process. The Supreme Court found no evidence that Westminster had considered the practicability of the move, especially regarding the best interests of the children affected. Nevertheless, the underlying policy remains intact, and like other large families subject to the cap, should Nzolameso move off the cap to work she would be hit by the two-child CTC limit.

Though family reunification with a spouse and/or children from abroad is not directly a benefits issue, the MIR for such cases was designed to forestall future recourse to welfare support. Again, the MIR has recognized negative effects for lower-income groups (*MM and Ors*, EWHC, paras. 112–13), notably women and minorities, and though designed as a measure to limit migration, it has had a significant impact on British citizens seeking family reunification (Middlesex University/JCWI 2015). The resultant discriminations were held to be justified by policy objectives, though fairness was also placed in question in relation to exclusion of the prospective earnings of an incoming spouse, to reliable third-party support in calculating income, and to the impact on children, often citizens themselves.

The Topology of Welfare–Migration–Asylum

Discriminatory effects have also arisen from the NRPF condition for non-citizen parents allowed to remain under Article 8. Here, a test-case challenge was stayed in March 2019 when the HO agreed to conduct an equality review of the policy. However, as noted above, guidance on its implementation has since been deemed unlawful, and related research reveals a pattern of disadvantage very similar to the effects of the benefit cap (Woolley 2019; Children's Society 2020). Of the estimated 90 per cent who apply to have the condition removed, 85 per cent are women and almost all are single parents, and again there are effects that cut across the citizen/non-citizen divide: 90 per cent of cases involve a British citizen child, almost always from a BME group.

Stratified entitlement, possible race and/or gender discrimination, and the impact on children also arose in relation to Zambrano carers (*Sanneh and Ors v SSWP* [2015] EWCA Civ 49, para. 120). In contrast to those who apply for leave under Article 8, these families cannot apply for the condition to be lifted. The outcome has been to confine Zambrano households to a lesser level of support available under S17 of the Children Act, and again the adults affected are mostly female lone parents. As with the NRPF condition, the measure has had the effect of withholding benefit rights from children who are British citizens.

A further instance concerned the removal of preferential rates for child asylum-seekers to a level of little more than half the standard benefit rates for children. A legal challenge based in part on discrimination as compared to children of nationals with full entitlement did not succeed. Indeed, prior to this case, asylum rates were cited in one of the benefit cap challenges (*SG and Ors v SSWP* [2014] EWCA Civ 156) as the marker below which a family will experience destitution. The disposable income of two of the capped households in the case roughly equalled asylum rates and thus '[did] not approach the level of destitution' (paras. 104–5) that would amount to breach of respect for private life.[5] However, asylum support has not been the yardstick normally applied as the guaranteed minimum for domestic welfare, and the comparison suggests a shifting standard that itself is far from stable.

All of these measures involve stratified rights to support that produce repeated patterns of discrimination against women, lone parents, large families, BME citizens and settled persons, and children. Each measure also has implications that cut across the citizen–non-citizen divide; this is one feature of the topology of a system that counterposes

THE TREATMENT OF CHILDREN

The treatment of children is implicated in all of the policies discussed so far in this chapter. Their treatment raises issues that warrant further comment, displaying contentious issues that recur across the fields of domestic welfare, migration, and asylum. Britain is a signatory of the Convention on the Rights of the Child (UNCRC), which requires that the best interests of the child be a primary consideration in all measures affecting them, though the convention has not been incorporated into domestic law. In fact, measures that seek to influence adult behaviour through negative effects on children have been a marked feature of the topology of the entire welfare–migration–asylum complex. In 2010 the government committed itself to due consideration of obligations to children in all new policy (JCHR 2011, 15), but the JCHR condemned the absence of any detailed compatibility exercise to assess the impact of the 2012 welfare reforms. The lowering of the benefit cap legislated in 2016 went ahead despite urging from a Supreme Court judge (*SG and Ors v SSWP* [2015] UKSC 16, para. 133) that the government review its effects on children. In fact, the reduced cap, along with the two-child CTC limit implemented in 2017, has been criticized for punishing a child for the actions (or lack thereof) of the parents (CPAG 2015).

We should therefore look again at the functioning of the benefit cap, now from the perspective of the treatment of children. The Children's Commissioner has questioned whether it is acceptable 'to treat child benefits as no more than a component of the family income' (*SG and Ors v SSWP* [2015] UKSC 16, para. 123), and children's advocates have argued that 'there is nothing fair about trying to balance to books on the back of poor children' (Kennedy et al. 2016, 37). The proffered justification was 'reversing the detrimental impact on families and children of benefit dependence' (*SG and Ors*, para. 104), even though 82 per cent of capped claimants were not required to work (WPC 2019a). One judge specifically questioned why the viability of a scheme directed at parents was 'so disproportionately dependent on child related benefits' (*SG and Ors*, para. 127).

The Topology of Welfare–Migration–Asylum

When a later case against the lowered cap centred on lone parents with a child under two considered whether there had been a breach of the UNCRC, parliamentary deliberation was taken as evidence that children's best interests *had* been considered at a primary level (*DA and Ors v SSWP* [2019] UKSC 21, para. 87), and it was not for the court to question the conclusion. A dissenting view from Lady Hale declared that the measure was not achieving its aims, was not fair, made few savings, and provided little evidence of attention to the risks of harm to young children; Lord Kerr asserted that the 'ephemeral aspirations' (para. 192) of policy were insufficient to displace the primary status to be accorded to the child's best interests.

The weighing of the child's best interests was also central in a challenge to the two-child limit for CTC. Here the judge found the differential treatment of the parents to be justified, but he also recognized the need to take the UNCRC into account, noting 'there was no consideration at all of whether it was fair to impose the consequences of the parents' choices (to have more children) on their children' (*SC and Ors* [2019] EWCA Civ 615, para 151). Again, the point at issue was the unfavourable treatment of children in order to motivate parents, and the judge pointed to a conflict between responding to the child's best interests and influencing parental behaviour (para. 156). However, this was seen to be a political question and (beyond the exemption noted above) not a proper matter for the court's intervention.

Children's treatment in consequence of measures directed at their parents has also arisen in various aspects of immigration policy. Welfare issues are prominent in this debate, and JCHR (2015) has noted the disproportionate impact of austerity measures both on children in low-income households *and* the children of migrants. In 2008 the reservation on the UNCRC for children subject to immigration control was lifted, and the 2009 Borders Citizenship and Migration Act has imposed a duty to treat the child's best interests as a primary consideration. Nevertheless, the JCHR has remarked on a deterioration in recent years and a focus on immigration control rather than children's rights, while the All Party Parliamentary Group (APPG 2013) has noted neglect to consider the best interests of the child in setting the MIR for partner visas. In relation to Zambrano cases, Baroness Hale has declared the aim of strengthening immigration control to be 'irrelevant to children who are not subject to it' (*HC v SSWP* [2017] UKSC 73, para. 51).

Nor does the lifting of the reservation on the UNCRC displace the stratified system of entitlement in relation to welfare. A parent without status may be allowed to remain where it 'would not be reasonable' to expect the child to leave (Yeo 2018a), and the basic principle is that a child should not be blamed for the conduct of a parent (*JO and Ors v SSHD* [2014] UKUT 00517 (IAC)). However, the NRPF condition can have a direct effect on children and has raised concerns over their inability to access free school meals or children's benefits (Taylor and Mohdin 2019). Though the condition can be lifted where the welfare of a child is at stake, onerous or unachievable evidential requirements have made this prohibitively difficult (Woolley 2019), hence the ruling on unlawful guidance, noted earlier. For Zambrano families confined to local authority assistance under S17 of the Children Act, one judge urged consideration of the impact of denying them support at a level commensurate with that of their peers (*HC v SSWP* [2017] UKSC 73, para. 46). The same argument applies to many children affected by the NRPF condition, and there is a parallel here with the children of benefit-capped households, who are denied access to benefits at the level of minimum need in order to incentivize their parents.

A harnessing of the position of children to influence the behaviour of parents is also apparent in aspects of asylum support and in the treatment of failed asylum-seekers. Asylum support rates have long been held below mainstream benefits, in part for fear of attracting 'non-genuine' claims (Home Affairs Committee 2013), and as part of a more general drive 'to demonstrate fairness to the taxpayer' (*Refugee Action v SSHD* [2014] EWHC 1033 (Admin), para. 26). The later removal of preferential rates for children was upheld by the High Court, given its 'legitimate aim' of discouraging economic migration (*Ghulam and Ors v SSHD* [2016] EWHC 2639 (Admin), para. 241). Changes under the 2016 act (yet to be implemented) will tighten access to support for failed asylum-seekers and their families and make that support more strongly conditional on cooperation with removal (Blanchard and Joy 2017; Harvey and Harper 2017, 356–7). These changes have been advanced despite objections that destitution is being used as a tool of control (Parliamentary Inquiry 2013), that this will drive families underground and/or increase demands on local authorities, and that families will opt for destitution before endangering their children by return (Still Human Still Here 2015).

In sum, reduced support for children is a topological feature of the governance of welfare, migration, and asylum. We have seen an erosion of benefits paid on behalf of children to incentivize their parents to work under the benefit cap and the two-child limit on CTC, as well as denial of Zambrano children's access to mainstream benefits in a drive against 'benefit tourism'. A similar logic is apparent in the imposition of an NRPF condition, the lowering of asylum support for children, and the rendering of failed asylum-seekers destitute with the aim of deterring arrival and encouraging departure.

DESTITUTION

Destitution is a more general issue that emerges from both welfare reform and immigration control. The definition applied by JRF (2018) is a lack of two or more essential items, and they estimate the make-up of destitute people in Britain to be 68 per cent British and 16 per cent migrant, with a further mixed group having 'complex needs' at 15 per cent of the total.[6] They calculate that 1.5 million people in the UK, including 365,000 children, were destitute at some point in 2017, 45 per cent lacking three or more items and 22 per cent having no income at all. The WPC (2019c) has expressed alarm at rising levels of destitution and argues that the DWP should develop an official measure.

An APPG report on hunger and food poverty concluded that the state had become a generator of destitution (APPG 2015), and a recurrent theme of commentary is that a guaranteed minimum income to be secured by welfare provision is no longer effective (Morris 2015; Church Action on Poverty 2015; WPC 2019a). This was implicitly acknowledged when the COVID-19 crisis prompted a temporary rise in basic UC and WTC rates. The roll-out of UC has forced many into debt, in a system reportedly beset by design flaws and causing immense hardship (Brown 2018; Alston 2018), with claimants having to choose between heating, eating, and paying their bills. The WPC reports 'harrowing stories of people going hungry, struggling to feed their children, and building up crippling rent arears' (WPC 2019a, 5). Even before the coronavirus crisis, Trussell Trust figures were showing a 73 per cent rise in the use of their food banks over five years, reaching 1.6 million (Trussell Trust 2019a). More than half this use was accounted for by benefit delays, errors, and sanctions – and note that the figures understate take-up by migrants from diverse religious backgrounds, who are more likely to apply to other outlets (Forrest 2014).

The five-week waiting period for UC has led to a heavy dependence on advances, which like hardship payments are repayable loans, and 47 per cent of UC claimants have a repayment debt of 20 per cent or more in place (Public Law Project, 2019), with more than half of these having further deductions relating to overpayment, social fund loans, hardship payments, and so on (Webster 2019). There were 228,000 sanctions in 2018, equivalent to 12.5 per cent of the total who fall under conditionality (Webster 2019); also, 31 per cent of sanctions exceed three months (Alston 2018). The WPC (2019b) has published a report substantiating claims that welfare reform has driven women to survival sex. The rate and number of sanctions has, however, been in decline (Webster 2020) – presumably in light of critical comment exposing what borders on a public scandal.

There has also been a fall in the take-up of hardship payments, with the result that claimants who are sanctioned under UC are often living off very low or zero income (Webster 2019a). Though take-up is falling, private debt has increasingly been incurred for payments to government organizations, and benefit-related problems are common (Barrett 2019). At the margins of the system are those who discontinue their claim when sanctioned, those who begin a UC claim but do not see it through to completion, and those who suffer 'digital exclusion' (Alston 2018). Arears and evictions are a generally observed feature among those who do secure a claim (PAC 2018; WPC 2019a), and they feed a visibly growing population in extreme destitution; there was a 169 per cent increase in rough sleeping between 2010 and 2018 (Mackley and Wilson 2018). Encampments of homeless people forcibly removed by local authorities have trebled in five years and are linked by charities to changes in the benefits system (Marsh and Greenfield 2019). The average age of death for rough sleepers is forty-seven, and their suicide rate is nine times that of the general population (Mackley and Wilson 2018). Furthermore, rough sleeping in the context of a pandemic poses significant health risks to the total population and has required urgent action from central and local governments.[7]

Though a direct connection between welfare reform, increasing destitution, and premature death has not been formally established, multiple press reports suggest an association,[8] and Dr Jay Watts, a consultant clinical psychologist, has stated that 'nearly everyone in

The Topology of Welfare–Migration–Asylum

the mental health field ... recognises the link between the current benefits system and suicide risk' (Watts 2018). Alston (2018) notes that a minister has been appointed for suicide prevention and that multiple organizations have instituted relevant training. In 2020 the NAO (2020) reported sixty-nine Internal Process Reviews by the DWP since 2014 relating to the death by suicide of a claimant, noting that this is 'highly unlikely' to represent the full number of such cases. In fact, the DWP has had no robust way of receiving, monitoring, or acting on such information – a situation it has now committed to address. However, these developments fall within the penumbra of a welfare system in which guaranteed minimum standards have fallen away, and they are echoed and amplified by the experience of migration and asylum.

The Windrush scandal unfolded at the interface between welfare and migration, and similar problems have arisen for children reaching adulthood with no immigration status, some of whom were born here and are entitled to register as citizens (Skehan et al. 2017; Coram 2017). Even those with the prospect of secure status (as with discretionary leave) can be rendered destitute by HO fees, which have trebled in five years (Noor 2019) – though the £1,000 fee for child registration has now been ruled unlawful for its failure to consider the best interests of the child (*Project for the Registration of Children As British Citizens & Ors v SSHD* [2019] EWHC 3536 (Admin)). Several groups survive on resources short of the welfare minimum, and as with the welfare reform there are degrees of destitution associated with different policy targets. The continuum includes refugees with full entitlement but problems in accessing mainstream benefits, reportedly driven to homelessness and even to the verge of suicide (Basedow and Doyle 2016). Exclusions from full entitlement have affected EEA jobseekers – who have been denied HB and targeted for removal when sleeping rough, Zambrano carers on S17 support, asylum-seekers on (reduced) survival rates, failed asylum-seekers on minimal cashless support, and migrants with leave to remain but NRPF. Others fall into the pool of undocumented persons, a growing proportion of whom have no income whatsoever (JRF 2018).

Even before the 2016 changes, the Home Affairs Committee (2013) concluded that all asylum-seekers and many recognized refugees experience destitution, but the situation for failed asylum-seekers is set to worsen. Access to support will be more tightly linked to cooperation with return, and care leavers will be especially vulnerable as the 2016 act excludes those with no immigration status from all forms of care-leaving provision (Harvey and Harper 2017, 388–9). Denied status and support, some will join a larger group of failed asylum-seekers whom a growing body of evidence (see Children's Commissioner 2015; Still Human Still Here 2015) suggests will opt for destitution rather than return. In many cases, removal is not viable because of lack of documentation and refusal by target destinations to accept returns (Blanchard and Joy 2017), a situation to be exacerbated when the onus of proof is shifted onto applicants, who lack the knowledge and resources to advance their case.

Reluctance to leave has been linked to a lack of faith in the asylum process, with its high level of success on appeal (Jesuit Refugee Service 2018). Once appeal rights are exhausted, and no further submissions are possible, then failed asylum-seekers unwilling to leave experience the most extreme forms of exclusion and destitution. The planned removal of a right of appeal against decisions on 'obstacles to departure' is a particular concern for support groups. The Red Cross (Blanchard and Joy 2017) reports that most of those denied support but unable or unwilling to depart live in limbo, with no control over their lives; some have considered suicide. Nearly half of refused asylum applicants have mental health problems that are worsened by their experience (Still Human Still Here 2015).

Hence, the rationale of 'incentivization' underpinning the welfare reforms and the deterrent features of immigration/asylum policy produce patterns of destitution linked to expectations of 'behavioural change'. Destitution has thus been harnessed as a device of governance; bare life has increasingly become a feature of mainstream administration. Across diverse policy areas we find that unsubstantiated assumptions shaping policy have created experiential exclusions imposed on disparate groups of people who live or are allowed to die not in discrete camps but in the interstices of our society.

CONCLUSION – THE TOPOLOGY OF WELFARE AND MIGRATION

The outsiders inside are a mixed group who may have fallen foul of either the welfare system or the migration/asylum system. In either case, they are subject to the law's capacity to stratify and divide and to the complex array of distinctions this produces. The disciplinary nature of the whole topology of welfare–migration–asylum is derived from conditions and requirements that permeate the system with a view to shaping behaviour in terms of incentives to work, the conduct of family life, and measures to deter arrival or encourage departure. Though a dominant discourse sets up lines of opposition between the welfare subject and various categories of migrant, while counterposing both to the hard-working taxpayer, we have seen notable overlaps in treatment and experience.

A topological approach serves to highlight the way a simple hierarchy between such groups can coexist with a system of folding and filtering, driven by a discourse of 'fairness' that shapes both the terms of welfare support and the conditions of entry and stay for migrants and asylum-seekers. Its translation into policy not only generates increasingly refined distinctions but also has exposed a variety of groups to a hostile environment, administrative error and formal or effective denial of access to justice. Recurrent effects are discriminatory outcomes for women, lone parents, large families, BME groups, and children, all groups that are disproportionately affected by the constraints of the benefit cap, the two-child limit, the family unification MIR, and the NRPF condition. Furthermore, both citizen sponsors and settled migrants on low incomes can be affected by family unification constraints, and both citizen and non-citizen children can be subject to public funds restrictions on migrant parents.

While some of the privileges of citizenship remain intact, and a hierarchy is still detectable, the provision of minimum levels of maintenance, let alone guaranteed social inclusion as a feature of 'full membership', has suffered substantial erosion. The particular impact on BME groups points to a failure to accommodate the changing make-up of the British citizenry, and is one instance of a stratifying dynamic within citizenship itself. Furthermore, a topological approach serves to foster awareness of the disciplinary devices of governance that increasingly determine the treatment of all vulnerable groups, and meanwhile, children emerge as the target of attempts to shape parental behaviour through various incentives or deterrents. Pushed to the outer limits of the system are welfare claimants falling victim to conditions and sanctions, migrants granted leave to remain but no welfare entitlement, refugees with problems accessing mainstream benefits, asylum-seekers on basic survival rates, and failed asylum-seekers and undocumented migrants with recourse only to charitable support. In this sense, bare life is not confined to 'the camp': it infiltrates the basic fabric of society, with effects for the total population that may yet be more fully revealed by the coronavirus crisis.

'The camp' serves as a provocative term for those who occupy an apparently rightless zone on the outskirts of society. However, within Britain's welfare–immigration–asylum complex, this zone is not a physical location, but a legal and experiential space. In fact, Agamben (1995, 122) observes that the point at which a decision on life becomes a decision on death no longer has a stable border, and in this context his reference to the 'metamorphoses and disguises' of 'the camp' becomes clearer. We see from the preceding account that in austerity Britain this space sits not outside but *within* society, at the end of a continuum in which the whittling away of rights in the name of control ends in destitution for those who are driven to the system's extremes. They are not without rights, but in a system dominated by conditions and filters, governed by harsh and error-prone administration, and offering little in the way of legal advice, the outsiders inside can find they have exhausted their access, and the outcome for some has been a life that is no longer worth living.

CONCLUSION

The Moral Economy of Welfare and Migration

This study has focused on the age of austerity proclaimed in the run-up to the 2010 general election and made concrete by the policies of the incoming Coalition government and its Conservative successors. While its most overt expression was a drive for deficit reduction, with a particular focus on welfare spending, austerity has run in parallel with a related commitment to bring net immigration down to the 'tens of thousands'[1] and to end the 'culture of dependency' for domestic welfare claimants and migrants alike. We have in consequence seen the launch of an ambitious reform and restructuring of welfare provision, a campaign to end the free movement of EEA nationals through Brexit, tighter conditions and controls for non-EEA migration, and the unleashing of a 'hostile environment' that has affected both regular and irregular migrants alike – all citing the protection of national resources and defence of the 'hardworking taxpayer'.

As a result, we have lived through a radical reconfiguration of our social structure and social rights, a shrinkage of the ideal of citizenship as social inclusion, a changed conception of the meaning and nature of membership in society, and a stepping back from movement toward a post-national or cosmopolitan ideal. Such contractions have all been advanced by an explicit desire 'to change the way we think about ourselves and our place in society' (Cameron 2010) – presented here as a form of moral economy that has been promoted and justified by a discourse imposed from above. The discourse with its accompanying measures has been subject to contestation on the basis of rationality, legality, and morality but has proved hard to dislodge. Indeed, it has taken the arrival of the coronavirus to reveal the full implications of a radical diminution of social rights and a failure to recognize the vital importance of migrant workers.

MORAL ECONOMY AS PRACTICE

The concept of moral economy has gone through several changes since it was adopted by Thompson (1971) in his analysis of riots and rebellion in eighteenth-century England as fuelled by a moral economy of the poor. In outlining his use of this term, Thompson posed the question of how behaviour is modified by custom, culture, and reason (78). That question holds significance beyond the specific context of his study and invites a more wide-ranging approach to moral economy and its associated value consensus. In such an approach, *moral* is not to be understood as an evaluative descriptor of a given economic structure, but serves rather to indicate that for effective social cohesion, an economic system must be grounded in some form of legitimizing principle. In Thompson's study such a principle was called into play in a movement to resist change, when traditional expectations of paternalism in pre-industrial society were exposed to the frictions of the marketplace. Contemporary applications of the idea of moral economy consider the reverse of this process, in that they recognize how a refashioning of public sentiment can be harnessed by attempts to legitimize change and an associated restructuring of social and economic relations.

Moral economy can in this sense be construed as a *practice*, and refers to the integration of economic relations with a set of governing principles in a dynamic relation that can run two ways. In Thompson's account, principles impinge on the practices of government and thought (Thompson 1971, 79) to constrain change 'from below'; but we can also find a shaping of public sentiment 'from above' that becomes part of the motor of change and fosters the necessary public support for radical policy intervention. Contemporary applications of the notion of moral economy thus conceive of a new form of moral embeddedness that looks to the role of the economy in the 'architecture of community' (Booth 1994, 663), such that reconfigured economic relations are reinforced by an associated value frame. This reversal is captured by Fassin's (2009a) speculative comment that if the moral economy of the poor has an opposite, it would be the moral economy of the masters. The effect is to introduce a purposive element to moral economy analysis and thus to focus attention on the embedding process itself.

For Fassin, moral economies represent the mental state of collectivities, but a dynamic approach is implicit in his definition of moral economy as 'the production, distribution, circulation and use of moral sentiments, emotions and values, norms and obligations in social space' (Fassin 2009a, 1254). Most contemporary writers in this field (e.g., Sayer 2007; Booth 1994; Clarke and Newman 2012) place a particular emphasis on the role of moral sentiments in the functioning of the economy and on the recognition that all economic practices carry an implicit moral conception of the interrelations involved – hence the associated claim that 'all economies ... are moral economies' (Booth 1994, 662). However, once we accept that economic practice, unless it is fundamentally coercive, will operate within the confines of an associated value frame, we can look to the legitimizing principles of any given socio-economic order, to ask: where are these principles given expression, how (and how far) are they established, how are they to be analysed, and how contested?

It is these reflections that have given shape to the present study, and they have directed attention to the justificatory discourse behind two central political concerns of the past decade – the control of both welfare spending and inward migration – and an implied connection between the two. If, as Munch (2012) has argued, political rhetoric shapes how problems are both perceived and tackled, then we must identify the socially patterned frameworks of meaning that lie behind specific policy initiatives, to ask how they are supported by distinctive values and sentiments. Attention would then focus on how and when social norms become the site of political intervention, thereby both shaping policy and carrying messages for public consumption, to become embedded in sentiments that also structure reason. This raises what Douglas (1986) has termed an epistemological issue; it also contains the solution to her own problematic of 'how institutions think', inviting attention to the construction of political discourse, the moral messages it contains, its translation into policy, and its implementation and effects in practice.

DISCOURSE: ITS ANALYSIS AND APPLICATION

Welfare provision has been a central focus of the present study, and its link with a moral economy approach lies in the recognition that a readiness to share, as implied by collective systems of protection against risk, will rest on the moral persuasiveness of the design and operation of welfare institutions (Mau 2003). Questions of financial contribution, personal desert, and social belonging are all called into play, and in this regard, the behavioural model of welfare dependency at the heart of recent reforms has invoked a set of principles based on individual accountability, responsibility, and self-reliance. Such principles have served to justify enhanced conditionality; extended 'activation' of previously protected groups; and disciplinary sanctions for failure to comply with requirements. A related orientation is apparent in the migration and asylum system, with its increased financial thresholds for entry to the territory, secure settlement, or family unification; its curtailment or removal of entitlement (e.g., for EEA migrants and Zambrano carers); its extension of the NRPF condition; and its erosion of rates for basic maintenance (e.g., for asylum-seekers and their children).

It was argued in earlier chapters that a composite discourse has been at work in relation to domestic welfare and migration, in that policies that seem 'hewn from the same rock' are now being applied across distinctive fields. While the citizen/non-citizen divide has traditionally been construed in binary terms, with citizenship seen as soft on the inside but hard on the outside (Bosniak, 2006, 4), there has been growing awareness of a continuum of legal statuses conferring only partial membership. Once the Marshallian (1992 [1950]) ideal of guaranteed social inclusion through social rights has in effect been renounced, and differential positions of entitlement and conditionality have been embedded in citizenship, then Fassin's (2012, 12) quest to 'seize morals at the point where they are articulated with politics' has added purchase. To extend Lockwood's (1996, 535) insight, the 'leading edge' of compromise between system integration (economic efficiency) and social integration (personal inclusion) in the management of domestic welfare and migration/asylum is driven in both fields by conceptions of merit and desert. The related framework of conditionality then appropriates the delivery of rights as a mode of control, in a retreat from both the guaranteed inclusion of Marshall's model and the cosmopolitan aspirations of a post-national society.

A starting point for analysis is therefore the political expression of the guiding principles for such a system, and their moral and practical justifications – broadly termed political discourse – whereby policy programmes are advanced in messages crafted for public consumption. So, while *rhetoric* shapes how problems are perceived and tackled (Munch 2012) and thereby becomes embedded in policies that fashion how institutions think (Douglas 1986), *discourse* operates on a grander ideological scale by bringing substantive meaning to abstract concepts (Freeden 1996, 2003). The broader political dynamic is therefore a battle over the socially legitimated meaning of key principles and how to translate them into practice, which in Freeden's terms means rendering the contestable incontestable in a process for creating 'social truths'. We have seen how one simple example has dominated Conservative discourse in relation to welfare – morality as fairness, which is then translated into responsibility and self-reliance, as well as protection for the hard-working taxpayer.

This approach has a close affinity with Laclau's (2014) conception of 'equivalential chains', whereby linked concepts and behaviours serve to unite or divide targeted social groups, so that – taking the example of welfare – morality, fairness, and responsibility are set against dependency, irresponsibility, and abuse. The discursive pattern for migration is remarkably similar – fairness, connectedness (to Britain), and contribution are set against exploitation, abuse, and illegality – but there have been few attempts to build equivalential chains across the welfare/migration divide, and the corresponding groups have instead been set in a zero-sum opposition. One interesting feature of discourse and policy for both welfare claimants and migrants, however, is the aim of behavioural change, which in turn rests on a particular model of agency governed by assumptions of irresponsibility and dependency in a 'something for nothing culture' (Cameron 2012a).

In fact, it is this behaviourism with its underpinning moral implications that provides the bridge from discourse to policy formulation and legitimation, by virtue of an associated effect on 'moral standing'. Here, for a fuller understanding, we can look to the operation of civic stratification. The key insight of Lockwood's (1996) model is that citizenship and its associated rights can function as a source of inequality; the dynamic aspect of his argument then looks to the expansion of rights through the possession of moral or material resources. He argues in particular that moral resources generate scope for enhanced entitlement, especially where a cause is taken up by civic activists and is amenable to pursuit through the courts and/or public campaigns. But when policy has been shaped by a moral economy infused with negative conceptions of individual agency resting on dependency, abuse, irresponsibility, or illegality, we can expect a corresponding erosion of moral standing that then serves to legitimate a contraction of rights.

THE EROSION OF MORAL STANDING

Conceptions of moral standing have a close link both with the idea of moral economy and with the argument that political rhetoric shapes how problems are perceived and tackled. Where the source of the problem is construed as behavioural (as with dependency, irresponsibility, abusive intent, etc.), the policy answer is likely to be disciplinary, and this has led to cuts, conditionality, activation, and incentivization in the case of welfare, and to cuts, conditionality, exclusions, and deterrence in the case of migration.

We have seen that early proposals for welfare reform counterposed rights and expectations in the statement that '80 percent of the system remains rights based, placing no real demand on its recipients' (SJPG 2007, 32). The implications were clear enough, and only made more so in subsequent references to behaviour and choices skewed by a system designed to pacify and not to incentivize (Duncan Smith 2014), to end the something-for-nothing culture of dependency (Cameron 2012a; Duncan Smith 2013), and to reduce dependency by increased conditionality (Cameron 2012). All such comments have underpinned a quest for behavioural change, which was to be achieved through disciplinary intervention against implied bad faith and abuse, and all have amounted to a discursive attack on the moral standing of claimants. This is made explicit in the language adopted to justify specific measures: examples abound of repeated reference to the need to enforce responsible behaviour – as with benefit sanctions, the benefit cap, abolition of the WRAG supplement, and the two-child limit on CTC.

The same language of responsibility, choice, and behavioural change appears again in relation to migration. We have noted a linkage between welfare and migration as 'two sides of the same coin', with an associated quest to 'end the something for nothing culture' among migrants as well as domestic welfare claimants (Cameron 2013). More specific charges followed as part of efforts to address the 'abuse of free movement' (Cameron 2014, 2015a) among EEA migrants and 'benefit tourism' among Zambrano carers. The expressed need for an elevated MIR for non-EEA partner visas was intended to prevent a burden on taxpayers, as were frozen asylum support rates. Failed asylum-seekers have been presented as illegal migrants (Home Office 2015), for whom support 'sends the wrong message', while the 'hostile environment' has sought to withhold

Conclusion 195

benefits and services from undocumented migrants as a means of compelling departure (Home Office 2016d).

All of the examples discussed – in relation to both domestic welfare and transnational migration – are part of an exercise in impugning the moral standing of the subject by assumptions of abusive or exploitative intent. They reflected a stated need to instil responsibility and to establish disciplinary measures to this end. The discourse is typically called into play both as a prelude to reductions in entitlements and as a justificatory rationale in the face of legal challenge, but it has the additional effect of disparaging those who claim any of the rights at issue. Such claims inevitably become tainted by assumed motivations of abuse propounded by the legitimating discourse, with the consequence that receipt of the right becomes stigmatizing. However, the main objective of the associated measures of contraction has been to maximize the delivery of rights as an opportunity for control, which operates by means of the nature of delivery and/or the conditions imposed on receipt.

PARADIGM CONSTRUCTION
AND BOUNDARY DRAWING

Munch (2012) sees welfare state change as entailing a symbolic struggle over both definition and legitimation, that is, a struggle over identifying and naming the 'problem' at issue, and over the rationale and justification for the proposed solution. In the examples noted earlier (and beyond the underlying drive for deficit reduction), the problem has been largely defined in behavioural terms, and this in turn has legitimated disciplinary or controlling devices intended to bring about desired change. Munch argues that institutions are held together by common ideas, guidelines, and principles, and we have seen that such linkages apply not just within the welfare system but across the entire welfare–migration–asylum complex. The appropriation of rights as a form of control is one feature of the emergent regime that relates to both welfare and migration, and in Munch's terms that regime can be construed as a paradigm, established as such when a vocabulary of ideas, concepts, and remedies spills over from one policy area to another. We have seen this process unfold in relation to the welfare–migration–asylum complex, driven by a dominant discourse based on the same key principles and sharing common elements across all three fields.

The principles of 'fairness' and protection of the hard-working taxpayer have been pursued by devices designed to engage behavioural change, whose combined effect can be seen as an attempt to shape the contours of society by expanding the linkage between rights and controls. The associated rhetoric has shaped public perceptions in seeking to justify reduced entitlement, and the result has been a formal system of stratified rights, underpinned by an informal system of moral desert. In the case of welfare, we see that citizenship has been stratified by measures of discipline and control geared toward the maximum extraction of labour. Across-the-board freezes have affected the entire benefit-dependent population, but this population is internally divided by the effect of sanctions and caps, and by differing degrees of conditionality, all sustained by the discourse of irresponsibility, perverse incentives, and allegations of abuse. Even the relief measures designed to offset the effects of the COVID-19 crisis have favoured large-scale businesses and previously secure workers.

Migrants are also clearly stratified, principally in terms of purpose of entry and conditions of stay, which together determine entitlements and rights. The system is governed by skill and salary thresholds, and outside of (pre-Brexit) EEA status most migrants are denied access to public funds until settlement. Asylum-seekers receive subsistence support, but this has been significantly reduced in recent years, driven by a logic of deterrence, and constraints are being planned to further limit support to failed asylum-seekers who are unable or unwilling to leave. Mirroring domestic welfare, the system as a whole is based on conditionality, sustained by assumptions of abuse, and shaped by deterrent measures, and though elements of citizen privilege remain, the same devices and techniques of control are in play. These are supported by similar discourses of merit and dismerit; moreover, they increasingly overlap and rest on an impoverished view of motivations and an inadequate appreciation of the complexities of intimate life.

The general orientation of policy is apparent in the discourse of fairness and responsibility, its motivational assumptions, and its intended behavioural effects, which operate with an impoverished conception of agency. But beyond the general design and purpose of policy measures, and their supporting discourse, the key to the whole regime is to be found in its complex system of classification and the boundary-drawing it entails. In Douglas's (1986) terms, this system provides an expression of 'how institutions think' and it both relies

Conclusion

on and promotes a distinctive epistemological viewpoint that serves as a guide to the details of policy design and implementation. In this way, Douglas observes, institutions create the very realities to which they apply – so to classify people in terms of the need for and purpose of policy intervention is to confirm them in a particular status that is predicated on a set of underpinning assumptions. The claims then made on behalf of policy turn the assumptions into reality, as 'institutions systematically direct individual memory and channel our perceptions into forms compatible with the relations they authorise' (Douglas 1986, 92).

This argument in effect provides a foundation for Munch's view that rhetoric shapes how problems are perceived and tackled, which in turn generates cognitive schema and symbolic boundaries that then become part of popular perceptions. For 'how can we possibly think of ourselves in society except by using the classifications established in our institutions?' (Douglas 1986, 99) – or, as Freeden (2003, 65) puts it with reference to political ideology, 'the map often becomes the reality itself'. Yet classifications driven by the dominant 'fairness' and 'responsibility' paradigm have generated a series of boundary problems, not least of which are questions about what counts as welfare (why not include corporate supports?), and who are its beneficiaries (why not include employers and landlords?).

The sanctions regime has raised boundary questions about interpretations of non-compliance, the provision of accurate information to claimants, the application of permissible easements according to circumstance, and assumptions of an adequate level of understanding. Similar questions apply to the operation of the WCA, including the capacity of its subjects to engage with the process, as well as its notoriously unreliable outcomes. Fairness itself has been declared 'emptied of content' (CPAG 2014), with the benefit cap raising questions about the appropriate comparator. Problems have also arisen regarding the distinction between worker and carer, both in relation to the age of the youngest child for lone parents, and carers in receipt of carer's allowance.

Other boundary problems arise from immigration policy. We have seen that conceptions of integration in relation to the MIR have been based on a narrow construal of financial resources rather than on social or moral criteria, while for EEA migrants there have been questions over interpretation of the genuine prospect of employment. The treatment of children has raised some rights-related issues about lower levels of support for some, often British citizen children, as in the case of Zambrano families and the NRPF rule, as well as practical difficulties over furnishing proof of destitution. Asylum support rates have prompted questions about the reduction of what had previously been deemed a minimum standard, while the portrayal of failed asylum-seekers as illegal migrants poses difficulties in determining obstacles to departure. We have also seen how migrants can be administered into irregular status through inadequate record-keeping (or, in the Windrush scandal, the destruction of records) and prohibitively high HO fees, and meanwhile, the whole welfare–migration–asylum complex is being undermined by poor decision-making and high rates of success on appeal.

CONTESTATION

We can now begin to see the substance of Freeden's (2003, 65) claim that ideologies are made up of fragmented facts and competing values, selected to establish an artificial order from a disjointed reality, while in Laclau's (2014) terms they can generate questionable chains of equivalence and difference. Yet their persuasiveness lies at the heart of the moral economy of welfare and migration, not least in setting domestic welfare claimants and incoming migrants in opposition to each other, as we saw in the dynamics of the referendum on EU membership. However, boundary problems have opened up possibilities for contestation, which have been documented in previous chapters in terms of rationality, legality, and morality. So, do policies deliver on their own objectives, and are they rationally based? Are their measures compatible with existing obligations enshrined in domestic and/or international law? Are the objectives and effects acceptable in terms of a broader conception of morality based on human flourishing, human dignity, and compassion? And what do we learn by considering the fields of welfare, migration, and asylum through this frame?

Rationality

Policy that is ideologically driven can still be empirically tested, in terms of both the effectiveness of its claims and what is left out of the picture, and for almost every measure in the welfare–migration–asylum complex we have seen evidence of perverse effects, failure to meet stated objectives, and/or flawed underlying assumptions.

Conclusion

The central claim of the welfare reforms has been a restoration of 'fairness': indeed, David Cameron (2012) ranked 'unfairness' with Beveridge's five great evils. Yet the changes have had a disproportionate effect on the poor, especially women, BME groups, large families, the disabled, and children. Sanctions have been undermined by poor understanding on the part of claimants, many of whom have mental health or behavioural problems; have led to increased destitution and homelessness; and have rebounded on local authorities that have already experienced huge budget cuts (Crewe 2016). The benefit cap was launched as a work incentive measure, yet it principally affects claimants who are not required to seek work, and it seeks to impose behavioural change on people with often limited control over their circumstances. The two-child limit on CTC's similarly involves a poor understanding of 'choice' and of family dynamics, while the imposition of the benefit cap on recipients of Carers Allowance relied on the implausible assumption that people providing thirty-five hours of care a week were available for work. This would disrupt the provision of care, at a subsequent cost to the state.

In the field of migration, a narrow focus on the sponsor's earnings in calculating the MIR denies a parent the support of their partner, which could release them from childcare constraints, free up their working time, and limit their call on public funds. EEA migrants have consistently been shown to contribute more to the exchequer than they receive in benefits and to claim out-of-work benefits at a lower level than their British counterparts. The Zambrano deterrent comes into play only *after* the situation it seeks to address and commonly results from a relationship breakdown. The NRPF condition limits access to childcare support (NRPF 2017) and thereby constrains availability for work, while the ten-year route to settlement is punitive in that it requires four formal extensions of stay, each with a prohibitively costly fee. There is no correlation between the level of asylum support and the number of asylum applications, and so no evidence of a deterrent effect, while removal of support from failed asylum-seekers has been shown to hinder managed removal and to drive them underground – a disturbing prospect in the context of a public health crisis. Here they meet with a 'hostile environment' whose efficacy has not been established and whose wider implications are only just becoming apparent – forcing costly compensations on the government (albeit criticized for a lack of adequacy and efficiency).

Legality

A rationality critique can be extended into the legal sphere, in that all British legislation is bound by pre-existing legal obligations – variously deriving from domestic law, EU law (pre-Brexit), and/or international law – to which policy is therefore expected to conform. We have as a result seen a wide range of legal challenges to the changes introduced in pursuit of austerity and immigration control, usually advanced through test-case campaigning by civic activists. Though few rights are absolute and there is considerable scope for deference to the executive and to parliamentary sovereignty, there have been some successes.

A challenge to the retrospective validation of the Work Programme Regulations succeeded under Article 6 of the ECHR (access to justice), thus validating a number of pending appeals against sanctions. Furthermore, all of the rights of the ECHR must be secured without discrimination, and this has been the basis for three different challenges to the benefit cap – albeit only succeeding on non-exemption of recipients of Carers Allowance. While the ECHR has the force of domestic law via the HRA, the UNCRC has not been incorporated in this way, and though several judges were convinced of its relevance to the legality of the cap, there was insufficient agreement to override the policy. However, other successes have been achieved through procedural challenges under domestic law, as with the failure to make reasonable adjustments in the conduct of the WCA under the PSED, and a reassertion of appeal rights for all DWP benefits on similar grounds. The DWP has also been found in error over a failure to apply its own regulations on appropriate easements in the sanctions regime, and incorrect interpretation of the UC regulations where two payments fall within one month, while the two-child limit on CTC was found to be irrational in relation to the sequencing of non-parental care.

We find a similar picture with respect to migration, though there was a rare finding of a breach of Article 3 – an absolute right – when the destitution entailed in delays over confirming a renewed asylum claim as 'fresh' was deemed inhuman and degrading. A challenge to the 'right to rent' rule initially succeeded on the grounds of discrimination, but this was deemed justifiable on appeal, while removal of EEA homeless migrants was found to be discriminatory under EU law. Guidance on when the NRPF condition should be lifted has been ruled unlawful in relation to article 3 (*W v SSHD* [2020] EWHC 1299

Conclusion

(Admin)), and discrimination was noted but deemed justifiable in relation to the MIR for family unification. The UNCRC did have some purchase in the latter case, and the UKSC found there had been inadequate attention to the impact on children. However, as with the benefit cap, the UNCRC did not prevail against the reduced level of support for citizen children of Zambrano carers. Access to justice was at issue in the attempt to impose a residence requirement on legal aid, ruled outside the power of LASPO, while there was a procedural success (albeit to little avail) over an error in the calculation of asylum rates. Removal of the right of appeal under new and reduced arrangements (yet to be implemented) may yet meet resistance through the courts.

Legal challenges in relation to both welfare reform and immigration controls have thus had some successes, and on rather similar grounds, but they have done little more than nibble at the edges of the emerging paradigm of contraction and control. However, challenges have sometimes served a further purpose: a judges' comments may stand outside the determining detail of a legal issue but, even so, express severe reservations about the nature of the measure at hand. In such instances, contestation shifts to the broader terrain of morality, significantly advanced by the civic activism of voluntary organizations.

Morality

If there is to be a challenge to the rhetoric underpinning the welfare–migration–asylum complex that does more than trim the edges of its extreme effects, this is likely to rest on morality. To use Fassin's distinction, epistemological change would require a *'moral* economy' to be established in opposition to the dominant 'moral *economy*' documented in these pages, and this reorientation potentially engages Booth's (1993) invitation to address the *telos* of economic thinking by asking what end or good the economy ought to serve.

The most overt approach of this kind sees the prevention of suffering and the meeting of basic survival needs as a moral absolute that contains its own imperative to act (Justfair 2014; Lambie-Mumford, Cooper, and Loopstra 2019): no one should want for food in a wealthy society where state power rests on an implied social contract to keep people free from hunger. Yet the state is now seen as a generator of destitution (APPG 2014), most notably in connection with the design flaws of UC, which have led to debt, arears, destitution, and homelessness (National Audit Office 2018). A UN report from the Special Rapporteur on Extreme Poverty (Alston 2018) describes a collapse of the idea of a guaranteed minimum, a system that drives people away from support, and a disciplinary approach that punishes the vulnerable. The punitive nature of reforms is captured by a sanctions system and a WCA imposed on people who may have little understanding of the process, a benefit cap on carers that has created hardship at no real benefit to the state (*Hurley and Ors v SSWP* [2015] EWHC 3382 (Admin), para. 75), a cap for lone parents that incentivizes work by removing benefits intended for children (*SG and Ors v SSWP* [2015] UKSC 16, para. 227), and a two-child tax credit limit that punishes children for the actions of their parents. Such criticisms all point to the use of disciplinary devices on people with limited capacity to respond, and this may be counterposed to the discourse of fairness and responsibility, summoning instead the ideals of human flourishing and human dignity (Justfair 2014; Lambie-Mumford, Cooper, and Loopstra 2019).

A further moral question arises in relation to what is owed to those outside of citizenship, especially when vulnerability and need are weighed in the balance against contribution and connectedness. An example is provided by the MIR for family unification, and campaigning has endeavoured to humanize debate by moving beyond crude economic criteria to social and moral issues, not least the impact on children. The treatment of EEA migrants (pre-Brexit) has been criticized for individualizing social security in a system ostensibly designed to collectivize risk, while the complete exclusion of some groups from mainstream benefit (as with Zambrano carers and the NRPF category) has been criticized for its impact on children. Yet as with the benefit cap, the children (often citizens) bear no responsibility for the situation in which they find themselves, nor do they have the capacity to respond to policy incentives or deterrents. Similar arguments can be applied to the erosion of asylum support – in particular, cuts to children's rates – while a broader view makes the point that adequate support is necessary for a humane and compassionate asylum system. The argument upholding support for 'fresh' claims by failed claimants has a more general relevance in the recognition that 'there are human beings behind each application' (*MK and AH v SSHD* [2012] EWHC 1896 (Admin), para. 183), who will often be extremely vulnerable: 'as a matter of fairness their rights must be upheld' (para. 184). This sense of absolute morality also extends to the treatment (and indeed

Conclusion 203

creation) of destitution, in that denial of support to enforce departure not only is of questionable efficacy but also creates a sense of dehumanization and abandonment, especially when so many aspects of the system have proved unreliable – as dramatically demonstrated by the Windrush scandal.

WELFARE–MIGRATION–ASYLUM
AS A COMPOSITE SYSTEM

Problems highlighted by the forms of contestation as just outlined often turn on issues of agency, raising questions about the rationality and relevance of behaviourism, the legality of its sometimes discriminatory effects, and the morality of often punitive measures when capacity to respond is in some way limited. Yet dominant conceptions of agency have an impact on the moral standing of the individuals concerned and have been central to the construction of a moral economy that operates across the whole welfare–migration–asylum complex.

We have therefore argued throughout this book that over the last decade the discourse and design underpinning welfare, migration, and asylum policy amounts to a composite moral economy built around a particular construal of fairness, responsibility, and resource protection. We have seen similarities in the rhetoric, principles, and devices of control as well as in the form and content of contestation. So although welfare claimants and transnational migrants have been set against each other in a discursive opposition, the treatment of the two groupings displays considerable common ground in that welfare serves as a pivotal site of control. However, while the concept of moral economy captures the principles, purpose, and portrayal of a given socio-economic regime, its concrete manifestations and effects require some further elaboration, and here the notion of topology can help to construct a model of the emergent landscape.

Civic stratification has been a central feature of this model, with reference both to the construction of a system for the differential allocation of rights and to a mapping of its concrete outcomes. Clearly, what has traditionally been viewed as a binary distinction (citizen and non-citizen) can now be more accurately construed as a continuum. Though a hierarchical element remains, Marshall's idealized conception of citizenship as guaranteed social inclusion has had ever less purchase, and his remark that a stratified status is creeping into citizenship is of increasing relevance (Marshall 1992[1950], 40). We have seen a use of the law to stratify and divide, and the appropriation of rights as a mode of control through a proliferation of subject positions shaped by repeated ideas, concepts, and devices, in a pervasive paradigm that has governed contraction of entitlement across the whole welfare–migration–asylum complex.

A particular construal of fairness as self-reliance, conditionality, and resource protection has driven the extraction of labour from expanding categories of welfare claimants; it has also been the basis of increasing attempts at selection and deterrence in relation to migration. But alongside the repeated themes and devices of control, and the pitting of migrants against welfare claimants as 'two sides of the same coin', there has been a blurring of the boundaries between them in terms of their treatment, experience, and effects. Among citizens, dependency is the principle division, and further distinctions have been imposed through graduated sanctions and conditions shaped by 'capacity' and 'availability', as well as through caps and limits determining levels of support. For migrants, divisions are governed by legal status as fashioned around thresholds and limits for entry, and by differential entitlement according to the purpose or basis of presence. The outcome has been a system for what Fassin (2009, 52) describes as the determination of who can live what kind of life and for how long, and this has produced extremes of destitution and exclusion at the outer limits for both groups.

The resultant hierarchy has generated areas of overlap in terms of the principles and behavioural assumptions underpinning control: welfare constraints have affected both domestic claimants and migrant groups, and policies designed to limit migration have also had an impact on citizens. So contractions in the domestic welfare regime affect settled migrants, refugees, and second- and third-generation BME groups, the MIR affects both migrant and citizen sponsors and their children, and constraints on Zambrano carers and the NRPF condition rebound on citizen children. Overlaps are also apparent in the poor evidence base of many policy measures, inadequate monitoring and administrative error, and repeated patterns of discrimination affecting women, lone parents, large families, and low-income and BME groups. It has also led to prejudicial treatment of children to influence parental action and to poor decision-making that results in high success rates on appeal.

All of these effects are part of a broader policy framework that amounts to a hostile environment for welfare claimants and migrants

Conclusion

alike. The term was introduced with specific reference to attempts to make life for undocumented migrants prohibitively difficult. It has now officially been relabelled the *compliant* environment. However, there remains an overarching hostility that continues to drive policy design, harsh administrative systems, and the absence of a duty of care, all with limited scope for redress. This system has pushed the most vulnerable to the very edges of protection and support – whether they are welfare claimants exposed to the design flaws of UC, those who exit the system for unknown destinations, homeless EEA migrants, Zambrano carers, families with NRPF, or failed asylum-seekers unable or unwilling to leave. Hence an emergent view of the state as a generator of destitution (APPG 2014), with negative effects shockingly reflected in rapidly escalating levels of homelessness (Jones 2018), and the appointment of a minister for suicide prevention. Agamben's evocative conception of 'bare life' in 'the camp' therefore has an intuitive resonance – not in the sense of a physical space, but rather as a legal and experiential space for those who live their lives *in* but not *of* society. The health consequences for the general population have yet to be fully revealed as the coronavirus crisis unfolds.

There is one other area of overlap in the welfare–migration–asylum complex. This is to be found where the system's perversities or contradictions open up avenues for challenge and contestation. While these challenges only rarely cross the lines between affected groups (though see the previous chapter for some examples), they have in common a role for civil society activists in seeking out situations that lend themselves to test-case treatment and public campaigns. In Lockwood's (1996) model of civic stratification, civic expansion (of entitlement to rights) can occur when groups accrue moral standing in society, or when civic activists effectively lend moral credence and bring public exposure to a cause. We have seen examples of this in the course of the present study – less in terms of expansion, but better construed as arresting contraction. There have been some successes, but the ability of such action to undermine the basic shape and underlying principles of the dominant moral economy is far from certain.

AN ALTERNATIVE MORAL ECONOMY?

Arguments identifying a breach of the citizen/non-citizen binary are not new. They have sometimes taken the form of post-national optimism about the expansion of universal principles that would support migrants' claims for rights and recognition within their host societies. However, it was argued earlier that a collapse of this binary in Britain is currently better understood in terms of the contraction of rights across the board, such that citizenship is no longer the marker of full inclusion (if indeed it ever was). Given this situation, it is significant that contestation in the fields of welfare *and* migration has looked to universal principles as the yardstick of inclusion, and this is perhaps the closest we come to an alternative *moral* economy. Some indications of this are apparent in a morality critique of contractions of both welfare and migrant rights, a critique guided by the principles of human dignity and human flourishing in combating suffering and need, and in which a claim to subsistence takes on the character of an absolute right.

In terms of legal purchase, the effect has been limited. The clearest victories have turned on access to justice, though the best interests of children has also had some effect, as with adjustments to the operation of the MIR for family unification and critical comment on the benefit cap. However, we have seen how the impact of universal principles can be constrained where qualified rights are at issue, for such rights leave scope for consideration of national interests and for bringing parliamentary sovereignty and policy objectives to bear. Successes have therefore been rather slight: discrimination with respect to the HRA has offered the most common challenge, but has often been deemed justifiable in terms of policy objectives. Other successes have largely related to administrative failure in terms of the government's own regulations, or other aspects of domestic law, as for example with easements in the sanctions regime, the UC assessment period, the two-child limit, and the setting of asylum rates.

The rationality critique has also had some purchase in securing adjustments to the operation of policy, but neither this nor the history of legal challenge has been sufficient to undermine the broader policy objectives and underlying epistemological assumptions of the dominant moral economy of welfare and migration. Lockwood's (1996, 532) central question of 'under which conditions inequality is tolerated or rejected' thus takes on a pressing contemporary relevance. One conclusion of the present study must be that the answer in part is dictated by the success of government discourse in embedding a particular view of socio-economic relations, their legitimizing 'moral economy', and the plausibility of the chains of equivalence and difference they construct. But if this is the case,

Conclusion

then a further question arises as to whether and how the discursive reality is amenable to reconfiguration.

We have seen that a dominant discourse nevertheless depends on boundary-drawing. This may be readily undermined, as with the neglect of corporations, landlords, and employers as welfare recipients; the view of migrants as abusers rather than contributors; the problematic carer/worker distinction for claimants of carers allowance and for lone parents with young children; questionable assessments of capability for work; and asylum-seekers as pursuing an absolute right to protection rather than disguised economic migration. All of these examples pose policy challenges that are passed over by the dominant rhetoric of 'fairness', activation, deficit reduction, and control. There is also scope for a focus on problems that cross the welfare/migration divide, such as the position of lone parents, BME groups, and children who repeatedly feature among the vulnerable. Two other recurring issues are the use of children to influence parental conduct and of destitution as a means of shaping behaviour. So chains of equivalence and difference *could* be constructed along different lines in such a way that welfare claimants and migrants would not be opposed in a binary divide, but instead would have a shared interest in a collective rather than individualized model of responsibility, so as to link fairness to need, vulnerability, or lack of capacity.

This redrawing of lines of equivalence and difference might seem unrealistic or unachievable, yet many of the key policies reviewed over the course of this study have been shown to be poorly grounded in terms of available evidence: they have failed to meet objectives, generated perverse effects, and/or conflicted with an established legal framework. Public opinion is not inured to unfairness, vulnerability, and human suffering, as we have seen in responses to the Windrush scandal, support for the Dubs amendment, and softening attitudes toward migration (Staton 2019). We have seen rapidly expanding volunteer support for food banks, disquiet over escalating levels of homelessness, and generous responses to media exposure of the extremes of the welfare and immigration regimes. Even so, an alternative master frame has failed to take hold; indeed, we have seen how a far-reaching policy paradigm has been able to sustain ill-founded policies, poor administrative systems, a weak evidential base, perverse effects, demonstrable discriminatory results, and limited access to justice, which at their worst produce destitution and death.

We can return again to Lockwood's (1996) framework and his question of why there is not more widespread 'legitimable discontent' (543). One factor is that receipt of a right can become stigmatizing, especially when linked to charges of abuse that erode the moral standing of recipients. Furthermore, policy often rests implicitly or explicitly on invidious comparisons between groups, as with the classic shirker/striver divide and the zero-sum picture of welfare and migration. We have seen piecemeal challenges to specific measures that have yielded some successes, and also moral disapprobation that has attracted judicial support but without meeting the legal threshold necessary to overturn policy. However, the paucity of critique that successfully combines welfare and migration issues is revealing, and shows the strength of the dominant paradigm and its success in dividing and ruling, especially when combined with the Brexit dilemma. Evidence points to the possibility of a new paradigm that would build equivalence across established boundaries of difference, to change the way institutions think, to reconfigure public discourse in terms of compassion and humanity, to build endorsement of a right to survival, and to redirect the *telos* of the economy.

CORONAVIRUS CRISIS: A PIVOTAL MOMENT

This has so far seemed beyond what can reasonably be hoped for, yet the fiscal response to the coronavirus pandemic is revealing in that it has demonstrated how quickly a dominant rhetoric – such as the primacy of deficit reduction – can be reversed, as rules that seemed written in stone were abandoned almost overnight. The onset of COVID-19 has made the dismal heritage of the austerity decade more visible: we entered the crisis with a tattered welfare safety net, high levels of labour market insecurity, a hole in local authority budgets, politically sanctioned hostility to migrant workers, and an underfunded health system facing recruitment problems. One immediate effect came when previously secure workers were confronted with the inadequacies of the welfare system on a personal level, and the speed at which the UC personal allowance was raised is notable – especially given the preceding four years of NGO campaigning against frozen rates. So we saw improved treatment for these workers within the UC system, while some were rescued from recourse by the job protection (furlough) scheme, highlighting the flaws in a discourse that sees unemployment as the result of a 'dependency culture'. But

Conclusion

for others, an increase in the UC allowance meant exposure to the benefit cap, which rendered them worse off under the crumbling rationale of incentivizing work – now the subject of a further legal challenge (Butler 2020a). The cap for affected households is almost £1,000 less than the £2,500 per month granted under the furlough scheme, and there have been calls for the cap to be suspended for at least the duration of the pandemic.

The furlough scheme was extended to the self-employed only after a threat of legal action, but for many the relief provided has amounted to only 80 per cent of a poverty wage. Meanwhile, the crisis has also made visible the exclusion of most 'non-standard' workers from access to sick pay. Even after entitlement was extended to this group, it was immediately apparent to most people (including the Secretary of State for Health and Social Care) that £94.25 per week was insufficient for basic maintenance. As a result, there has been evidence that key workers feel compelled to work when sick – 47 per cent of the self-employed and 51 per cent of atypical workers (Booth 2020a) – thus endangering themselves and others, and in some cases ending in death (Busby 2020a). Add to this a pattern of vulnerability revealed by the unequal impact of COVID-19 on front-facing workers, notably in the health service, care work, and transport, and falling disproportionately on BAME workers, the 'low skilled', and migrants. One result has been to enhance the moral standing of these groups, while the pattern of deaths suggests that it is *inequality* itself that kills, with lower-paid men representing the most vulnerable group (Barr and Inman 2020).

The creation of a flexible workforce was one of the early objectives of UC (Duncan Smith 2014). Accordingly, unemployed claimants could be required to accept zero-hours employment, while the generally punitive operation of the system pushed others into reluctant self-employment, the 'last refuge of the desperate' (Clark 2014a; see also Inman 2019). Taxi drivers, delivery drivers, care workers, and cleaners have since become part of the front line in a pandemic against which they were offered inadequate protection. Vulnerability to the virus has been linked in part to occupation, and in this regard, the disproportionate effect on BAME workers is shockingly apparent: black male workers have four times the death rate of their white counterparts (Booth and Barr 2020). They account for 94 per cent of drivers in London (Booth 2020a) and make up 20 per cent of the 1.2 million NHS staff (Siddique 2020), while 12.8 per cent of the Pakistani and Bangladeshi workforce are in public transport (Booth and Barr 2020).

Some of these workers will be second and third generation immigrants holding British citizenship, but others are first generation arrivals, and one further effect of the crisis has been to highlight the need for migrant workers to keep the country and the health system running. A total of 20 per cent of key workers were born outside the UK, amounting to 30 per cent work in the food industry; nearly 25 per cent work in health and social care; and 20 per cent work in transport (Farquharson, Rasul, and Sibieta 2020). Furthermore, 28 per cent of NHS doctors and 13.1 per cent of all NHS staff are not UK-born (Baker 2019), though the number of nurses joining the health service from EU countries has more than halved since the referendum (Baker 2019), and vacancies are running at 43,000, or 12 per cent (Mitchell 2019). The NHS's reliance on non-British workers has exposed the inequity of the health surcharge for non-EEA migrants – a charge of £400 per person per year, that rose to £625 in October 2020, which post-Brexit will also apply to EEA migrants. Workers already pay into the system through their taxes and national insurance, though in response to COVID-19, doctors, nurses, and paramedics were granted a one-year exemption, which the British Medical Association and Royal College of Nurses argued should be extended to care workers. Given the high levels of public sympathy, and in the face of pressure from politicians and professional bodies – sometimes expressed in terms of morality – the surcharge has now been dropped for all NHS and care workers (Proctor 2020).

Meanwhile, the care sector has 122,000 vacancies and a non-UK workforce of around 17 per cent, nearly half of whom come from EU countries (Skills for Care 2019). Along with the role of other 'low skilled' key workers in the pandemic, this has raised questions about the impact of withdrawal from the EU's freedom-of-movement regime. The Immigration and Social Security Co-ordination (EU Withdrawal) Bill 2019–21, which will end free movement for EEA nationals, has now passed through Parliament. It relies mainly on salary and skills thresholds to regulate migration from the EU and lowers the skilled worker minimum-income threshold from £30,000 to £25,600, with some flexibility for shortage occupations (Gower and Kennedy 2020). However, two thirds of those classed as key workers during the pandemic would not qualify (*Guardian* 2020a), and this comes at a time when polls indicate widespread public sympathy for such workers. Though this arguably has challenged the context and tone of the immigration debate (Katwala, Rutter et al. 2020), and notably the income threshold for a Tier 2 visa has been reduced from £30,000 to £25,600. Nevertheless, both the planned visa scheme and the continuing health surcharge for most arrivals maintain a distinction between 'deserving' and 'undeserving' migrants.

The depth and scale of cuts to local authorities' funding is another aspect of austerity more fully exposed by the crisis. Those cuts have rebounded on the ability to provide social care, support for the vulnerable, offer protection for workers, and provision for the homeless. Despite additional funds, several authorities are on the brink of bankruptcy (Butler and Syal 2020), but following an effort to get 90 per cent of the homeless off the streets, advance spending from the rough sleepers budget has been made available to construct an exit strategy. The crisis has also exposed the plight of those lawfully present but falling under the NRPF condition (see Gower 2020), and of others with uncertain status and hence cut off from support. The vulnerability of these groups has been the subject of an open letter to Boris Johnson from more than fifty charities,[2] though he seemed ignorant of the NRPF policy when questioned by the Work and Pensions Committee (Honeycombe-Foster 2020). Exclusions from support have a knock-on effect in relation to homelessness, since the costs of accommodating those without entitlement may well fall on struggling local authorities, though undocumented migrants will tend to avoid all contact with officialdom. This poses a particular health hazard, and while treatment for the coronavirus has been declared free of charge, undocumented migrants will fear being diagnosed with a different condition and confronted with a bill (or possibly deportation).

Experience of COVID-19 also poses problems for the government that go beyond negotiating a course through the crisis, not least of these being the implicit challenge to some of their core ideological positions. If public spending is no longer taboo, if deficit reduction is no longer a determinant of policy, and if migrants are now valued as an essential resource, what will happen to the discursive reality constructed and sustained over the last decade? A punitive approach to unemployment becomes less sustainable, the rationale for the benefit cap and the two-child limit loses its credibility, and anti-immigrant rhetoric loses its force. Indeed, many of the vulnerabilities created or exacerbated by austerity measures have been made more apparent as the destruction of the safety net threatens mainstream workers, homelessness emerges as a problem for public health, and the crisis illuminates the extent to which all our fates are interlinked. There are already signs of a shift in public sentiment (Butler 2020b).

In fact, morality and rationality have often come together in critical responses, with respect to measures to incentivize work when work is not feasible, to 'low-skilled' key workers who feel compelled to work but unable to protect themselves, to a health surcharge for workers who are putting themselves at risk, to the inequitable pattern of vulnerability to the virus, to the plight of those destitute or homeless, and to the dilemma of migrant groups without entitlements. All these examples make an alternative *moral* economy seem more feasible, and indeed more rational, as unanticipated funds of public sympathy and gratitude are tapped, as previously marginal groups accrue improved moral standing, and as it becomes increasingly apparent that the well-being of each is the only route to the well-being of all.

The experience of the crisis means that some of the measures most obviously required to restore the strength of the social fabric are now self-evident (see Economic Affairs Committee 2020). These include adequate coverage for the unemployed and removal of unrealistic job-search requirements; abolition of the benefit cap and the two-child CTC limit; fuller adherence to the principle of the best interests of children; improved entitlement and conditions for atypical workers; recognition and facilitation of the role of 'low skilled' migrant labour; restoration of the old terms of Discretionary Leave, which did not carry the NRPF condition; humanitarian treatment for failed asylum-seekers unable to leave; and a cessation of policies that create homelessness and destitution. All of these elements emerge as both a rational and a moral response to the crisis, and it may yet be a drive for self-preservation on the part of a more affluent and securely placed majority that provides a spur for the creation of a moral economy in which care for the vulnerable takes a more central place, as essential to the protection of all.

Notes

INTRODUCTION

1 Financial penalties for failure to meet conditions.
2 Varying from 6.1 per cent in the North East to 2.6 per cent in the South West (Office for National Statistics 2019a).
3 Total self-employment is 15 per cent of all employment (Inman 2019).
4 A further six-month extension was announced in March 2021.
5 If born in the UK to a parent with permanent residence.
6 Having a parent or grandparent whose citizenship was acquired within the UK.
7 The term 'outsider within' was coined by Patricia Hill Collins (1986).

CHAPTER ONE

1 Founded by Ian Duncan Smith, later secretary of state for work and pensions.
2 The six are Job Seekers Allowance, Housing Benefit, Working Tax Credit, Child Tax Credit, Employment Support Allowance (for the disabled), and Income Support (for the economically inactive). A list of benefit changes under the coalition is provided by the New Policy Institute (NPI) (2013). For a list of changes under the Conservative government's Welfare and Work Act see Spencer (2016).
3 Recipients of the Working Tax Credit are exempt.
4 A bill to prohibit this possibility failed to complete passage through Parliament in the 2018–19 session and will make no further progress.
5 For example, by the Social Security Advisory Committee and the Social Mobility and Child Poverty Commission.

214   Notes to pages 37–82

6 £0.8bn from official error and £1.6bn from claimant error.

7 See for example MA *and Ors v* SSWP [2014] EWCA Civ 13.

8 £500 per week for a workless family and £350 for a single adult, lowered in 2016 to £384.62 and £257.69 outside London and £442.31 and £296.35 inside.

9 The amount of earnings permitted before a resultant loss of in-work benefit.

10 See, for example, CPAG 2016a and JRF 2018a.

11 Article 1 Protocol 1 – the peaceful enjoyment of possessions, which has been found to apply to Social Security entitlement.

12 The age was lowered to three in 2016.

13 Later revised upwards to 3,789–4,305.

CHAPTER TWO

1 For changes under the coalition government see New Policy Institute (2013); for subsequent changes see GPAG (2016).

2 Tightened conditions for entry and residence, a raised minimum income threshold for family unification, increased civil society checks on immigration status, and so on.

3 See CPAG intervention in SG *and Ors v* SSWP [2015] UKSC 16 (CPAG 2014).

4 As in the landmark case on destitute asylum-seekers (*Adam, Tesema and Limbuela v* SSHD [2005] UKHL 66).

5 A sponsor in this context is the person applying for entry permission for a family member.

CHAPTER THREE

1 Elisabeta Dano and Florin Dano v Sozialgericht Leipzig (Germany), C-333/13, and *Nazifa Alimanovic et al. v Jobcenter Berlin Neukölln*, C-67/14

2 David Cameron held the worst house-building record since 1923 (Yeung 2016).

3 An estimated 2 per cent of total claims.

4 For a list of changes under the Coalition, see NPI (2013), and under the Welfare and Work Act, see Spencer (2016).

5 For example, differential requirements for participation in the Work Programme.

Notes to pages 82–104

6 Currently being phased in, to integrate Job Seekers Allowance, Housing Benefit, Working Tax Credit, Child Tax Credit, Employment Support Allowance (for the disabled), and Income Support (for the economically inactive).
7 See note 4.
8 Notably the *Alimanovic* case (C-67/14), which upheld a denial of social assistance after six months' unemployment.
9 Immigration (European Economic Area) (Amendment) Regulations 2014 (SI 2014/1511) and SI (2014/2761)
10 The main working-age benefits are JSA (for unemployment), ESA (for disability), and Income Support (for the economically inactive).
11 This is not, of course, a full expression of the tax/benefit picture. For more details, see Markaki and Vargas-Silva (2017).
12 On perceptions of benefit fraud, see Grice (2013), and on migrant access to welfare, see Duffy and Frere-Smith (2014, Chapter 3).
13 See Graham (2015) for a Factcheck and compare with Beckford (2016) for a tabloid press report.
14 This concept (Foster 1965) has been applied in anthropological studies of societies in which a belief that the resources available are finite produces fragile and shifting patterns of alignment among social groups.
15 Though Scotland and Northern Ireland supported Remain (Sensier and Devine 2017).
16 An electoral unit of average population 7,000, analysed by Becker, Fetzer, and Novy (2016) for four cities.
17 Prior support for the UK Independence Party or the British National Party.
18 Notably, the Scottish vote (62 per cent Remain) displayed a different pattern of response.

CHAPTER FOUR

1 Here meaning means-tested working-age benefits.
2 Now replaced by the Youth Obligation Scheme and the Work and Health Programme.
3 Expected to report in the course of 2022.
4 Revised under the coalition government but subject to controversy.
5 54 per cent of fit-for-work appeals were upheld between July and September 2014.
6 £26,000 in 2012, lowered in 2016 to £23,000 for London and £20,000 elsewhere.

216 Notes to pages 107–154

7 With exceptions for PhD-level jobs and shortage occupations.
8 Article 8 of the ECHR.
9 Though note that CPAG has successfully challenged the genuine-prospect-of-work test for retained workers, which was found to be unlawful (*KH v Bury MBC and SSWP* (2020) UKUT 50 (AAC)).
10 For 2012–16 the latter outnumbered the former by 5:1 (APPG 2017).
11 The HO has recently been in error over returns to Afghanistan.
12 S55 of 2009 Borders Citizenship and Immigration Act, and the PSED.

CHAPTER FIVE

1 Median income was £27,195 at time of writing. Qualifying income for settlement was reduced to £25,600 in December 2020.
2 See *MM and Ors v SSHD* [2013] EWHC 1900 (Admin), para. 107(i). Lesser requirements apply to sponsors on disability benefits.
3 Article 8, ECHR.
4 Supplied by the centre's director.
5 Rates were standardized at £36.62 per week, meaning a fall of £16.34 for those under sixteen.
6 In Europe since 20 March 2016, and under fifteen, or under eighteen and accompanying a younger sibling.
7 A camp for those seeking transit to Britain.
8 81 per cent of destitution appeals succeeded in 2011–12 and 68 per cent in 2015–16 (ASAP 2015).
9 The first Commonwealth arrivals travelled on HMT *Empire Windrush*.
10 As in the Windrush cases.
11 Supports recommended after the 2018 review have been deemed a 'drop in the ocean' (Fouzder 2019).

CHAPTER SIX

1 A think tank allied to the Conservative Party, in which Iain Duncan Smith (later the secretary of state for work and pensions) was active.
2 Combining six working-age benefits.
3 Equivalent to net average earnings and excluding benefits available to the working population.
4 Effective for new claims from April 2017.
5 Likely to be in a different (cheaper) area.

CHAPTER SEVEN

The title of this chapter echoes Hill Collins's (1986) conception of the 'outsider within'. My own focus differs from her 'standpoint' orientation, but it reflects the spirit of her argument, in which attention to multiple 'outsider' positions can illuminate the unstable nature of dichotomies and intersecting patterns of disadvantage, discrimination, and exclusion.

1 Ex-minister for families and children.
2 Neil Couling denies official targets but shows evidence of a target culture; see Couling 2013, and Domokos and Wintour 2013.
3 As with heightened sanctions.
4 Freedom from inhuman and degrading treatment.
5 Under Article 8 of the ECHR.
6 One-third migrant.
7 Some local authorities are struggling with the financial impact of the crisis (see Bounds and Tighe 2020)
8 See for example Bulman and Polianskaya (2017), Bulman (2018), Butler and Pring (2016).

CONCLUSION

1 Net migration peaked at 336,000 in 2016 (Sumption and Vargas-Silva 2019), but the target was abandoned in December of 2018.
2 Available at https://www.jesuit.org.uk/open-letter-prime-minister.

References

Adkins, Lisa. 2017. 'Disobedient Workers, the Law, and the Making of Unemployment Markets'. *Sociology* 51(2): 290–305.

Adler, Michael. 2016. 'A New Leviathan'. *Journal of Law and Society* 43(2): 19–227.

– 2015. 'Benefit Sanctions and the Rule of Law'. UK Administrative Justice Institute. 14 October 2015. https://ukaji.org/2015/10/14/benefit-sanctions-and-the-rule-of-law.

Advertising Standards Authority. 2019. 'Ruling on Department of Work and Pensions in Association with Associated Newspapers'. 6 November 2019. https://www.asa.org.uk/rulings/department-for-work-and-pensions-G19-1021769.html.

Agamben, Giorgio. 1998. *Homo Sacer* [1995]. Stanford: Stanford University Press.

Aitkenhead, Decca. 2013. 'Sarah Teather: I'm Angry There Are No Alternative Voices on Immigration'. *The Guardian,* 13 July 2013.

Alexander, Jeffery. 2006. *The Civil Sphere.* Oxford: Oxford University Press.

Allbeson, Janet. 1996. *Failing the Test.* London: National Association of Citizens Advice Bureaus.

Allen, Kate, and Larry Elliott. 2016. 'Britain at Bottom of League as Real Wages Decline by 10%'. *The Guardian,* 27 July 2016.

Alston, Philip. 2018. 'Statement on Visit to the United Kingdom, by Professor Philip Alston, United Nations Special Rapporteur on Extreme Poverty and Human Rights'. Office of the High Commissioner, 16 November 2018. https://www.ohchr.org/en/NewsEvents/Pages/DisplayNews.aspx?NewsID=23881&LangID=E.

Amelina, A. 2020. 'European Welfare between Complex Regulatory Frameworks and Mobile Europeans' Experience of Social (In)security'. In *Boundaries of European Social Citizenship*, edited by Anna Amelina, Emma Carmel, Anna Runfors, and Elisabeth Scheibelhofer, 1–18. London: Routledge.

Amnesty International. 2016. *Cuts That Hurt*. London: Amnesty International UK.

Anderson, Bridget. 2019. 'New Directions in Migration Studies: Towards Methodological De-nationalism'. *Comparative Migration Studies* 7: 36. https://10.1186/s40878-019-0140-8.

– 2013. *Us and Them*. Oxford: Oxford University Press.

Anderson, Bridget, Nandita Sharma, and Cynthia Wright. 2009. 'Editorial: Why No Borders?' *Refuge* 26(3): 5–15.

Anti-Slavery. 2019. 'UK Survivors Win Right to Long Term Support'. *Anti-Slavery.* 2 July 2. www.antislavery.org/win-uk-slavery-survivors.

APPG (All Party Parliamentary Group). 2017. *Refugees Welcome.* London: Barrow Cadbury Trust.

– 2014. 'Feeding Britain: A Strategy for Zero Hunger in England, Wales, Scotland and Northern Ireland'. *Feeding Britain*, 8 December 2014. https://feedingbritain.org/wp-content/uploads/2019/01/feeding_britain_report_2014-2.pdf.

– 2013. 'Report of the Inquiry into New Family Migration Rules'. June 2013. http://appgmigration.org.uk/wp-content/uploads/2012/11/APPG_family_migration_inquiry_report-Jun-2013.pdf.

Arendt, Hannah. 1979. *The Origins of Totalitarianism* [1948]. New York: Harcourt Brace.

ASAP (Asylum Support Appeals Project). 2015. 'A Decade of Disbelieving'. Asylum Support Appeals Project, October 2015. https://www.asaproject.org/uploads/ASAP-Summary-A-Decade-of-disbelieving-destitution-Oct-2015.pdf.

– 2015a. 'Response to "Reforming Support for Failed Asylum Seekers and Other Illegal Migrants"'. Asylum Support Appeals Project, 7 September 2015. http://www.asaproject.org/uploads/ASAP-response-to-HO-Consultation-on-Asylum-Support-7-9-15.pdf.

– 2013. 'Response to "Transforming Legal Aid: Delivering a More Credible and Efficient System."' http://www.asaproject.org/uploads/ASAP-response-to-Legal-Aid-consultation.pdf.

Atkins, Judi. 2010. 'Moral Argument and the Justification of Policy'. *British Journal of Politics and International Relations* 12(3): 408–24.

References 221

Baker, Carl. 2019. *NHS Staff from Overseas: Statistics*. London: House of Commons Library, BP 7783.

Ball, James. 2013. 'Iain Duncan Smith Rapped by Watchdog for Misusing Benefit Cap Statistics'. *The Guardian*, 9 May. https://www.theguardian.com/politics/2013/may/09/iain-duncan-smith-benefits-cap-statistics.

Barbulescu, Roxana, and Adrian Favell. 2019. 'Commentary: A Citizenship without Social Rights? Freedom of Movement and Changing Access to Welfare Rights'. *International Migration* 58(1): 151–65.

Barr, Caelainn, and Phillip Inman. 2020. 'Lowest Paid Men More Likely to Die from Virus'. *The Guardian*, 12 May.

Barr, Jonathan, Elena Magini, and Michela Meghnani. 2019. *Trends in Economic Activity across the OECD*. Paris: Organisation for Economic Co-operation and Development.

Barrett, Claer. 2019. 'On the Frontline with Those Tackling the UK's Debt Crisis'. *Financial Times,* 27 April.

Basedow, Josephine, and Lisa Doyle. 2016. *England's Forgotten Refugees*. London: Refugee Council.

Bauman, Zygmunt. 2003. *Wasted Lives: Modernity and Its Outcasts*. Cambridge: Polity Press

Beattie, Jason. 2014. '27 Bishops Slam David Cameron'. *Daily Mirror*, 19 February. https://www.mirror.co.uk/news/uk-news/27-bishops-slam-david-camerons-3164033.

Beatty, Christina, and Stephen Fothergill. 2016. *The Uneven Impact of Welfare Reform*. Sheffield: Sheffield Hallam, Centre for Regional Economic Social Research.

Beck, Ulrich. 2006. *Cosmopolitan Vision*. Cambridge: Polity Press.

Beck, Ulrich, and Natan Sznaider. 2006. 'Unpacking Cosmopolitanism for the Social Sciences'. *British Journal of Sociology* 57(1): 1–23.

Becker, Sascha O., Thiemo Fetzer, and Dennis Novy. 2016. *Who Voted for Brexit? A Comprehensive District-Level Analysis*. Working Paper no. 305. Warwick: Centre for Competitive Advantage in the Global Economy.

Beckford, Martin. 2016. '£866 Million … That Is the Eye-Watering Sum You Pay in Benefits to Out of Work EU Migrants in Just One Year'. *Mailonline*, 28 February. http://www.dailymail.co.uk/news/article-3467563/886million-eye-watering-sum-pay-benefits-work-EU-migrants-just-one-year.html.

Beitz, Charles R. 1983. 'Cosmopolitan Ideals and National Sentiment'. *Journal of Philosophy* 80(10): 591–600.

Benhabib, Seyla. 2004. *The Rights of Others*. Cambridge: Cambridge University Press.

Bhambra, Gurminder, and John Holmwood. 2018. 'Colonialism, Postcolonialism, and the Liberal Welfare State'. *New Political Economy* 23(5): 574–87.

Blanchard, Catherine, and Sarah Joy. 2017. *Can't Stay Can't Go*. London: Red Cross.

Bommes, Michael, and Andrew Geddes, eds. 2000. *Immigration and Welfare: Challenging the Borders of the Welfare State*. London: Routledge.

Booth, Robert. 2020. 'Revenue Teams Catch Only One in Eight Firms Paying Illegally Low Wages'. *The Guardian*, 8 January.

– 2020a. 'Chancellor Faces Legal Action over Lack of Help for the Self-Employed'. *The Guardian*, 23 March.

Booth, Robert, and Caelainn Barr. 2020. 'Black People Four Times More Likely to Die from Coronavirus'. *The Guardian*, 8 May.

Booth, William J. 1994. 'On the Idea of the Moral Economy'. *American Political Science Review* 88(3): 653–67.

– 1993. 'A Note on the Idea of the Moral Economy'. *American Political Science Review* 87(4): 949–54.

Bosniak, Linda. 2006. *The Citizen and the Alien*. Princeton: Princeton University Press.

Bottomore, Tom. 1992. 'Citizenship and Social Class: Forty Years On'. In *Citizenship and Social Class*, edited by Tom Bottomore, 55–93. London: Pluto Press.

Bounds, Andy, and Chris Tighe. 2020. 'Struggling Councils to Receive Extra £1Bn but Press for More'. *Financial Times*, 19 April.

Bourquin, Pascale, Jonathan Cribb, Tom Waters, and Xiaowei Xu. 2019. *Living Standards, Poverty, and Inequality in the UK: 2019*. London: Institute for Fiscal Studies.

Bradshaw, Jonathan. 2015. 'The Erosion of the UK Safety Net'. Discover Society, 3 January. https://discoversociety.org/2015/01/03/the-erosion-of-the-uk-safety-net.

Broad, Rose, and Nick Turnbull. 2019. 'From Human Trafficking to Modern Slavery: The Development of Anti-Trafficking Policy in the UK'. *European Journal on Criminal Policy and Research* 25: 119–33.

Brokenshire, James. 2014. 'Levels of Support to Asylum Seekers Provided by the Home Office'. Home Office, 11 August. http://www.nrpfnetwork.org.uk/Documents/Home%20Office%20letter%20asylum%20support%20August%202014.pdf.

References

Brown, Thomas. 2018. 'Welfare Changes: Impact on Family Life'. Parliament.uk, 25 October. https://researchbriefings.parliament.uk/ResearchBriefing/Summary/LLN-2018-0111#fullreport.

Bruzelius, Cecilia. 2019. 'Freedom of Movement, Social Rights, and Residence-Based Conditionality in the European Union'. *Journal of European Social Policy* 29(1): 70–83.

Brysk, Alison, and Gershon Shafir. 2004. *People Out of Place*. London: Routledge.

Bulman, May. 2018. 'Universal Credit Claimants Driven to Consider Suicide over Stress Caused by Welfare Reform'. *The Independent*, 16 November. https://www.independent.co.uk/news/uk/home-news/universal-credit-benefits-suicide-stress-mental-health-welfare-conservatives-report-a8636661.html.

Bulman, May, and Alina Polianskaya. 2017. 'Attempted Suicides by Disabled Benefit Claimants More than Double after Introduction of Fit-to-Work Assessments'. *The Independent*, 28 December. https://www.independent.co.uk/news/uk/home-news/disability-benefit-claimants-attempted-suicides-fit-to-work-assessment-i-daniel-blake-job-centre-dwp-a8119286.htm.

Busby, Mattha. 2020. 'Government Reduces Minimum Salary for Migrants to Settle in UK'. *The Guardian, 24 October.*

– 2020a. 'Sick Cleaner Toils for Five Days before Dying'. *The Guardian*, 5 May.

– 2019. 'Immigration Check Outcry Sees Officers Removed by Councils'. *The Observer*, 24 February.

Butler, Patrick. 2020. 'Judge Me Fairly: Plea of Man Who Died after Benefits Cut'. *The Guardian*, 28 February.

– 2020a. 'Single Mother on Universal Credit Challenges Sunak's "Perverse" Benefit Cap'. *The Guardian*, 18 May.

– 2020b. 'Support for Welfare and Migration Growing'. *The Guardian*, 29 November.

– 2019. 'Slow Response to Universal Credit Errors "Bizarre" Says Council'. *The Guardian*, 7 May.

– 2019a. 'Tories Ditch Ineffective Three Year Sanction'. *The Guardian*, 10 May.

– 2019b. 'Poor Universal Credit Advice Costs Claimants Thousands, MPS Say'. *The Guardian*, 23 July 2019.

– 2014. 'Foodbank Issues Parcels for Those Too Poor to Heat Dinner'. *The Guardian*, 20 January.

224 References

Butler, Patrick, and John Pring. 2016. 'Suicides of Benefit Claimants Reveal DWP Flaws, Says Inquiry'. *The Guardian*, 14 May.

Butler, Patrick, and Jennifer Rankin. 2019. 'Surge in EU Citizens Unfairly Refused Access to Universal Credit'. *The Guardian*, 5 August.

Butler, Patrick, and Rajeev Syal. 2020. 'Councils Face £5Bn Funding Shortfall'. *The Guardian*, 27 April.

Butterworth, Jonathan, and Jamie Burton. 2013. 'Equality, Human Rights, and Public Service Spending Cuts'. *Equal Rights Review* 11: 26–45.

Cameron, David. 2015. 'PM Speech on Immigration'. *Gov.uk*, 21 May. https://www.gov.uk/government/speeches/pm-speech-on-immigration.

– 2015a. 'The Prime Minister Delivered His Speech on Europe at Chatham House, Setting Out the Case for EU Reform'. *Gov.uk*, 10 November. https://www.gov.uk/government/speeches/prime-ministers-speech-on-europe.

– 2014. 'Speech to the Conservative Party Conference 2014'. Conservative.home, 1 October. https://www.conservativehome.com/thetorydiary/2014/10/full-text-of-david-camerons-party-conference-speech.html.

– 2014a. 'We are Building an Immigration System That Puts Britain First'. *The Telegraph*, 28 July. http://www.telegraph.co.uk/news/uknews/immigration/10995875/David-Cameron-Were-building-an-immigration-system-that-puts-Britain-first.html.

– 2014b. 'Why the Archbishop of Westminster Is Wrong about Welfare'. *The Telegraph*, 18 February. http://www.telegraph.co.uk/news/politics/david-cameron/10646421/David-Cameron-Why-the-Archbishop-of-Westminster-is-wrong-about-welfare.html.

– 2014c. 'David Cameron's EU Speech'. *BBC News*, 28 November. http://www.bbc.co.uk/news/uk-politics-30250299.

– 2013. 'David Cameron's Immigration Speech'. *Gov.uk*, 25 March. https://www.gov.uk/government/speeches/david-camerons-immigration-speech.

– 2013a. 'Queen's Speech 2013'. *The Guardian*, 8 May. http://www.theguardian.com/politics/2013/may/08/queens-speech-2013-full-text.

– 2013b. 'Free Movement within Europe Needs to Be Less Free'. *Financial Times*, 26 November 2013. https://www.ft.com/content/add36222-56be-11e3-ab12-00144feabdco?mhq5j=e2.

– 2012. 'David Cameron's Conservative Party Speech: In Full'. *The Telegraph*, 10 October 2012. http://www.telegraph.co.uk/news/politics/

conservative/9598534/David-Camerons-Conservative-Party-Conference-speech-in-full.html.

– 2012a. 'Prime Minister's Message on "Welfare Reform"'. Gov.uk, 1 March.https://www.gov.uk/government/news/prime-ministers-message-on-welfare-reform.

– 2011. 'Conservative Party Conference 2011: David Cameron's Speech in Full'. *The Telegraph*, 5 October 2011. https://www.telegraph.co.uk/news/politics/conservative/8808521/Conservative-Party-conference-2011-David-Camerons-speech-in-full.html.

– 2011a. 'David Cameron on Immigration: Full Text of the Speech'. *The Guardian*, 14 April 2011. http://www.theguardian.com/politics/2011/apr/14/david-cameron-immigration-speech-full-text.

– 2011b. 'Prime Minister's Speech on Immigration'. *Gov.uk*, 10 October. https://www.gov.uk/government/speeches/prime-ministers-speech-on-immigration.

– 2011c. 'PM's Speech on the Fightback after the Riots'. *Gov.uk*, 15 August. https://www.gov.uk/government/speeches/pms-speech-on-the-fightback-after-the-riots.

– 2010. 'David Cameron's Conservative Conference Speech in Full'. *The Telegraph*, 6 October. https://www.telegraph.co.uk/news/politics/david-cameron/8046342/David-Camerons-Conservative-conference-speech-in-full.html.

– 2010a. 'Prime Minister's Speech on the Economy'. *Gov.uk,* 7 June. https://www.gov.uk/government/speeches/prime-ministers-speech-on-the-economy.

– 2009. 'The Age of Austerity'. Conservative Party speeches, 26 April. http://conservative-speeches.sayit.mysociety.org/speech/601367.

Carmel, Emma, and Bozena Sojka. 2020. 'Beyond Welfare Chauvinism and Deservingness: Rationales of Belonging as a Conceptual Framework for the Politics and Governance of Migrants Rights'. *Journal of Social Policy.* doi:10.1017S0047279420000379.

Committee on Economic, Social and Cultural Rights (CESCR). 2009. 'General Comment No. 20: Non Discrimination in Economic, Social and Cultural Rights' (art. 2, para. 2, of the International Covenant on Economic, Social and Cultural Rights), 2 July 2009, E/C.12/GC/20. https://www.refworld.org/docid/4a60961f2.html.

– 1990. 'General Comment No. 3: The Nature of States Parties' Obligations'. (art. 2, para. 1, of the Covenant)'. 14 December 1990, E/1991/23. https://www.refworld.org/docid/4538838e10.html.

References

Chakrabortty, Aditya. 2014. 'Cut Benefits? Yes, Let's Start with Our £85Bn Corporate Welfare Handout'. *The Guardian*, 7 October.

Chauvin, Sébastien, and Blanca Garces-Mascarenas. 2012. 'Beyond Informal Citizenship'. *International Political Sociology* 6(3): 241–59.

Children's Commissioner. 2015. 'Response to Home Office Consultation'. September. https://www.childrenscommissioner.gov.uk/wp-content/uploads/2017/06/UK-Childrens-Commissioners-Response.pdf.

The Children's Society. 2020. *A Lifeline for All*. London.

Chu, Ben. 2014. 'Why Osborne's Headline-Grabbing Claims Are Wrong'. *Independent on Sunday*, 7 October.

Church Action on Poverty. 2015. 'Restoring Faith in the Safety Net'. June. https://www.church-poverty.org.uk/restoring-faith-in-the-safety-net.

Church Action on Poverty and Oxfam. 2013. *Walking the Breadline*. Oxford: Oxfam.

Clark, Tom. 2014. 'Self-Employment Surge across UK Hides Real Story behind Up-Beat Job Figures'. *The Guardian,* 6 May.

– 2014a. 'Unwilling Freelancers Give the Lie to Unemployment Statistics'. *The Guardian*, 29 October.

Clarke, John, and Janet Newman. 2012. 'The Alchemy of Austerity'. *Critical Social Policy* 32(3): 299–319.

Clarke, Stephen, and Nye Cominetti. 2019. 'Setting the Record Straight'. Resolution Foundation. January. https://www.resolutionfoundation.org/app/uploads/2019/01/Setting-the-record-straight-full-employment-report.pdf.

Clasen, Jochen, and Daniel Clegg. 2007. 'Levels and Levers of Conditionality: Measuring Change within Welfare States'. In *Investigating Welfare State Change*, ed. Jochen Clasen and Nico A. Siegel. Cheltenham: Edward Elgar.

Collinson, Alex. 2017. 'Working People are Struggling to Pay for Food'. Trades Union Congress, 7 September. https://www.tuc.org.uk/blogs/working-people-are-struggling-pay-food-britain-needs-pay-rise.

Collinson, Patrick. 2018. 'Low Earners Gain Little from Hammond's £3 Billion Tax Giveaway'. *The Guardian*, 29 October. https://www.theguardian.com/uk-news/2018/oct/29/low-earners-gain-little-from-hammonds-3bn-tax-giveaway.

Conservative Party. 2008. *Responsibility Agenda, Work for Welfare*. Policy Green Paper no. 3. London.

Cooper, Jacquie, Stuart Campbell, Dhiren Patel, and Jon Simmons. 2014. *The Reason for Migration and Labour Market Characteristics of UK Residents Born Abroad*. Occasional Paper no. 110. London: Home Office.

References

Corporate Watch. 2017. 'The Hostile Environment'. 8 April. https://corporatewatch.org/the-hostile-environment-turning-the-uk-into-a-nation-of-border-cops-2.

Coram Children's Legal Centre. 2015. 'Response to Consultation on Reforming Support for Failed Asylum Seekers'. London.

– 2017. *This Is My Home*. London.

Coughlan, Sean. 2019. 'Food Bank Supplies Help Record Numbers'. *BBC News*, 25 April. https://www.bbc.co.uk/news/education-48037122.

Couling, Neil. 2013. 'Conditionality and Sanctions: Report to the Secretary of State for Work and Pension'. *Gov.uk*, May. https://assets.publishing.service.gov.uk/government/uploads/system/uploads/attachment_data/file/199242/sanctions-report.pdf.

Cowburn, Ashley. 2018. 'Benefit Fraud Witch-Hunt: 280,000 Public Tip-Offs Led to No Action Taken Due to Lack of Evidence'. *The Independent*, 15 January.

CPAG (Child Poverty Action Group). 2019. 'Child Poverty in Working Families on the Rise'. 28 March. https://cpag.org.uk/news-blogs/news-listings/child-poverty-working-families-rise.

– 2018. 'Submission to the WPC Sanctions Inquiry'. 8 June. https://cpag.org.uk/policy-and-campaigns/briefing/submission-benefit-sanctions.

– 2018a. 'Budget 2018'. 29 October. https://cpag.org.uk/news-blogs/news-listings/budget-2018-universal-credit-moves-welcome-root-and-branch-change-must-come.

– 2017. 'Broken Promises'. March. http://www.cpag.org.uk/sites/default/files/Broken%20promises%20FINAL%20for%20website.pdf.

– 2016. 'Exceptions to the Limiting of the Individual Child Element of the Child Tax Credit and the Child Element of Universal Credit to a Maximum of Two Children'. November. http://www.cpag.org.uk/sites/default/files/Two%20child%20limit%20consultation_CPAG%20response.pdf.

– 2016a. 'Universal Credit: Cuts to Work Allowances'. May. https://cpag.org.uk/sites/default/files/CPAG%20Briefing%20Universal%20Credit%20work%20allowances.pdf.

– 2015. 'The Welfare Reform and Work Bill: Does It Comply with Human Rights?' November. https://cpag.org.uk/sites/default/files/CPAG-submission-JCHR-Welfare-Reform-and-Work-Bill-2015-Nov2015.pdf.

– 2014. 'Benefit Cap – CPAG Intervention – R(SG and others) v SSWP Formerly JS and Others'. 10 April. https://cpag.org.uk/sites/default/files/CPAG%20Supreme%20Court%20skeleton%20argument%20R%28SG%20and%20others%29%20vs%20SSWP.pdf.

Crawley, Heaven, and Jessica Hagen-Zanker. 2019. 'Deciding Where to Go'. *International Migration* 57(1): 20–35.

Credit-Connect. 2019. 'Citizens Advice Says Report Undermines Efforts to Make Collections Less Punitive'. 19 September. https://www.credit-connect.co.uk/consumer-news/local-authority-collections/citizens-advice-says-report-undermines-efforts-to-make-collections-less-punitive.

Crewe, Tom. 2016. 'The Strange Death of Municipal England'. *London Review of Books* 38(24): 6–10.

CRISIS. 2017. 'Detention and Removal of Migrant Rough Sleepers Must Stop'. 16 June. https://www.crisis.org.uk/about-us/media-centre/detention-and-removal-of-migrant-rough-sleepers-must-stop.

Curtice, John, Miranda Phillips, and Elizabeth Clery, eds. 2016. *British Social Attitudes: The 33rd Report*. London: NatCen.

De Agostini, Paola, John Hills, and Holly Sutherland. 2014. *Were We Really All in It Together?* CASE Working Paper no. 10. London: London School of Economics.

Dean, Hartley. 2012. 'The Ethical Deficit of the UK's Proposed Universal Credit'. *The Political Quarterly* 83(2): 353–59.

Deckard, Natalie D., and Alison Heslin. 2016. 'After Post-National Citizenship'. *Sociology Compass* 10(4): 294–305.

Department for Communities and Local Government. 2011. *Vision to End Rough Sleeping*. London: HM Government.

Department of Social Security. 1998. *New Ambitions for Our Country*. Cm 3805. London: HMSO.

Desira, Chris. 2017. 'Home Office Makes Changes to Appendix FM Minimum Income Rule Following MM Case'. *Free Movement*, 10 August.https://www.freemovement.org.uk/home-office-makes-changes-appendix-fm-minimum-income-rule-following-mm-case.

Devlin, Ciaran, Olivia Bolt, Dhiren Patel, David Harding, and Ishtiaq Hussain. 2014. *Impact of Migration on UK Native Employment*. Occasional Paper no. 109. London: Home Office/Department for Business Innovation and Skills.

Disability Rights UK. 2019. '9 Out of 10 Work and Health Programme Participants Do Not Have a Job Outcome'. 31 May. https://www.disabilityrightsuk.org/news/2019/may/9-out-10-work-and-health-programme-participants-do-not-have-job-outcome.

Dominiczak, Peter. 2015. 'David Cameron Facing Row with Church'. *The Telegraph*, 15 January. http://www.telegraph.co.uk/news/politics/david-cameron/11349601/David-Cameron-facing-row-with-Church-as-he-profoundly-disagrees-with-Archbishops-attack.html.

References   229

- 2013. 'We Will Block Benefits to New EU Migrants Says Cameron'. *The Telegraph,* 18 December. http://www.telegraph.co.uk/news/uknews/immigration/10524285/We-will-block-benefits-to-new-EU-migrants-says-Cameron.html.

Domokos, John, and Patrick Wintour. 2013. 'Jobcentre Scorecard Shows How Areas Are Performing on Stopping Benefits'. *The Guardian,* 28 March 2013. https://www.theguardian.com/society/2013/mar/28/jobcentre-scorecard-areas-stopping-benefits.

Dorling, Danny. 2016. 'Brexit: The Decision of a Divided Country'. Editorial. *BMJ* 354: i3697.

Dorling, Danny, Ben Stuart, and Joshua Stubbs. 2016. 'Brexit, Inequality, and the Demographic Divide'. 22 December. https://blogs.lse.ac.uk/politicsandpolicy/brexit-inequality-and-the-demographic-divide.

Douglas, Mary. 1986. *How Institutions Think.* Syracuse: Syracuse University Press.

Düvell, Franck, and Bill Jordon. 2002. 'Immigration, Asylum, and Welfare: The European Context'. *Critical Social Policy* 22: 498–517.

Duffy, Simon. 2014. *Counting the Cuts.* Sheffield: Centre for Welfare Reform.

Duffy, Bobby, and Tom Frere-Smith. 2014. 'Perceptions and Reality: Public Attitudes to Immigration'. Ipsos MORI Social Research Institute. January. https://www.ipsos.com/sites/default/files/publication/1970-01/sri-perceptions-and-reality-immigration-report-2013.pdf.

Duncan Smith, Iain. 2016. 'Speech on Why the EU Is a Force for Social Injustice. Full Text'. *Conservative Home,* 10 May. https://www.conservativehome.com/parliament/2016/05/iain-duncan-smith-speech-on-why-the-eu-is-a-force-for-social-injustice-full-text.html.

- 2014. 'Iain Duncan-Smith's Speech on Welfare Reform: Full Text'. *The Spectator,* 23 January. https://www.spectator.co.uk/article/iain-duncan-smith-s-speech-on-welfare-reform---full-text.

- 2014a. 'Jobs and Welfare Reform: Getting Britain Working'. *Gov.uk,* 8 April. https://www.gov.uk/government/speeches/jobs-and-welfare-reform-getting-britain-working.

- 2013. 'Iain Duncan Smith's Conservative Party Conference Speech'. 1 October. http://www.conservativepartyconference.org.uk/Speeches/2013_Iain_Duncan_Smith.aspx. https://www.theguardian.com/politics/2013/oct/01/benefit-reforms-iain-duncan-smith-unemployed.

- 2012. 'Welfare Reforms Realised'. *Gov.uk,* 8 March. https://www.gov.uk/government/news/iain-duncan-smith-welfare-reforms-realised.

230 References

Dustmann, Christian, and Tommaso Frattini. 2014. 'The Fiscal Effects of Immigration to the UK'. *The Economic Journal* 124(580): 593–43.

DWP (Department of Work and Pensions). 2020. 'Benefit Cap: Data to February 2020'. https://www.gov.uk/government/collections/benefit-cap-statistics.

– 2018. Central Freedom of Information Team. 'Freedom of Information Request Ref. FOI 2998 + IR 414'. 1 August. https://www.whatdotheyknow.com/request/494836/response/1201245/attach/2/FoI%202998%20IR%20414%20Reply.pdf?cookie_passthrough=1.

– 2015. 'Tackling Fraud Error and Debt in the Benefits and Tax Credits System'. *Gov.uk*. March. https://assets.publishing.service.gov.uk/government/uploads/system/uploads/attachment_data/file/417718/tackling-fraud-error-debt-benefit-tax-system.pdf.

– 2015a. 'Benefit Cap: Thousands Move into Work or Off Housing Benefit'. *Gov.uk*, 14 May. https://www.gov.uk/government/news/benefit-cap-thousands-move-into-work-or-off-housing-benefit.

– 2013. 'Jobseekers Allowance: Overview of Sanctions Rules'. *Gov.uk*, 10 September. https://www.gov.uk/government/publications/jobseekers-allowance-overview-of-sanctions-rules.

– 2013a. 'Accelerating Action to Stop Rogue EU Benefit Claims'. *Gov.uk*, 18 December. https://www.gov.uk/government/news/accelerating-action-to-stop-rogue-eu-benefit-claims.

– 2013b. 'Tough New Migrants Benefits Rules Come into Force Tomorrow'. *Gov.uk*, 31 December. https://www.gov.uk/government/news/tough-new-migrant-benefit-rules-come-into-force-tomorrow.

– 2012. 'Access to Benefits for Those Who Will Have a "Zambrano" Right to Work and Reside'. *Gov.uk,* October. https://www.gov.uk/government/uploads/system/uploads/attachment_data/file/220217/eia-zambrano-right-to-reside-and-work.pdf.

– 2010. *21st Century Welfare*. Cm 7971. London: HMSO.

– 2010a. *Universal Credit: Welfare That Works*. Cm 7957. London: HMSO.

Dwyer, Peter, and Sharon Wright. 2014. 'Universal Credit, Ubiquitous Conditionality, and Its Implications for Social Citizenship'. *Journal of Poverty and Social Justice* 22(1): 27–35.

Economic Affairs Committee. 2020. *Universal Credit Isn't Working*. London: HMSO, HL 105.

The Economic Voice. 2014. 'Church Leaders Call National Fast for Nation's Hungry'. 20 February. https://www.economicvoice.com/church-leaders-call-national-fast-for-uks-hungry-end-hunger-fast-campaign-planned-for-lent.

References

The Economist. 2014. 'How Much Tax Goes on Welfare?' 8 November.

Elgot, Jessica. 2017. 'Dubs Amendment Child Refugee Places Left Unfilled'. *The Guardian*, 24 October. https://www.pressreader.com/uk/the-guardian/20171024/281827169011133.

Elson, Diane. 2012. 'The Reduction of the UK Budget Deficit: A Human Rights Perspective'. *International Review of Applied Economics* 26(2): 177–90.

Emirbayer, Mustafa, and Ann Mische. 1998. 'What Is Agency?' *American Journal of Sociology* 103(4): 962–1023.

European Commission in the UK. 2013. 'Getting the Facts Straight: EU Right to Reside in Another Member State'. 18 February. http://web.archive.org/web/20130607025834/http://blogs.ec.europa.eu:80/ECintheUK/getting-the-facts-straight-eu-rights-to-reside-in-another-member-state-eu-benefit-claimants-and-nhs-treatment-entitlement.

Evans, Liam. 2019. 'No "DSS" Discrimination'. *Turn2us*, 13 March. https://www.turn2us.org.uk/About-Us/News/%E2%80%98No-DSS-discrimination.

Evason, Eileen, and Kevin Higgins. 2019. 'Welfare Reform Mitigation in Northern Ireland'. *Poverty* 164: 17–18.

Faist, Thomas. 2013. *Transnational Social Protection: An Emerging Field of Study*. COMCAD Working Papers No. 113, Bielefeld University.

– 2009. 'The Transnational Social Question'. *International Sociology* 24(1): 7–35.

Farnsworth, Kevin. 2013. 'Bringing Corporate Welfare In'. *Journal of Social Policy* 42(1): 1–22.

Farquharson, Christine, Imran Rasul, and Luke Sibieta. 2020. *Differences between Key Workers*. IFS Briefing Note BN285. London: Institute of Fiscal Studies.

Fassin, Didier. 2012. *Humanitarian Reason*. Berkeley: University of California Press.

– 2010. 'Ethics of Survival'. *Humanity* 1(1): 81–95.

– 2009. 'Another Politics of Life Is Possible'. *Theory, Culture, and Society* 26(5): 44–60.

– 2009a. 'Moral Economies Revisited'. *Annales, Histoire, Sciences Sociales* 64(6): 1237–66.

– 2005. 'Compassion and Repression'. *American Anthropological Association* 20(3): 362–87.

Favell, Adrian. 2014. 'The Fourth Freedom'. *European Journal of Social Theory* 17(3): 275–87.

Field, Frank, and Andrew Forsey. 2016. 'Wild West Workplace: Self-Employment in Britain's Gig Economy'. *Frankfield.co.uk*. September. http://www.frankfield.co.uk/upload/docs/Wild%20West%20Workplace.pdf.

Finn, Dan. 2011. 'Welfare to Work after the Recession'. *Social Policy Review* 23: 127–46.

Finn, Dan, and Jo Goodship. 2014. *Take-Up of Benefits and Poverty*. London: Centre for Economic and Social Inclusion.

Fletcher, Del Roy, and Sharon Wright. 2018. 'A Hand Up or a Slap Down: Criminalising Benefit Claimants in Britain via Strategies of Surveillance, Sanctions, and Deterrence'. *Critical Social Policy* 38(2): 323–44.

Flynn, Don. 2005. 'New Borders, New Management: The Dilemmas of Modern Immigration Policy'. *Ethnic and Racial Studies* 28(3): 463–90.

Forkert, Kirsten. 2017. *Austerity as a Public Mood*. Lanham: Rowman and Littlefield.

Forrest, Adam. 2014. 'Muslim Groups Are Putting Their Faith in Food Banks to Help Tackle Poverty'. *The Guardian*, 2 April 2014. https://www.theguardian.com/society/2014/apr/02/muslim-groups-food-banks-tackle-poverty.

Foster, George M. 1965. 'Peasant Society and the Image of Limited Good'. *American Anthropologist* 67(2): 293–315.

Foucault, Michel. 1991. 'Governmentality'. In *The Foucault Effect*, edited by Graham Burchell, Peter Miller, and Colin Gordon, 85–104. Hemel Hempstead: Harvester Wheatsheaf.

Fouzder, Monidipa. 2019. 'LASPO Review: The Profession Reacts'. *Law Gazette*, 7 February 2019. https://www.lawgazette.co.uk/law/laspo-review-the-profession-reacts/5069191.article.

Freeden, Michael. 2003. *Ideology: A Very Short Introduction*. Oxford: Oxford University Press.

– 1996. *Ideologies and Political Theory*. Oxford: Oxford University Press.

Freeman, Gary. 1986. 'Migration and the Political Economy of the Welfare State'. *Annals of the American Academy of Political and Social Science* 485(1): 51–63.

Full Fact. 2019. 'Poverty in the UK: A Guide to the Facts and Figures'. 27 September. https://fullfact.org/economy/poverty-uk-guide-facts-and-figures.

Gabbatt, Adam. 2011. 'Iain Duncan Smith Appeals to Businesses to Employ Young Britons'. *The Guardian*, 1 July. https://www.theguardian.com/politics/2011/jul/01/duncan-smith-appeals-businesses-employ-young-britons.

References

Geddes, Andrew. 2003. 'Migration and the Welfare State in Europe'. *The Political Quarterly* 74(1): 150–62.

Gentleman, Amelia. 2018. 'Shameful: Widespread Outrage over Man Denied NHS Cancer Care'. *The Guardian*, 12 March.

– 2012. 'GP's Call for Work Capability Assessment to be Scrapped'. *The Guardian*, 23 May.

Giddens, Anthony. 1979. *Central Problems in Social Theory*. London: Macmillan.

Glennie, Alex, and Jenny Pennington. 2013. *In Transition: Romanian and Bulgarian Migration to the UK*. London: Institute for Public Policy Research.

Goodrick, Jean. 2019. 'Benefits System Set Up for Cruelty Not Efficiency'. *The Guardian* [letter], 24 April.

Goodwin, Matthew, and Oliver Heath. 2016. 'The 2016 Referendum, Brexit, and the Left Behind'. *The Political Quarterly* 87(3): 323–32.

Gower, Melanie. 2020. *Coronavirus: Calls to Ease NRPF Conditions*. London: House of Commons Library, CBP 8888.

– 2019. *Should Asylum Seekers Have Unrestricted Rights to Work in the UK?* London: House of Commons Library, BP 1908.

– 2016. *Calls to Change Overseas Domestic Worker Conditions*. London: House of Commons Library, BP 4786.

– 2015. *Immigration and Asylum: Changes Made by the Coalition Government 2010–15*. London: House of Commons Library, SN/HA/5829.

– 2015a. *Asylum Support: Accommodation and Financial Support for Asylum-seekers*. London: House of Commons Library, BP 1909.

– 2014. *The Financial Requirement for Partner Visas*. London: House of Commons Library, SN/HA/06724.

Gower, Melanie, and Steven Kennedy. 2020. *The Immigration and Social Security Co-ordination (EU Withdrawal) Bill 2019–21*. London: House of Commons Library, CBP 8706.

Gower, Melanie, Douglas Pyper, and Wendy Wilson. 2015. *The Immigration Bill 2015–16*. London: House of Commons Library, CBP 07304.

Graham, Edward. 2013. 'ESA and Sanctions – More Hard Times Ahead'. Child Poverty Action Group. 21 February, issue 232. http://www.cpag.org.uk/content/esa-and-sanctions-%E2%80%93-more-hard-times-ahead.

Graham, Georgia. 2015. Fact Check: 'Do 43 Per Cent of EU Migrants Claim Benefits?' *Channel 4 News*, 10 November. https://www.channel4.com/news/factcheck/fact-check-43-eu-migrants-claim-benefits.

Grant, Aimee. 2013. 'Welfare Reform, Increased Conditionality, and Discretion: Jobcentre Plus Advisers' Experiences of Targets and Sanctions'. *Journal of Poverty and Social Justice* 21(2): 165–76.

Green, Damian. 2010. 'Speech to the Royal Commonwealth Society'. 7 September, 2010. https://www.gov.uk/government/speeches/immigration-damian-greens-speech-to-the-royal-commonwealth-society.

Grice, Andrew. 2015. 'Refugee Crisis: Tim Farron Accuses Government of Cutting Financial Support for Asylum Seekers'. *The Independent*, 23 October. http://www.independent.co.uk/news/uk/politics/refugee-crisis-tim-farron-accuses-government-of-cutting-financial-support-for-asylum-seekers-a6706612.html.

– 2013. 'Voters "Brainwashed by Tory Welfare Myths" Shows New Poll'. *The Telegraph,* 4 January. http://www.independent.co.uk/news/uk/politics/voters-brainwashed-by-tory-welfare-myths-shows-new-poll-8437872.html.

Grierson, Jamie. 2019. 'Number of EU Immigrants Falls as More Come from Rest of World'. *The Guardian*, 29 November.

– 2018. 'UK Offers "Calais Leave" to Children Denied Asylum'. *The Guardian*, 14 September.

Griffiths, Tom, and Terry Patterson. 2014. 'Work Capability Assessment Concerns'. *Journal of Poverty and Social Justice* 22(10): 59–70.

The Guardian. 2020. 'The Government Is Playing Catch-Up' [editorial]. 21 March.

– 2020a. 'The Government View on Covid-19 and Migration' [editorial]. 18 May.

– 2011. 'Bank Reforms How Much Did We Bail Them Out and How Much Do They Still Owe?' [datablog]. 12 November. http://www.the guardian.com/news/datablog/2011/nov/12/bank-bailouts-uk-credit-crunch.

Guentner, Simon, Sue Lukes, Richard Stanton, Bastian A. Vollmer, and Jo Wilding. 2016. 'Bordering Practices in the UK Welfare System'. *Critical Social Policy* 36(3): 391–411.

HM Treasury. 2014. Press release: 'Millions Start Receiving Breakdown of How Their Tax Is Spent'. *Gov.uk*, 2 November. https://www.gov.uk/government/news/millions-start-receiving-break-down-of-how-their-tax-is-spent.

Hall, Stuart. 1996. 'Race, Articulation, and Societies Structured in Dominance' [1978]. In *Black British Cultural Studies: A Reader,* edited by Houston A. Baker Jr., Manthia Diawara, and Ruth H. Lindeborg, 16–60. Chicago: University of Chicago Press.

References

Hammar, Tomas. 1990. *Democracy and the Nation State*, Aldershot: Avebury.

Harris, Neville. 2008. 'From Unemployment to Active Jobseeking'. In *A European Work-First Welfare State*, edited by Sara Stendahl, Thomas Erhag, and Stamatia Devetzi, 49–77. Gothenburg: Centre for European Research.

Harvey, Alison, and Zoe Harper. 2017. *A Guide to the Immigration Act 2016*. London: Bloomsbury.

Hill, Amelia. 2019. 'Home Office Chaos Leads to Illegal Detentions'. *The Guardian*, 29 April.

Hill Collins, Patricia. 1986. 'Learning from the Outsider Within: The Sociological Significance of Black Feminist Thought'. *Social Problems* 33(6): 14–32.

Hitlin, Steven, and Stephen Vaisey. 2013. 'The New Sociology of Morality'. *Annual Review of Sociology* 39: 51–68.

HM Treasury. 2014. 'Public Expenditure Statistical Analysis 2014'. *Gov. uk*, July 17, 2014. https://www.gov.uk/government/statistics/public-expenditure-statistical-analyses-2014.

Home Affairs Committee. 2019. *EU Settlement Scheme*. London: HMSO, HC 1945.

– 2018. *The Windrush Generation*. London: HMSO, HC 990.

– 2013. *Asylum*. London: HMSO, HC 71.

Home Office. 2017. 'Refugee Leave. Version 4.0'. *Gov.uk*, 2 March. https://www.gov.uk/government/uploads/system/uploads/attachment_data/file/597990/Refugee-Leave-v4.pdf.

– 2016. 'Reforming Support for Migrants without Immigration Status'. *Gov.uk*, January, 2016. https://assets.publishing.service.gov.uk/government/uploads/system/uploads/attachment_data/file/494240/Support.pdf.

– 2016a. 'Impact Assessment: Reforming Support for Failed Asylum Seekers and Other Migrants without Immigration Status'. IA No: HO0195. *Gov.uk*, 28 January. https://assets.publishing.service.gov.uk/government/uploads/system/uploads/attachment_data/file/497333/2016-01-29_Immigration_Bill_-_support_-_revised_impact_assessment.pdf.

– 2016b. 'Immigration Act 2016 Factsheet – Support for Certain Categories of Migrant'. *Gov.uk*, July. https://www.gov.uk/government/uploads/system/uploads/attachment_data/file/537248/Immigration_Act_-_Part_5_-_Support_for_Certain_Categories_of_migrants.pdf.

– 2016c. 'Immigration Rules Part 9: Grounds for Refusal'. *Gov.uk*, 25 February, updated 20 February. https://www.gov.uk/guidance/immigration-rules/immigration-rules-part-9-grounds-for-refusal.

236 References

- 2016d. 'Immigration Act: Overview'. *Gov.uk*, 12 July. https://www.gov. uk/government/publications/immigration-bill-2015-overarching-documents/immigration-bill-201516-overview-factsheet.
- 2015. 'Reforming Support for Failed Asylum Seekers and Other Illegal Migrants'. *Gov.uk*, August. https://assets.publishing.service.gov.uk/ government/uploads/system/uploads/attachment_data/file/451088/ Reforming_support_for_failed_asylum_seekers_and_other_illegal_ migrants_-_Consultation_Document.pdf.
- 2015a. 'Reforming Support for Failed Asylum Seekers and Other Illegal Migrants: Response to Consultation'. *Gov.uk*, November. https://assets. publishing.service.gov.uk/government/uploads/system/uploads/ attachment_data/file/473284/Response_to_Consultation.pdf.
- 2015b. 'Explanatory Memorandum to the Asylum Support (Amendment No. 3) Regulations 2015 No. 1501'. 8 July. http://www. legislation.gov.uk/uksi/2015/1501/pdfs/uksiem_20151501_en.pdf.
- 2012. 'Changes to Family Migration Rules: Impact Assessment'. *Gov.uk*, 6 December. https://assets.publishing.service.gov.uk/government/uploads/ system/uploads/attachment_data/file/257357/fam-impact.state.pdf.
Honeycombe-Foster, Matt. 2020. 'Johnson Hints at a Review of No Recourse to Public Funds Policy after "Jaw-Dropping" Committee Grilling'. *Civil Service World*, 28 May. https://www.civilserviceworld. com/articles/news/johnson-hints-review-no-recourse-public-funds-policy-after-%E2%80%98jaw-dropping%E2%80%99-committee.
Honneth, Axel. 1995. *The Struggle for Recognition*. Cambridge: Polity Press.
Hood, Andrew, and Paul Johnson. 2014. 'What Is Welfare Spending?' Institute for Fiscal Studies, 4 November. http://www.ifs.org.uk/ publications/7424.
House of Commons. 2017. 'Privatisation of Job Centre Call Centres'. Early Day Motion, EDM 681. Parliament UK, 29 November. https:// edm.parliament.uk/early-day-motion/51086/privatisation-of-job-centre-call-centres.
House of Commons. Hansard. 2013. Parliament UK, 18 December, col. 802–55. https://publications.parliament.uk/pa/cm201314/cmhansrd/ cm131218/debtext/131218-0003.htm.
- 1995. 18 July, col. 1027. https://publications.parliament.uk/pa/ cm199495/cmhansrd/1995-07-18/Writtens-5.html.
- 1995. 11 December, col. 699–808. https://api.parliament.uk/historic-hansard/commons/1995/dec/11/asylum-and-immigration-bill.

References

237

House of Lords Secondary Legislation Scrutiny Committee. 2017. '30th Report of Session 2016–17'. HL Paper 148. Parliament UK, 30 March 30. https://publications.parliament.uk/pa/ld201617/ldselect/ldsecleg/148/148.pdf.

Hutton, Will. 2020. 'This Tory Budget Is Keynes Reborn'. *The Observer*, 15 March 15.

– 2014. 'Cameron's Tax Credo Is Incoherent, Immoral and Economically Illiterate'. *The Observer*, 2 November 2014.

Huysmans, Jef. 2008. 'The Jargon of Exception'. *International Political Sociology* 2(2): 165–83.

IFS (Institute for Fiscal Studies). 2014. *Living Standards, Poverty, and Inequality in the UK*. London: Institute for Fiscal Studies.

– 2011. *Child and Working Age Poverty from 2010–2020*. York: Joseph Rowntree Foundation.

ILPA (Immigration Law Practitioners Association). 2015. 'Immigration Bill: ILPA Briefing for House of Commons Report and Third Reading, 1 December 2015'. 27 October. http://www.ilpa.org.uk/resources.php/31585/immigration-bill-ilpa-briefing-for-house-of-commons-report-and-third-reading-1-december-2015.

Inman, Phillip. 2020. 'Bold Move to Help Firms and Households'. *The Guardian*, 21 March.

– 2019. 'British Jobs Machine May Not Be Working the Way People Want It To'. *The Guardian*, 23 September.

– 2019a. 'Migrants Saved Us from a Post-Brexit Downturn'. *The Observer*, 13 October.

– 2019b. 'Has the Age of Austerity Really Come to an End?' *The Guardian*, 5 September.

– 2016. 'Flexibility Is the New Injustice Inflicted on the Working Class'. *The Observer*, 22 May.

JCHR (Joint Committee on Human Rights). 2015. *Compliance with the UNCRC*. HL paper no. 144, HC 1016. London: HMSO.

– 2013. *The Implications for Access to Justice of the Government's Proposals to Reform Legal Aid*. HL Paper 100, HC 766, London: HMSO

– 2011. *Legislative Scrutiny: Welfare Reform Bill*. HL Paper 233, HC 1704. London: HMSO.

JCWI (Joint Council for the Welfare of Immigrant). 2015. *No Passport Equals No Home*. London.

– 2012. *United by Love, Divided by Law*. London.

Jenkins, Ciaran. 2013. 'Bed Tax Forces People out of Homes.' *Channel 4 News*, 23 January. http://www.channel4.com/news/bed-tax-forces-people-out-of-homes.

Jessop, Bob. 1999. 'The Changing Governance of Welfare'. *Social Policy and Administration* 33: 348–59.

Jesuit Refugee Services. 2018. *Out in the Cold*. London: Jesuit Refugee Services.

Jones, Owen. 2018. 'The Wetherspoon Ban on Homeless People Reveals Our Rotten Social Order'. *The Guardian*, 7 August.

Jowit, Juliette. 2013. 'Strivers v. Shirkers: The Language of the Welfare Debate'. *The Guardian*, 8 January. https://www.theguardian.com/politics/2013/jan/08/strivers-shirkers-language-welfare.

JRF (Joseph Rowntree Foundation) and New Policy Institute. 2018. *Destitution in the UK 2018*. York.

– 2018a. *Budget 2018*. 12 October. https://www.jrf.org.uk/report/budget-2018-tackling-rising-tide-work-poverty.

– 2016. *The EU Referendum and UK Poverty*. York.

– 2014. *A Minimum Income Standard for the UK*. York.

– 2014a. *Housing Benefit Size Criteria*. York.

– 2014b. *UK without Poverty*. York.

– 2014c. *Welfare Sanctions and Conditionality in the UK*. York.

Justfair. 2014. *Going Hungry? The Human Right to Food*. London.

Kaleeli, Homa. 2014. 'Benefit Fraud: The Facts and Figures'. *The Guardian*, 21 October.

Katwala, Sunder, Jill Rutter, Steve Ballinger, Bobby Duffy, and Kirstie Hewlett. 2020. *The Reset Moment: Immigration in the New Parliament*. London: British Future and the Policy Institute.

Keegan, William. 2014. 'The Conservatives' Real Deficit Problem Is a Lack of Shame'. *Independent on Sunday*, 7 October 2014.

Keen, Richard, and Ross Turner. 2016. *Statistics on Migrants and Benefits*. London: House of Commons Library, BP 7445.

Kennedy, Steven. 2015. *People from Abroad: What Benefits Can They Claim?* London: House of Commons Library, BP 06847.

– 2015a. *Welfare Reform and Work Bill*. London: House of Commons Library, CBP 079252.

– 2015b. *Measures to Limit Migrants' Access to Benefits*. London: House of Commons Library, BP 06889.

Kennedy, Steven, Alex Bate, and Richard Keen. 2017. *The Two Child Limit in Tax Credits and Universal Credit*. London: House of Commons Library, CBP 7935.

References 239

Kennedy, Steven, Richard Keen, and Andrew Mackley. 2017. *Work Capability Assessment*. London: House of Commons Library, CDP-2017-0254.

Kennedy, Steven, Chris Murphy, and Wendy Wilson. 2016. *Welfare Reform and Disabled People*. London: House of Commons Library, CBP 7571.

Kennedy, Steven, Wendy Wilson, Vyara Apostolova, and Richard Keen. 2016. *The Benefit Cap*. London: House of Commons Library, CBP 06294.

Kentish, Benjamin. 2017. 'Brexit: Deportations of EU Citizens Soar since Referendum'. *The Independent*, 10 September. https://www.independent.co.uk/news/uk/politics/brexit-latest-eu-citizens-deportations-rise-uk-home-office-referendum-a7935266.html.

Khan, Sadiq. 2020. 'A Once-in-a-Generation Responsibility to Beat This Crisis Confronts Us'. *The Observer*, 22 March.

Kirkup, James, and Robert Winnett. 2012. 'Theresa May Interview: We're Going to Give Illegal Migrants a Really Hostile Reception'. *The Telegraph*, 25 May. https://www.telegraph.co.uk/news/uknews/immigration/9291483/Theresa-May-interview-Were-going-to-give-illegal-migrants-a-really-hostile-reception.html.

Koenoenen, Jukka. 2017. 'Differential Inclusion of Non-Citizens in a Universalistic Welfare State'. *Citizenship Studies* 22(1): 53–69.

Kofman, Eleonore. 2002. 'Contemporary European Migrations, Civic Stratification, and Citizenship'. *Political Geography* 21(8): 1035–54.

Kofman, Eleonore, Annie Phizacklea, Parvati Raghuram, and Rosemary Sales. 2000. *Gender and International Migration*. London: Routledge.

Kramer, Dion. 2015. 'Had They Only Worked One Month Longer! An Analysis of the Alimanovic Case [2015] C-67/14'. *European Law* [blog], 27 September. https://europeanlawblog.eu/2015/09/29/had-they-only-worked-one-month-longer-an-analysis-of-the-alimanovic-case-2015-c-6714.

Laclau, Ernesto. 2014. *The Rhetorical Foundations of Society*. London: Verso.

Laenen, Tijs, Frederica Rossetti, and Wim Van Oorschot. 2019. *Why Deservingness Theory Needs Qualitative Research*. SPSW Working Paper no. CeSo/SPSW/2019-1. Leuven: Centre for Sociological Research.

Lakhani, Beth. 2009. 'Lone Parents: The Move from IS to JSA'. Child Poverty Action Group, 1 February, issue 208. https://cpag.org.uk/welfare-rights/resources/article/lone-parents-move-jsa.

Lambie-Mumford, Hannah, Niall Cooper, and Rachel Loopstra. 2019. *Why End UK Hunger?* Salford: Church Action on Poverty.

Lamont, Michele, and Virag Molnar. 2002. 'The Study of Boundaries in the Social Sciences'. *Annual Review of Sociology* 28: 167–95.

Landolt, Patricia, and Luin Goldring. 2015. 'Assembling Non-Citizenship through the Work of Conditionality'. *Citizenship Studies* 19(8): 853–69.

Lemos, Sara, and Jonathan Portes. 2008. 'New Labour? The Impact of Labour from Central and European Countries on the UK Labour Market'. Bonn: IZA Institute of Labour Economics, Discussion paper no. 3756.

Liberty. 2013. 'Liberty's Submission to the All Party Group on Immigration's Inquiry into the New Family Migration Rules'. January. https://www.libertyhumanrights.org.uk/sites/default/files/changes-to-immigration-rules-briefing-on-family-migration-inquiry-jan-2013.pdf.

Lockwood, David. 1996. 'Civic Integration and Class Formation'. *British Journal of Sociology* 47(3): 531–50.

Local Government Association. 2019. 'Loan Sharks Warning as Debt Enquiries Hit Record High'. 10 August,2019. https://www.local.gov.uk/loan-sharks-warning-debt-enquiries-hit-record-high.

Local Government Association, Welsh Local Government Association, Convention of Scottish Local Authorities, Association of Directors of Children's Services, and No Recourse to Public Funds. 2015. 'Reforming Support for Failed Asylum Seekers and Other Illegal Migrants – Response to Consultation'. September. https://adcs.org.uk/assets/documentation/ADCS_LGA_WLGA_COSLA_NRPF_response_Home_Office_consultation_reforming_asylum_support.pdf.

Loopstra, Rachel, Aaron Reeves, Martin McKee, and David Stuckler. 2015. 'Punitive Approaches to Unemployment Benefit Recipients'. Oxford: University of Oxford, Sociology Working Paper no. 2015–1.

Lukes, Steven. 2010. 'The Social Construction of Morality'. In *Handbook of the Sociology of Morality*, edited by Steven Hitlin and Stephen Vaisey, 549–560. New York: Springer.

Luqmani, Thompson, and Partners. 2014. 'Immigration Act 2014: Part 2 – Appeals'. https://www.luqmanithompson.com/immigration-act-2014-part-2-appeals.

MAC (Migration Advisory Committee). 2014. *Migrants in Low-Skilled Work*. London: Home Office.

Mackley, Andrew, and Wendy Wilson. 2018. *Street Homelessness*. London: House of Commons Library, CBP 0099.

References

Manchester Citizens Advice Bureau. 2013. *Punishing Poverty.* Manchester.

Marsh, Sarah. 2018. 'Windrush Citizens Awaiting Rulings Still Sleeping Rough'. *The Guardian*, 22 May.

Marsh, Sarah, and Patrick Greenfield. 2019. 'Removal of Homeless Camps Trebles as Charities Warn of Out of Control Crisis'. *The Guardian*, 18 June.

Marshall, Thomas H. 1992. *Citizenship and Social Class* [1950]. In Thomas H. Marshall and Tom Bottomore, *Citizenship and Social Class*. London: Pluto Press.

Mason, Rowena. 2015. 'Make Up for Benefit Cuts by Working More Hours'. *The Guardian*, 21 December 2015. https://www.theguardian. com/society/2015/dec/21/universal-credit-benefit-cuts-work-allowance.

– 2014. 'Osbourne Accused of Using New Tax Statements as "Political Propaganda"'. *The Guardian*, 3 November.

Massey, Doreen, and Michael Rustin. 2014 'Whose Economy?' *Soundings* 57 (Summer): 170–91.

Markaki, Yvonne, and Carlos Vargas-Silva. 2017. 'How Immigrants Affect Public Finances'. *Fullfact*, 5 June. https://fullfact.org/immigration/ how-immigrants-affect-public-finances.

Mau, Steffen. 2003. *The Moral Economy of Welfare States.* London: Routledge.

May, Theresa. 2017. 'The Shared Society: Prime Minister's Speech at the Charity Commission Annual Meeting'. *Gov.uk*, 9 January. https://www. gov.uk/government/speeches/the-shared-society-prime-ministers-speech- at-the-charity-commission-annual-meeting.

– 2016. 'Statement from the New Prime Minister Theresa May'. *Gov.uk*, 13 June. https://www.gov.uk/government/speeches/statement-from-the- new-prime-minister-theresa-may.

– 2016a. 'Read in Full: Theresa May's Conservative Conference Speech on Brexit'. *The Independent*, 5 October. https://www.independent. co.uk/news/uk/politics/theresa-may-speech-tory-conference-2016-in-full- transcript-a7346171.html.

– 2015. 'Theresa May's Speech to the Conservative Party Conference – in Full'. *The Independent*, 6 October. http://www.independent.co.uk/news/ uk/politics/theresa-may-s-speech-to-the-conservative-party-conference- in-full-a6681901.html.

Mayblin, Lucy. 2016. 'Complexity Reduction and Policy Consensus: Asylum Seekers, the Right to Work, and the "Pull Factor" Thesis in the UK Context'. *British Journal of Politics and International Relations* 18(4): 812–28.

References

Mayblin, Lucy, and Poppy James. 2017. *Asylum and Refugee Support*. Coventry: University of Warwick.

McCann, Kate, and Robert Mendick. 2018. 'Home Office Destroyed Windrush Migrants' Records in 2010, Leaving Amber Rudd to Clear Up May's Mess'. *The Telegraph*, 17 April. https://www.telegraph.co.uk/politics/2018/04/17/home-office-destroyed-windrush-migrants-records-2010-leaving.

McGuinness, Terry. 2017. *The UK Response to the Syrian Refugee Crisis*. London: House of Commons Library, BP 06805.

– 2017a. *Deportation of Foreign National Offenders*. London: House of Commons Library, BP 8064.

McInnes, Roderick. 2018. *Benefit Upratings 2019*. London: House of Commons Library, CBP 8458.

– 2014. *Statistics on Migrants and Benefits*. London: House of Commons Library, SNO 6955.

– 2014a. *Benefit Upratings 2015*. London: House of Commons Library, SNO 7054.

McKenzie, Lisa. 2017. 'The Class Politics of Prejudice: Brexit and the Land of No-Hope and Glory'. *British Journal of Sociology* 68(1): 265–80.

McKinney, C.J. 2020. 'Asylum Backlog Continues to Rise'. *Free Movement*, 27 February. https://www.freemovement.org.uk/asylum-backlog-continues-to-rise.

– 2019. 'Half of All Immigration Appeals Now Succeed'. *Free Movement*, 13 June. https://www.freemovement.org.uk/half-of-all-immigration-appeals-now-succeed.

Metcalf, David. 2016. 'Work, Immigration, and the Labour Market'. London: London School of Economics, July, 2016. https://assets.publishing.service.gov.uk/government/uploads/system/uploads/attachment_data/file/541805/MAC_presentation-immigrationandlabourmarket.pdf.

Mezzadra, Sandro, and Brett Neilson. 2012. 'Between Inclusion and Exclusion'. *Theory, Culture, and Society* 29(4–5): 58–75.

Middlesex University/JCWI. 2015. *Family Friendly?* London: Office of the Children's Commissioner.

Migrant Rights Network. 2014. 'Creating a "Hostile Environment" for Migrants in the UK'. MRN briefing paper, 6 February. https://www.migrantsrights.org.uk/wp-content/uploads/publications/MRN_briefing-Immigration_Bill-House_of_Lords-Feb_2014.pdf.

Millar, Jane. 2018. *Women, Work, and Welfare: Conditionality and Choice*. Institute for Policy Research. Bath: University of Bath.

References

Milligan, Brian. 2014. 'The Truth about Welfare Spending: Facts or Propaganda'. *BBC news*, 4 November. http://www.bbc.co.uk/news/business-29898083.

Mitchell, Gemma. 2019. 'NHS Nurse Vacancies in England Rise to More than 43,000'. *Nursing Times*, 8 October.

Monaghan, Angela. 2014. 'Self-Employment at Highest Level for 40 Years'. *The Guardian*, 21 August 2014.

Moore, Stan. 2018. 'Hostile Environments Go Way Beyond Immigration'. *The Guardian* [letter], 1 May 2018.

Morris, Juliet. 2015. 'Hunger and Food Poverty: All-Party Parliamentary Group Inquiry'. Local Government Information Unit, 20 January. https://www.wirralintelligenceservice.org/media/1858/hunger-and-food-poverty-all-party-parliamentary-group-inquiry.pdf.

Morris, Lydia. 2010. *Asylum, Welfare, and the Cosmopolitan Ideal: A Sociology of Rights*. London: Routledge.

– 2007. 'New Labour's Community of Rights: Welfare, Immigration, and Asylum'. *Journal of Social Policy* 36(1): 39–57.

– 2003. 'Managing Contradiction: Civic Stratification and Migrants' Rights'. *International Migration Review* 37: 74–100.

– 2002. *Managing Migration: Civic Stratification and Migrants' Rights*. Abingdon: Routledge.

– 2002a. 'Britain's Immigration and Asylum Regime: The Shifting Contours of Rights'. *Journal of Ethnic and Migration Studies* 28(3): 409–25.

– 1998. 'Governing at a Distance: Rights and Controls in British Immigration'. *International Migration Review* 32(4): 949–73.

– 1997. 'A Cluster of Contradictions'. *Sociology* 31(2): 241–59.

– 1994. *Dangerous Classes: The Underclass and Social Citizenship*. London: Routledge.

Morris, Lydia, and Trevor Llewellyn. 1991. *Social Security Provision for the Long-Term Unemployed*. A report for the Social Security Advisory Committee. London: HMSO.

Morrisens, Ann, and Diane Sainsbury. 2005. 'Migrants' Social Rights, Ethnicity, and Welfare Regimes'. *Journal of Social Policy* 34(4): 637–60.

Munch, Richard. 2012. *Inclusion and Exclusion in the Liberal Competition State*. Abingdon: Routledge.

Murphy, Carole. 2018. *A Game of Chance: Long-Term Support for Survivors of Modern Slavery*. London: Centre for the Study of Modern Slavery, St. Mary's University.

Murphy, Chris, and Richard Keen. 2016. *Abolition of the ESA Work Related Activity Component*. London: House of Commons Library, CBP 7649.

NAO (National Audit Office). 2020. *Information Held by the DWP on Deaths by Suicide of Benefit Claimants.* London: National Audit Office, HC 79.

– 2018. *Rolling Out Universal Credit.* London: National Audit Office, HC 1123.

– 2016. *Benefit Sanctions.* London: National Audit Office, HC 628.

– 2016a. *Contracted Out Health and Disability Assessments.* London: National Audit Office, HC 609.

NatCen. 2013. 'British Social Attitudes 2013: Attitudes to Migration'. http://www.bsa.natcen.ac.uk/media/38108/immigration-bsa31.pdf.

Noor, Poppy. 2019. 'Leave to Remain but No Home to Remain In'. *The Guardian,* 1 August.

Norval, Aletta J. 2000. 'Review Article: The Things We Do with Words–Contemporary Approaches to the Analysis of Ideology'. *British Journal of Political Science* 30: 313–46.

NPI (New Policy Institute). 2013. *Monitoring Poverty and Social Exclusion,* York: JRF.

NRPF (No Recourse to Public Funds Network). 2018. 'Assessing and Supporting Families Who Have No Recourse to Public Funds'. 13 April. http://guidance.nrpfnetwork.org.uk/reader/practice-guidance-families.

– 2017. 'Childcare Changes Will Not Benefit NRPF Families'. 23 May. http://www.nrpfnetwork.org.uk/News/Pages/childcare.aspx.

– 2016. 'Further Amendments Made to Local Authority Support in Immigration Bill'. 23 March. http://www.nrpfnetwork.org.uk/News/Pages/local-authority-support-update.aspx.

Nussbaum, Martha. 2007. *Frontiers of Justice.* Cambridge, MA: Belknap Press.

O'Brien, Charlotte. 2016. 'Hand to Mouth Citizenship'. *Journal of Social Welfare and Family Law* 38(2): 228–45.

– 2015. 'The Pillory, the Precipice, and the Slippery Slope'. *Journal of Social Welfare and Family Law* 37(1): 111–36.

The Observer. 2019. 'One Nation? Not the Vision PM Set Out in Queen's Speech'. Comment and Analysis, 22 December.

O'Carroll, Lisa. 2019. 'Brexit Confusion Could Hit EU Tenants in UK'. *The Guardian,* 4 April 2019.

O'Connor, Sean, and Jim Packard. 2016. 'Number of EU Nationals Working in the UK Reaches Record Level'. *The Financial Times,* 18 May. https://www.ft.com/content/ac4f8ace-1cf6-11e6-b286-cddde55ca122.

Oakley, Matthew. 2014. *Independent Review of the Operation of the Jobseekers Allowance Sanctions.* London: OGL.

References

OBR (Office for Budget Responsibility). 2019. 'An OBR Guide to Welfare Spending'. 4 May. https://obr.uk/forecasts-in-depth/brief-guides-and-explainers/an-obr-guide-to-welfare-spending.

– 2015. *Economic and Fiscal Outlook*. London: HMSO, Cm 9024.

– 2013. *Fiscal Sustainability Report*. London: HMSO.

ONS (Office for National Statistics). 2020. 'Young People Not in Employment Education or Training'. *Gov.uk*, 27 February. https://www.ons.gov.uk/employmentandlabourmarket/peoplenotinwork/unemployment/datasets/youngpeoplenotineducationemploymentortrainingneettable1.

– 2019. 'Labour Market Economic Commentary: September 2019'. www.ons.gov.uk/employmentandlabourmarket/peopleinwork/employmentand employeetypes/articles/labourmarketeconomiccommentary/september 2019.

– 2019a. 'Regional Labour Market Statistics in the UK: December, 2019'. *Gov.uk*. https://www.ons.gov.uk/employmentandlabourmarket/people inwork/employmentandemployeetypes/bulletins/regionallabourmarket/ december2019.

Ormston, Rachel, and John Curtice, eds. 2015. *British Social Attitudes: The 32nd Report*. London: NatCen.

Osborne, George. 2015. 'Summer Budget 2015 Speech'. *Gov.uk*, 8 July. https://www.gov.uk/government/speeches/chancellor-george-osbornes-summer-budget-2015-speech.

– 2012. 'Autumn Statement 2012: Chancellor's Statement'. *Gov.uk*, 5 December. https://www.gov.uk/government/speeches/autumn-statement-2012-chancellors-statement.

Oxfam. 2014. *Multiple Cuts for Poorest Families*. Oxford.

– 2013. *Walking the Breadline*. Oxford: Oxfam

– 2012. *The Perfect Storm*. Oxford.

Oxford Economics. 2018. 'The Fiscal Impact of Immigration on the UK'. June. https://www.oxfordeconomics.com/recent-releases/8747673d-3b26-439b-9693-0e250df6dbba.

Public Accounts Committee. 2019. 'Windrush Generation and the Home Office'. HC 1518. Parliament UK, 6 March. https://publications.parliament.uk/pa/cm201719/cmselect/cmpubacc/1518/1518.pdf.

– 2018. 'Universal Credit'. HC 1183. Parliament UK, 26 October https://publications.parliament.uk/pa/cm201719/cmselect/cmpubacc/1183/1183.pdf.

– 2017. *Benefit Sanctions*. London: HMSO, HC 775.

Palmer, Ellie. 2010. 'The Child Poverty Act 2010'. *European Human Rights Law Review* 10(2): 303–15.

Parkin, Elizabeth. 2015. *The Work Capability Assessment for Employment and Support Allowance*. London: House of Commons Library, CBP 07182.

Parliamentary Inquiry. 2013. 'Report of the Parliamentary Inquiry into Asylum Support for Children and Young People'. January. Circulated by the Children's Society. https://www.childrenssociety.org.uk/sites/default/files/tcs/asylum_support_inquiry_report_final.pdf.

Partington, Richard. 2019. 'UK Wage Growth Slows Again but Jobs Hit New High'. *The Guardian*, 17 December.

— 2019a. 'Surprise as Inflation Remains at Lowest Level for Three Years'. *The Guardian*, 17 October.

— 2019b. 'Net Migration to UK from EU Falls to Lowest in 10 Years'. *The Guardian*, 28 February.

— 2017. 'Brexit Vote Has Cost Each Household More than £600 a Year, Says NIESCR'. *The Guardian*, 1 November 2017.

— 2017a. 'Brexit Will Hit North of England Hardest Says Thinktank'. *The Guardian*, 9 November. https://www.theguardian.com/business/2017/nov/09/brexit-will-hit-northern-england-economy-hardest-ippr-north-thinktank.

Partington, Richard, and Phillip Inman. 2020. 'Voters Will Be Disappointed by Sunak's Spending'. *The Guardian*, 13 March.

Peers, Steve. 2016. 'Brexit Briefing: Rights of Entry and Residence'. *Free Movement*, 17 May. https://www.freemovement.org.uk/brexit-briefing-rights-of-entry-and-residence.

Pettinger, Trejvan. 2016. 'What Does the Government Spend Its Money On?' *EconomicsHelp*, 24 November. http://www.economicshelp.org/blog/142/economics/what-does-the-government-spend-its-money-on.

Polanyi, Karl. 1957. *The Great Transformation*. Boston: Beacon Press.

Politowski, Ben, and Melanie Gower. 2016. *The £35,000 Salary Requirement to Settle in the UK*. London: House of Commons Library, CBP 7264.

Portes, Jonathan. 2016. 'How Small Is Small? The Impact of Immigration on UK Wages'. National Institute of Economic and Social Research, 17 January. http://www.niesr.ac.uk/blog/how-small-small-impact-immigration-uk-wages#.WFQJTLmQKCk.

— 2015. 'Benefit Tourism – the Facts'. *The Guardian*, 14 October.

— 2015a. 'The Coalition Government's Record on Immigration'. National Institute of Economic and Social Research, February 23, 2015. http://www.niesr.ac.uk/blog/coalition-government%E2%80%99s-record-immigration.

— 2013. 'A Crisis over the UK's Benefits Bill for EU Migrants? What Crisis?' *The Guardian*, 6 March.

References

247

Poverty and Social Exclusion Project. 2013. 'The Impoverishment of the UK: PSE UK First Results: Living Standards'. 28 March. http://www.poverty.ac.uk/sites/default/files/attachments/The_Impoverishment_of_the_UK_PSE_UK_first_results_summary_report_March_28.pdf.

Prince, Rosa. 2010. 'David Cameron: Net Immigration Will Be Capped at Tens of Thousands'. *The Telegraph*, 10 May. https://www.telegraph.co.uk/news/politics/6961675/David-Cameron-net-immigration-will-be-capped-at-tens-of-thousands.html.

Proctor, Kate. 2020. 'PM in U-turn on Surcharge for Foreign NHS Workers'. *The Guardian*, 22 May.

Public Law Project. 2019. 'Do Benefit Sanctions Breach Article 3?' 29 May. https://publiclawproject.org.uk/uncategorized/do-benefit-sanctions-breach-article-3-echr.

Pyper, Douglas. 2018. *Employment Status*. London: House of Commons Library, CBP 8045.

Rawnsley, Andrew. 2020. 'The Coronavirus Crisis Ignites a Bonfire of Conservative Party Orthodoxies'. *The Observer*, March 22, 2020.

Red Cross. 2017. *Can't Stay, Can't Go*. London.

– 2015. *Poor Health, No Wealth*. London.

Reed, Isaac Ariail, and Michael Weinman. 2019. 'Agency, Power, Modernity: A Manifesto for Social Theory'. *European Journal of Culture and Political Sociology* 6(1): 6–50.

Refugee Action. 2017. *Slipping through the Cracks*. London.

– 2014. 'Refugee Action Briefing on Early Day Motion 99 – High Court Judgment on Asylum Support'. October. https://www.refugee-action.org.uk/wp-content/uploads/2014/10/briefing_on_Early_Day_Motion_99.pdf.

Refugee Children's Consortium. 2015. 'House of Commons Committee Stage Briefing Amendment 223 – Welfare of Separated and Unaccompanied Young People'. Children's Society, November. https://www.childrenssociety.org.uk/sites/default/files/RCC_Schedule%203WelfareofUnaccompaniedYoungPeople_HoCCS_Nov15_FINAL.pdf.

Refugee Council. 2015. 'Response to Asylum Support Consultation'. Refugee Council, September. http://web.archive.org/web/20160826105836/https://www.refugeecouncil.org.uk/assets/0003/5789/Refugee_Council_response_to_asylum_support_consultation.pdf.

Refugee Council and Refugee Action. 2006. *Inhumane and Ineffective – Section 9 in Practice*. London: Refugee Council.

Rethink Mental Illness. 2017. 'It's Broken Her'. https://www.rethink.org/media/2585/its-broken-her-pip-report.pdf.

Rodger, John. 2003. 'Social Solidarity, Welfare, and Post-Emotionalism'. *Journal of Social Policy* 32(3): 403–21.

References

Rowthorn, Robert. 2015. *Costs and Benefits of Large-Scale Immigration.* London: Civitas.

Ruhs, Martin, and Carlos Vargas-Silva. 2015. 'The Labour Market Effects of Immigration'. *Migration Observatory*, 15 April. https://migrationobservatory.ox.ac.uk/resources/briefings/election-2015-briefing-immigration-and-jobs-the-labour-market-effects-of-immigration.

Ryan, Frances. 2019. 'This Man Had to Fight for Benefits Just Before He Died'. *The Guardian*, 23 April.

Safe Passage. 2018. 'Hundreds More Children Now Eligible for Dubs Scheme'. 20 December. https://www.safepassage.org.uk/news/hundreds-more-children-now-eligible-for-dubs-scheme-following-home-office-decision-to-scrap-the-cut-off-date.

Sainsbury, Diane. 2012. *Welfare States and Immigrant Rights.* Oxford: Oxford University Press.

Sayer, Andrew. 2011. *Why Things Matter to People.* Cambridge: Cambridge University Press.

– 2007. 'Moral Economy as Critique'. *New Political Economy* 12(2): 261–70.

– 2005. *The Moral Significance of Class.* Cambridge: Cambridge University Press.

– 2000. 'Moral Economy and Political Economy'. *Studies in Political Economy* 61 (Spring): 79–103.

Schmuecker, Katie. 2017. 'Keeping More of What You Earn'. Joseph Rowntree Foundation, 22 October. https://www.jrf.org.uk/report/keeping-more-what-you-earn.

Scott, James C. 1976. *The Moral Economy of the Peasant.* New Haven: Yale University Press.

Scottish Government. 2019. 'Treating Everyone with Dignity and Respect: Social security Charter'. *Gov.scot*, 11 January. https://www.gov.scot/news/treating-everyone-with-dignity-and-respect.

Sen, Amartya. 2005. 'Human Rights and Capabilities'. *Journal of Human Development* 6(2): 151–62.

Sensier, Marianne, and Fiona Devine. 2017. 'Social Mobility and Brexit'. Economics Discussion Paper Series. Manchester: University of Manchester, EDP-1709.

Sentamu, John, ed. 2015. *On Rock or Sand? Firm Foundations for Britain's Future.* London: Society for Promoting Christian Knowledge.

Shapiro, Susan. 2005. 'Agency Theory'. *Annual Review of Sociology* 31: w263–84.

References

Shue, Henry. 1996. *Basic Rights*. Princeton: Princeton University Press.

Shutes, Isabel. 2016. 'Work-Related Conditionality and the Access to Social Benefits of National Citizens, EU and Non-EU Citizens'. *Journal of Social Policy* 45(4): 691–707.

Siddique, Haroon. 2020. 'BAME Health Staffs Sacrifice Shames Hostile Environment'. *The Guardian*, 4 April.

Sigona, Nando. 2015. 'Campzenship'. *Citizenship Studies* 19(1): 1–15.

Sikka, Prem. 2015. 'Tax Cheats Cost Far More than Benefit Cheats'. *Leftfootforward*, 7 February. http://leftfootforward.org/2015/02/tax-cheats-cost-far-more-than-benefits-cheats-yet-far-fewer-are-prosecuted.

Simmons, David. 2010. 'Universal Credit: Universal Panacea'. Child Poverty Action Group, 1 December 2010, Issue 219. https://cpag.org.uk/welfare-rights/resources/article/universal-credit-universal-panacea.

Simpson, Mark. 2020. 'The Social Security Response to COVID-19: Read the Small Print'. *Discover Society*, 2 April 2020. https://discoversociety.org/2020/04/02/the-social-security-response-to-covid-19-read-the-small-print.

Sinfield, Adrian. 2013. 'On Bringing Corporate Welfare In'. *Journal of Social Policy* 42(1): 31–8.

SJPG (Social Justice Policy Group). 2007. *Breakthrough Britain*. London: Centre for Social Justice.

– 2006. *Breakdown Britain*. London: Centre for Social Justice.

Skeggs, Beverley. 2014. 'Struggles for Value'. *British Journal of Sociology* 63(3): 472–90.

Skehan, Anna, Baljeet Sandhu, Lisa Payne, and Edward Wake Smith. 2017. *Precarious Citizenship*. London: Migrant and Refugee Children's Legal Unit.

Skills for Care. 2019. *The State of the Adult Social Care Sector and Workforce in England*. Leeds.

SMCPC (Social Mobility and Child Poverty Commission). 2014. 'Child Poverty Strategy Consultation Response'. *Gov.uk*, 9 June 2014. https://www.gov.uk/government/publications/response-to-the-consultation-on-the-child-poverty-strategy.

Smith, Helena. 2015. 'Shocking Image of Drowned Syrian Boy Shows Tragic Plight of Refugees'. *The Guardian*, 2 September. https://www.theguardian.com/world/2015/sep/02/shocking-image-of-drowned-syrian-boy-shows-tragic-plight-of-refugees.

Sodha, Sonia. 2016. 'Will Theresa May's "Just About Managing" Families Fall for the Rhetoric?' *The Guardian*, 21 November.

Soysal, Yasemin. 2012. 'Citizenship, Immigration, and the European Social Project'. *British Journal of Sociology* 63(1): 1–21.

– 1994. *Limits of Citizenship*. Chicago: University of Chicago Press.

Spencer, Mike. 2016. 'Changes in the Welfare Reform and Work Act 2016'. Child Poverty Action Group, 1 June, Issue 252. https://cpag.org.uk/welfare-rights/resources/article/changes-welfare-reform-and-work-act-2016.

Sparrow, Andrew. 2015. 'Peers Vote to Delay Tax Credit Cuts and Protect Those Who Lose Out'. *The Guardian*, 26 October. https://www.theguardian.com/politics/blog/live/2015/oct/26/tax-credit-cuts-debate-hancock-tells-peers-not-to-trigger-constitutional-crisis-politics-live?page=with%3Ablock-562e5665e4b005d7733de37d.

SSAC (Social Security Advisory Committee). 2014. *The Housing Benefit (Habitual Residence) Amendment Regs 2014 (S.I. 2014 No. 539): SSAC Report*. London.

– 2014a. *The Cumulative Impact of Welfare Reform*. Occasional Paper no. 12. London.

– 2006. *Sanctions in the Benefit System*. Occasional Paper no. 1. London.

Staton, Bethan. 2019. 'Attitudes towards Immigration Soften – but It's Still Complicated'. *The Financial Times*, 22 November. https://www.ft.com/content/a8007652-0b97-11ea-b2d6-9bf4d1957a67.

Standing, Guy. 2011. *The Precariat*. London: Bloomsbury.

Steensland, Brian. 2006. 'Cultural Categories and the American Welfare State'. *American Journal of Sociology* 111(5): 1273–326.

Still Human Still Here. 2015. 'Response to Home Office Consultation'. August 2015. https://stillhumanstillhere.files.wordpress.com/2009/01/response-to-the-consultation-on-reforming-support-for-failed-asylum-seekers.pdf.

Stone, John. 2016. 'More than Half of Appealed "Fit-to-Work" Decisions Found to Be Wrong'. *The Independent*, 10 March.

Sturge, Georgina. 2019. *Asylum Statistics*. London: House of Commons Library, SNO 1403.

Sumption, Madeleine, and Szilvia Altorjai. 2016. *EU Migration, Welfare Benefits, and EU Membership (Pre-Referendum)*. Oxford: Migration Observatory.

Sumption, Madeleine, and Carlos Vargas-Silva. 2019. 'Net Migration to the UK'. Migration Observatory, 26 July. https://migrationobservatory.ox.ac.uk/resources/briefings/long-term-international-migration-flows-to-and-from-the-uk.

Swales, Kirby. 2016. *Understanding the Leave Vote*. London: NatCen.

References

Syal, Rajeev. 2019. 'Benefit Cap: Single Mothers Make Up 85% of Those Affected'. *The Guardian*, 4 January.

Taylor, Diane, and Aamna Mohdin. 2019. 'British Children in Poverty Denied Basic Benefits by Home Office, Report Finds'. *The Guardian*, 14 June.

Taylor-Gooby, Peter. 2016. 'The Divisive Welfare State'. *Social Policy and Administration* 50(6): 712–33.

Taylor-Gooby, Peter, Bjorn Hvinden, Steffen Mau, Benjamin Leruth, Mi Ah Schoyen, and Adrienn Gyory. 2019. 'Moral Economies of the Welfare State: A Qualitative Comparative Study'. *Acta Sociologica* 62(2): 119–34.

Thompson, Edward P. 1971. 'The Moral Economy of the English Crowd in the Eighteenth Century'. *Past and Present* 50 (Feb): 76–136.

Titmus, Richard. 1970. *The Gift Relationship*. London: Allen and Unwin.

Tooze, Adam. 2020. 'Covid-19 Means That It's Not the Economy Anymore, Stupid'. *The Guardian*, 21 March.

Townsend, Mark, and Michael Savage. 2019. 'Foster Agencies Add Pressure on UK to Take Child Refugees'. *The Observer*, 29 December.

Trades Union Congress (TUC). n.d. 'Managing Migration Better for Britain'. 30 October. https://www.tuc.org.uk/sites/default/files/ManagingmigrationbetterforBritain.pdf.

– 2016. 'Living on the Edge'. London: Trades Union Congress, December, 2016. https://www.tuc.org.uk/sites/default/files/Living_On_The_Edge_2016.pdf.

Travis, Alan. 2016. 'Fear of Immigration Drove Leave Victory – Not Immigration Itself'. *The Guardian*, 25 June 25.

– 2016a. 'Are EU Migrants Really Taking British Jobs and Pushing down Wages?' *The Guardian*, 20 May. https://www.theguardian.com/politics/2016/may/20/reality-check-are-eu-migrants-really-taking-british-jobs.

Travis, Alan, and Shiv Malik. 2013. 'European Watchdog Accuses Britain of Shameful Rhetoric on Migrants'. *The Guardian*, 29 March.

Trussell Trust. 2019. 'Steep Increase in People Needing Foodbanks for Past 5 Years'. 13 November. https://www.trusselltrust.org/2019/11/13/april-sept-2019-foodbank-figures.

– 2019a. 'End of Year Stats'. April. https://www.trusselltrust.org/news-and-blog/latest-stats/end-year-stats.

Turner, Bryan S. 1993. 'Outline of a Theory of Human Rights'. *Sociology* 27(3): 485–512.

Tweedy, John, and Alan Hunt. 1994. 'The Future of the Welfare State'. *Journal of Law and Society* 21(3): 288–316.

Van Houtum, Henk, and Ton Van Naerssen. 2002. 'Bordering, Ordering, and Othering'. *Journal of Economic and Social Geography* 93(2): 125–36.

Van Oorschot, Wim. 2008. 'Solidarity towards Immigrants in European Welfare States'. *International Journal of Social Welfare* 17(1): 3–14.

Van Oorschot, Wim, Femke Roosma, Bart Meuleman, and Tim Reeskens, eds. 2017. *The Social Legitimacy of Targeted Welfare*. Cheltenham: Edward Elgar.

Vargas-Silva, Carlos, and Madeleine Sumption. 2019. *The Fiscal Impact of Immigration in the UK*. Oxford: University of Oxford, Migration Observatory.

Valluvan, Sivamohan, and Virinder S. Kalra. 2019. 'Racial Nationalism: Brexit, Borders, and Little Englander Contradictions'. *Ethnic and Racial Studies* 42(14): 2393–412.

Viney, Melissa. 2014. 'Almost Every Day One of My Clients Said They Felt Suicidal'. *The Guardian*, 5 November.

Virdee, Satnam, and Brendan McGeever. 2017. 'Racism, Crisis, and Brexit'. *Ethnic and Racial Studies* 41(10): 1802–19.

Wadsworth, Jonathan. 2015. 'Immigration and the UK Labour Market'. London: Centre for Economic Performance, London School of Economics, Paper EA 019.

Walker, Amy. 2020. 'South East Gained Half of New Jobs in England in Past 10 Years'. *The Guardian*, 21 February.

Walker, Peter. 2020. 'Brexit Bill: Tories Block Child Refugee Rights'. *The Guardian*, 1 January.

Warrell, Helen. 2014. 'EU Migrants Pay £20Bn More in Taxes Than They Receive'. *Financial Times*, 5 November. https://www.ft.com/content/c49043a8-6447-11e4-b219-00144feabdco.

Watts, Jay. 2018. 'Angered by the Damage That Austerity Does to the Poor'. *The Guardian* [letter], 11 November. https://www.theguardian.com/society/2018/nov/19/angered-by-the-damage-that-austerity-does-to-the-poor.

Webster, David. 2020. *Benefit Sanctions Statistics: February 2020*. Glasgow: University of Glasgow.

– 2019. 'Benefit Sanctions Statistics, May, 2019'. Child Poverty Action Group. 4 June. https://cpag.org.uk/policy-and-campaigns/briefing/david-webster-glasgow-university-briefings-benefit-sanctions.

– 2019a. 'Proportion of Sanctioned Universal Credit Claimants Receiving a Hardship Payment'. *Wordpress*, 8 July. https://suwn.files.wordpress.com/2019/07/19-05-uc-hardship-payments-d.webster.pdf.

References

253

– 2017. 'Benefit Sanctions Statistics: JSA, ESA, Universal Credit, and Income Support for Lone Parents'. 13 December. Glasgow: University of Glasgow. https://cpag.org.uk/policy-and-campaigns/briefing/david-webster-glasgow-university-briefings-benefit-sanctions.

– 2016. 'Explaining the Rise and Fall of JSA and ESA Sanctions 2010–16'. Child Poverty Action Group, 3 October. http://www.cpag.org.uk/sites/default/files/uploads/16-08%20Supplement%20-%20Reasons%20for%20rise%20%20fall%203%20Oct%2016.docx.

– 2015. 'Benefit Sanctions: Britain's Secret Penal System'. Centre for Crime and Justice Studies, 26 January. https://www.crimeandjustice.org.uk/resources/benefit-sanctions-britains-secret-penal-system.

– 2013. 'Jobseekers Allowance Sanctions and Disallowances'. *Working Brief* 233: 6–7.

Wiggan, Jay. 2012. 'Telling Stories of 21st Century Welfare'. *Critical Social Policy* 32(3): 383–405.

Williams, Martin. 2015. 'Kapow to GPOW'. London: CPAG, July 2015. http://www. cpag.org.uk/sites/default/files/CPAG-*Kapow-to-the-GPOW*-0715.pdf.

Women's Budget Group. 2017. *The Impact of Austerity on Black and Minority Ethnic Women in the UK*. London: Runnymede Trust.

Woolley, Agnes. 2019. 'Access Denied'. *Frontline Network*, 17 June. https://www.frontlinenetwork.org.uk/resources/news-and-views/2019/06/access-denied-the-cost-of-the-no-recourse-to-public-funds-policy.

WPC (Work and Pensions Committee). 2020. 'DWP's Response to the Coronavirus Outbreak'. 22 June. https://publications.parliament.uk/pa/cm5801/cmselect/cmworpen/178/17802.htm.

– 2019. *Universal Credit: Tests for Managed Migration*. London: House of Commons Library, HC 2091.

– 2019a. *The Benefit Cap*. London: House of Commons Library, HC 1477.

– 2019b. *Universal Credit and 'Survival Sex'*. Second Report of Session 2019–20, HC 83.

– 2019c. *Welfare Safety Net*. 28th Report of Session 2017–19, HC 1539.

– 2018. *Benefit Sanctions*. London: House of Commons Library, 19th Report of Session 2017–19, HC 955.

– 2016. *In-Work Progression in Universal Credit*. London: House of Commons Library, HC 549.

– 2015. *Benefit Sanctions Policy beyond the Oakley Review*. London: House of Commons Library, HC 814.

Wright, Sharon. 2016. 'Conceptualising the Active Welfare Subject: Welfare Reform in Discourse, Policy, and Lived Experience'. *Policy and Politics* 44(2): 235–52.

– 2012. 'Welfare-to-Work, Agency, and Personal Responsibility'. *Journal of Social Policy* 41(2): 309–28.

Wright, Sharon, Del Roy Fletcher, and Alasdair B.R. Stewart. 2020. *Social Policy Administration* 54: 278–94.

Wright, Dan, and Callum Masters. 2018. *Families Hit by Crippling Cost of Living*. York: Joseph Rowntree Foundation.

Yeo, Colin. 2018. 'What Are the 10 and 20 Year Rules on Long Residence?' *Free Movement*, 26 June. https://www.freemovement.org.uk/what-are-10-20-year-rules-on-long-residence-immigration-rules-paragraph-276-continuous-lawful-residence.

– 2018a. 'Can Children and Parents Apply to Remain after Seven Year Residence?' *Free Movement*, 28 November. https://www.freemovement.org.uk/can-children-and-parents-apply-to-remain-after-seven-years-residence.

– 2018b. 'Briefing: What Is the Hostile Environment, Where Does It Come from, Who Does It Affect?' *Free Movement*, 1 May 2018. https://www.freemovement.org.uk/briefing-what-is-the-hostile-environment-where-does-it-come-from-who-does-it-affect.

– 2017. 'Everything You Need to Know about the "Hostile Environment" for Immigrants'. *Free Movement,* 29 May. https://www.freemovement.org.uk/hostile-environment-affect.

– 2016. 'Inspection Report on the Hostile Environment Finds Hundreds Wrongly Denied Services'. *Free Movement*, 14 October. https://www.freemovement.org.uk/inspection-report-on-hostile-environment-finds-hundreds-wrongly-denied-services.

– 2014. 'Outcome of MM Minimum Income Case in Court of Appeal'. *Free Movement*, 11 July. https://www.freemovement.org.uk/outcome-of-mm-minimum-income-case-in-court-of-appeal.

Yeung, Peter. 2016. 'David Cameron Built the Fewest Houses of Any Prime Minister since 1923'. *The Independent*, 19 July. http://www.independent.co.uk/news/uk/politics/david-cameron-housing-housebuilding-prime-minister-england-john-healey-a7144646.html.

Yuval-Davis, Nira, Georgie Wemyss, and Kathryn Cassidy. 2019. *Bordering*. Cambridge: Polity.

– 2017. 'Introduction to the Special Issue: Racialized Bordering Discourses on European Roma'. *Ethnic and Racial Studies* 40(7): 1047–57.

References

LEGAL CASES CITED

Zambrano v ONEM C-34/09

Case C-292/89 [1991] ECR I-00745 (Antonissen)

Adam, Tesema and Limbuela v SSHD [2005] UKHL 66

MK *and* AH *v* SSHD [2012] EWHC 1896

Reilly and Wilson v SSWP [2012] EWHC 2292

Elisabeta Dano and Florin Dano v Sozialgericht Leipzig (Germany),
C-333/13

JS *and Ors v* SSWP [2013] EWHC 3350

Reilly and Wilson v SSWP [2013] UKSC 68

MM *and Ors v* SSHD [2013] EWHC 1900

MM *and* DM *v* SSHD [2013] EWCA Civ 1565

Gudanaviciene v Lord Chancellor [2014] EWCA Civ 1622

JO *and Ors v* SSHD [2014] UKUT 00517 (IAC)

MA *and Ors v* SSWP [2014] EWCA Civ 13

PLP *v* SSJ [2014] EWHC 2365

Refugee Action v SSHD [2014] EWHC 1033

Reilly and Hewstone v SSWP [2014] EWHC 2182

SG *and Ors v* SSWP [2014] EWCA Civ 156

GS *(India) and Ors v* SSHD [2015] EWCA

Hurley and Ors v SSWP [2015] EWHC 3382

Nzolameso v City of Westminster [2015] UKSC 22

Ors v SSWP [2015] EWCA Civ 49

SG *and Ors v* SSWP [2015] UKSC 16

Sanneh and Ors v SSWP [2015] EWCA Civ 49

Nazifa Alimanovic et al v Jobcenter Berlin Neukölln [2015] C-67/14

Ghulam and Ors v SSHD [2016] EWHC 2639

KS *v* SSWP [2016] UKUT 269 AAC

MB *and Ors v* SSWP [2016] UKUT, 372 AAC

Public Law Project v Lord Chancellor [2016] UKSC 39

ZAT *and Ors v* SSHD [2016] EWCA Civ 810

CJ *and* SG *v* SSWP [2017] UKUT 0324

DA *and Ors v* SSWP [2017] EWHC 1446

Gureckis and Ors v SSHD [2017] EWHC 3298

HC *v* SSWP [2017] UKSC 73

Help Refugees v SSHD [2017] EWHC 2727

MM *and Ors* [2017] UKSC

RR *v* SSWP *(UC)* [2017] UKUT 459 (AAC)

TM *v* SSHD [2018] UKUT 299 (IAC)

256 References

DA and Ors v ssWP [2018] EWCA Civ 504
SC and Ors v ssWP [2018] EWHC 864
K and AM v SSHD [2018] EWHC 2951
DA and Ors v ssWP [2019] UKSC 21
JCWI v SSHD [2019] EWHC 452
Johnson and Ors v ssWP [2019] EWHC 23
SC and Ors [2019] EWCA Civ 615
NN and LP v SSHD [2019] EWHC 1003)
Project for the Registration of Children As British Citizens & Ors v SSHD
     [2019] EWHC 3536 (Admin)
KH v Bury MBC and ssWP (2020) UKUT 50 (AAC)
W v SSHD [2020] EWHC 1299 (Admin)
W (by litigation friend J) v SSHD [2020] EWHC 1299 (Admin)

Index

absolute right, 47, 111, 200, 206, 207

abuse: assumptions of, 15, 99, 108, 116, 162, 165, 195, 196; of asylum system, 19, 25–6, 112, 132, 171; of free movement, 24, 73, 81, 88, 93, 161, 194; taxpayers and, 33

administrative errors, 22, 26, 175–7, 198, 206

Agamben, Giorgio, 26, 167–8, 169, 188, 205

agency, 25, 27; conceptions of, 142–5, 149, 159–60, 196; embodiment and interconnected, 152–4, 157, 164; identity and intersubjectivity and, 155–6; legal judgements and individual, 145–6, 150–2, 160; moral standing and, 165, 166, 193, 203; policy and, 161–5; reflexive, 150–1, 158

AIRE Centre (Advice on Individual Rights in Europe), 87, 127, 162

All Party Parliamentary Group (APPG), 112, 125–6, 183

Anderson, Bridget, 9, 11, 77, 98, 170

appeal, right of, 70, 113, 140, 153, 159; destitution and, 176, 200, 216n8; no/denial of, 114–16, 134–5, 136–7; removal of, 134, 186,

201; successful, 104, 132, 175–6, 186, 198, 204, 215n5

Arendt, Hannah, 54, 167–8

Asylum and Immigration Act (1999), S4 support, 113, 131–6, 140

asylum policy, 115, 119–20, 175, 186; agency and, 163–4; rationality and morality critiques, 129–33, 136, 203; reforming, 133–5

asylum-seekers: daily allowance, 4; decision-making, 166; genuine *versus* false, 65, 112; minor-age, 116, 131, 216n6; resettlement scheme, 111–12; rights, 62, 69, 124, 163; support rates, 112–13, 129–30, 172, 179, 182, 194, 198, 216n5; support system, 14–15, 71, 115–16, 202. *See also* failed asylum-seekers; welfare–migration–asylum complex

austerity decade, 7, 8, 16, 98, 116, 145; COVID-19 and, 208, 211; deficit reduction and, 3–4, 84, 90, 189; immigration controls, 12, 15, 167; moral economy of, 5, 31, 51, 139

banks, bailouts, 49

bare life, 26, 167–9, 186, 187, 205

battlefields of change, concept, 21, 22, 97–9, 117

Beck, Ulrich, 19, 55, 91

Becker, Sascha O., 91

behavioural change, 111, 133, 146, 171, 186; through discipline and control, 26, 194, 195–6, 199, 202; policies aimed at, 142, 143, 159–60, 166; schemes seeking, 101, 150, 151, 187

behaviours, 78–9, 106, 147, 155, 193; assumptions, 48, 98, 108, 113, 115, 204; parental, 169, 180–1, 182, 187, 207; sanctions and conditionality and, 100–3, 172, 194; welfare dependency and, 100. *See also* mental health problems; responsibility

benefit cap, 7, 13, 32, 39, 108, 159, 199, 212; discrimination and, 177–8; ECHR and, 200; household limits, 148, 209, 214n8, 215n6; lone parents and, 43, 61, 105, 155–6, 202; treatment of children and, 180–1

benefit entitlement, 8, 86, 90, 153, 176; EEA nationals and, 83–5

benefit tourism, 14, 15, 19, 68, 86, 88–9, 93; Zambrano carers and, 127, 128, 140, 163, 166, 183, 194

black and minority ethnic (BME), 42, 137, 173, 178–9, 199, 204, 209

Booth, Robert, 29–30, 47, 49, 120, 201

bordering practices, 12, 20, 63

Borders, Citizenship and Immigration Act (2009), 115, 126, 130, 134, 181

boundaries and boundary-drawing, 109, 170, 207, 208; blurring of, 23, 55, 114, 204; of desert, 75, 100–3, 112; of entitlement, 96, 98, 106; hierarchical, 10, 63; margins of, 105; moral, 28, 68; policy design

and, 20, 95, 196–7; problematic, 101, 104, 116, 117, 198; stratified, 111, 112; symbolic, 77, 98, 197

Brexit, 3, 18, 83, 94; Leave and Remain supporters, 24, 81, 89–92, 95, 215n19; promises of, 93; right to freedom of movement and, 53, 189

Cameron, David, 51–2, 87, 89, 214n2; austerity campaign, 4–5, 34, 167; morality and fairness speeches, 17, 24, 32–3, 73, 78–81, 84, 199; 'moral mission' of welfare reform, 19, 29, 45, 58, 80; and Remain (in the EU), 5, 90, 92–3

capability, 152–3, 207; limited, 39, 69, 148, 172. *See also* Work Capability Assessment (WCA)

care-leaving, 114–15, 133, 186

carers, 107, 154, 199, 210; single-parent, 156, 157; worker distinction, 104–5, 197, 207. *See also* Zambrano carers

Carers Allowance, 154, 199, 200

CARIN-criteria, 99

category and circumstance distinction, 106, 107

chains of equivalence: construction of, 48; and difference, 19, 35, 79, 80, 81, 198, 206–7; Laclau's concept, 19, 23, 34–5, 193

Chauvin, Sébastien, 121, 140

Child Poverty Action Group (CPAG), 37, 43, 105, 216n9

children, treatment of, 127, 181–3, 197–8, 200; differential or pre-judicial, 26, 128, 179, 204

Children Act (1989), 133; S17 support of, 109–10, 115, 127, 134, 179, 182, 185

Children's Commissioner, 115, 126, 180

Index

259

children's rights, 70, 71, 136, 181;
asylum-seekers and, 130–1, 134,
179; citizenship registration, 179,
185; and related benefits, 61,
102–3, 105, 108, 155–6, 202;
Zambrano, 109–10, 126–9, 163
Child Tax Credit (CTC) two-child limit,
13, 18, 32, 39, 61, 148, 163, 199,
200; discrimination and, 178; legal
challenges to, 102–3, 157–9; treatment of children and, 180–1, 183
citizen/non-citizen divide, 11, 69, 98,
187, 192; assemblage, 121–2;
discriminatory effects, 177, 179;
inclusion and exclusion and, 168,
170, 205–6
citizenship, 10, 14, 76, 196, 202;
British, 19, 53, 70–1, 210; divisions, 169; effective, 127; EU,
61–2; exclusion and, 167–8; full
membership of, 167–8; 'good', 11,
83; inequality, 20, 61, 77; inner
logic of, 65; registration of children
for, 185; rights, 19–20, 53–5, 59,
69, 72, 122, 193; social inclusion
and, 16, 53, 55–7, 167, 187, 189,
192, 203, 206; topological
approach to, 170–1
civic activists, 58, 119, 140–1, 193,
201; asylum advocacy groups, 129,
130–1, 134, 135, 163; legal test-case
campaigns, 125, 146, 200, 205;
Lockwood's term, 65, 122; moral
standing and, 35, 36, 71, 205
civic expansion, 58, 65–6, 72, 88, 205
civic stratification, 18, 23, 25, 26, 99,
203; boundaries and behaviours
and, 100–3, 116; conditionality
and, 101, 105, 117; discourse of
dependency and, 45, 48; domestic
welfare and, 58–60; (in)formal
dimensions of, 24, 64–7, 73, 77,

87; gendered aspect, 61; inclusion
and exclusion thresholds and, 96,
106–7; Lockwood's concept, 20,
35, 49, 57–8, 122, 193; migration
and, 61–3; non-EEA nationals and,
96, 109; political rhetoric and,
94, 98
civil society organizations, 21, 47, 69
Coalition government (2010), 4, 13,
17, 31, 44, 78, 147; austerity under,
16, 33, 116, 189
collectivities, 10–11, 63, 74, 75, 97,
190
community, 53, 77, 83, 132, 167; role
of the economy, 30, 190; of value,
68, 76, 98, 170
compassion, 27, 47, 121, 124, 127,
133, 208; repression and, 119,
129, 139–40
compliant environment. See hostile
environment
conditionality, 11, 16, 26, 67, 109;
control and, 10, 18, 71, 122, 123,
192, 196; ESA claimants and,
103–4, 152–3; income thresholds
and, 107, 129; increased, 31–2, 40,
88–9, 94, 143; migrant rights and,
56–8, 111, 196; for non-citizens,
121–2; out of work and in-work,
13, 18, 100–3, 172; sanctions and,
41, 52, 88, 149, 174, 184; single
parents and, 104, 157
Conservative Party, 3, 12–13, 17, 59,
123, 193; Brexit and, 93, 95;
conference speeches, 31–3, 78–81;
responsibility agenda, 29, 82
contestation, forms of, 21–2, 99, 106,
110, 121, 198, 203; institutional,
114, 116, 117
context creation, term usage, 144,
149–50
coronavirus. See COVID-19

Index

cosmopolitan ideal, 19–20, 23, 55–6, 189

Council Tax Benefit (CTB), 32, 38, 46, 82

COVID-19, 3, 101, 128, 134, 189, 208–12; business subsidy, 60, 102, 196; 'low-skilled' workers and, 65, 68, 107, 209–10; NHS staff, 8, 210; rise in benefits, 4, 7, 38, 47, 60, 102, 148, 183; wage subsidy, 33

culture of dependency, 33, 43, 48, 51, 67–8, 82, 93, 208; culture of responsibility and, 23, 31, 58, 98; end to, 189, 194; low-pay support and, 101–2

DA and Ors v SSWP, 105, 156–7, 181

death rates, 184, 209

debt: collection, 46; national, 4; personal, 38, 183–4; reduction, 33, 124

decision-making: of asylum-seekers, 163, 166, 176; poor-quality, 101, 104, 105, 112, 117, 136, 198, 204

deficit reduction, 34, 48, 123, 143; austerity drive and, 4, 84, 90, 189; COVID-19 and, 208, 211; policy, 3, 24, 73; welfare reform and, 16, 38

delivery of rights, 20, 88, 192, 195

Department of Work and Pensions (DWP), 6, 39, 44, 110, 174, 183; administrative failures, 175, 185, 200; appeals, 153, 159

desert, 74–5, 100–3, 137, 169, 196; conceptions of, 15, 32, 88, 105, 129, 139; entitlement and, 77, 87, 98; inclusion and, 170; moral economy of, 15, 121, 139; responsibility and, 127

destitution, 14, 46, 87, 164, 183–6, 204; appeals, 176, 200, 216n8; creation of, 117, 169, 175, 201, 202, 205, 207; enforced, 26, 138;

failed asylum-seekers and, 111, 114–15, 132, 134–5, 166, 183, 212; as a mode of control, 173, 174, 182, 188; proof of, 198; Windrush migrants and, 137

dignity, 50, 135, 136, 198, 202, 206

disability benefits, 32, 39, 61, 103–4, 148, 156; agency and, 153, 154

Discretionary Leave, 176, 212

discrimination, 7, 26, 69, 87, 106, 157, 206; children's rights and, 71, 110, 117; crossover effects, 177–80, 187, 204; disabled people and, 104, 154; ECHR articles and, 42, 200–1; enjoyment of rights and, 64–5; gender, 105, 155–6, 158, 179; 'right to rent' and, 63, 71, 137, 173, 200

domestic violence, 43, 87, 155

domestic welfare: boundaries and behaviours, 100–3; civic stratification and, 58–61; claimants, 8–9, 11, 24, 68, 81, 88, 142; controls, 57; dependency, 18, 85, 94, 123; erosion of, 56; and migration link, 51–3, 71–2, 89, 194–5, 204–5; policies, 16–17, 82–3, 192. See also welfare–migration–asylum complex

Dorling, Danny, 89, 90, 92

Douglas, Mary, 100, 101, 105, 107, 112; on 'how institutions think', 20, 24, 97–8, 117, 191, 196–7

Duncan Smith, Iain, 78, 92, 216n1

East European migrants, 15, 66, 84, 92

economic policy, 47, 49

Emirbayer, Mustafa, 144, 160

Employment and Support Allowance (ESA), 13, 32, 103, 148, 152–3, 154, 215n11

employment rates, 6, 39–40, 86, 162

Employment Skills and Enterprise Scheme, 44, 149
English Poor Law (1834), 12
Equality Act (2010), 104, 106, 137, 152
equivalential chains. *See* chains of equivalence
European Convention on Human Rights (ECHR), 42–3, 66, 106, 128, 155; Article 3, 69, 71, 132, 138, 176, 200; Articles 6 and 8, 70–1, 105, 200
European Court of Justice, 10
European Economic Area (EEA) migrants, 3, 52, 57, 175, 194; benefit rights, 77, 108–10, 111, 196; fiscal costs and contributions, 85–6, 199; free movement of, 8, 10, 18, 77–8, 83, 108, 189; health surcharge, 210, 211, 212; homelessness, 71, 87, 162, 205; jobseekers, 84–5, 109, 185; moral standing of, 88–9; treatment of, 202. *See also* non-European Economic Area (EEA) migrants
exclusion, 11, 109, 120, 126, 186, 204; hostile environment and, 137–8; inclusion and, 26, 57, 96, 106–7, 124, 167–9, 170; isolationism and, 111, 115; from mainstream benefits, 127, 128, 163, 185, 202

failed asylum-seekers, 124, 135, 142, 194, 202; appeals, 176, 186; destitution, 111, 132, 166, 183, 185–6; hostile environment and, 173, 199; reforming support for, 133–4, 212; support system, 8, 18, 62, 71, 113–14, 131, 164, 172, 196; treatment of children and, 133, 182; unable or unwilling to leave, 186, 198, 205, 212
fairness, 90, 93, 102, 116, 138, 187, 203–4; benefit cuts and, 37–8; Cameron's speeches on, 17, 24, 32–3, 73, 78–81, 199; desert and, 137; income and, 107, 108; legal judgements and, 43–5, 110, 128, 132, 177–8; morality and, 23, 34, 46, 193; and responsibility, 5, 8, 19, 81, 82, 83, 110, 196–7, 202; securing, 48; to taxpayers, 33, 34, 43, 100, 104, 112, 147, 155, 182, 196
Faist, Thomas, 9–10
family life, 110, 125–7, 163, 165, 187; right to, 107, 129
family (re)unification, 8, 18, 112, 124, 187, 192, 214n2; MIR and, 62, 65, 107–8, 125–6, 136, 163, 178, 202
Fassin, Didier, 168–9, 192, 204; on compassion and repression, 139–40; moral economy concept, 21, 25, 74, 119–20, 121, 190, 201
First Tier Tribunal (FtT), 151–2
'flexible' labour, 6, 157, 209; market, 40, 52, 68, 88–9, 103, 106
food banks, 45, 47, 58–9, 183, 207
forced labour, 44
formal entitlements, 20, 24, 77, 82, 185; civic stratification and, 57–8, 64
fraud, 31, 33, 34, 37, 65, 147; task force on, 174
Freeden, Michael, 41, 50, 76, 80, 193; on ideology, 19, 23, 33–6, 37, 78, 197, 198
free movement, 62, 94–5, 111, 120; abuse of, 24, 73, 79, 81, 84, 88, 93, 161, 194; concessions on, 89; of EEA citizens, 8, 10, 18, 77–8, 83, 108, 189; end to, 3, 210

Garces-Mascarenas, Blanca, 121, 140

gender: discrimination, 105, 149, 155–6, 158, 179; protections and treatment, 63–4; use of public services and, 60–1

genuine-prospect-of-work test, 84, 86–7, 216n9

Giddens, Anthony, 144, 160

Goldring, Luin, 121–2, 140, 170

Goodwin, Matthew, 73, 91–2

governmentality, 23, 57, 62, 71

Gross Domestic Product (GDP), 8, 49, 85

guaranteed minimum, 13, 69, 70, 76, 202; abolition of, 16, 27, 103, 157, 183, 185

Gureckis and Ors v SSHD, 87, 162

Hale, Lady, 127–8

Hammar, Tomas, 61

Harris, Neville, 12

HC v SSWP, 109, 127, 172, 181, 182

health system. *See* National Health Service (NHS)

Heath, Oliver, 73, 91–2

hierarchy, 9, 170–1, 172, 187, 204

Hill Collins, Patricia, 217n

Hitlin, Steven, 28, 98

homelessness, 3, 27, 114, 184, 199; COVID-19 and, 211–12; EEA migrants, 71, 87, 162, 200, 205; Windrush migrants and, 137–8

Home Office (HO), 15, 107, 114–15, 132–5, 162; administrative errors, 176, 177, 216n11; asylum support rates, 112–13; fees, 185, 198; Windrush scandal, 137, 177

hostile environment, 18, 26, 169, 189; for undocumented migrants, 4, 8, 16, 25, 62, 124, 137–8, 173–5, 194–5, 205

housing benefit (HB), 7, 32, 48, 162, 172; cuts, 37, 38, 46, 82, 87

humanitarianism, 119–20, 121

human rights, 8, 22, 72, 97, 110, 115, 117; citizenship and, 53–6; universal, 41, 53, 57, 65, 69, 70. *See also* European Convention on Human Rights (ECHR)

Human Rights Act (HRA), 42–3, 69–70, 200, 206

hunger, 45, 183, 201. *See also* food banks

Hurley and Ors v SSWP, 104, 154, 202

identity, 93, 95, 155–6

ideology, 19, 23, 33–6, 49, 78, 197, 198

illegal migrants. *See* undocumented migrants

Immigration Acts: of 1971, 14; of 2014 and 2016, 14, 17, 111, 113, 131, 133, 164, 167

immigration controls, 3, 14–15, 23, 62, 80, 167, 171–2; Brexit and, 90; Cameron's arguments on, 51–2; children and, 128, 135, 181; legal challenges to, 110–11, 200, 201; reduction target, 123, 189, 217n1; welfare entitlement and, 76

immigration policy, 14, 18, 64, 110, 161, 181, 197–8; contestation and conditionality, 21, 119, 123–5

inclusion: civic, 66; exclusion and, 26, 96, 106–7, 124, 167–9, 170; trans-national and national, 97; universal principles of, 205–6; welfare, 52, 77, 116, 123. *See also* social inclusion

income thresholds, 15, 107, 124, 210–11, 214n2. *See also* minimum income requirement (MIR) individualization, 10, 75, 83, 97, 109, 111, 202; model of responsibility, 11, 142–3, 207

inequality, 10, 95, 122, 206; civic stratification and, 20, 61, 66, 77, 81, 193; economic, 53, 90, 143; income, 90, 92; rights and, 57–8; social, 9, 59, 209

insider/outsider divide, 168, 169, 170, 186, 188, 217n

institutional battlefield, 24, 99–100, 101, 105, 117–18

institutions, 97–9, 144, 195–6

International Covenant on Economic, Social and Cultural Rights (ICESCR), 42, 66

involuntary economic inactivity, 6

in-work benefits, 13, 18, 60, 81, 88, 102, 172

Javid, Sajid, 3

job-search requirements, 12–13, 100, 105, 147, 212; and legal challenges, 150, 151–2

Job Seekers Act (1995), 12

Job Seekers Allowance (JSA), 13, 39, 60, 62, 215n11; for EEA migrants, 84, 86, 109; sanctions, 12, 47, 103

Johnson, Boris, 18, 211

Joint Committee on Human Rights (JCHR), 177, 180, 181

Joint Council for the Welfare of Immigrants (JCWI), 21, 125–6

JS and Ors v SSWP, 155, 178

just about managing (JAM), 93

justice, access to, 153, 201, 206, 207; in Article 6 of the ECHR, 70, 71, 200; failure of, 26, 136; rights of, 133, 138

Kerr, Lord, 156, 181

kinship care, 103

Labour government, 15

labour market, 12, 39, 51, 65, 76, 98, 208; access to, 15, 61–2, 83; damage to, 80; 'flexible', 40, 52, 68, 88–9, 103, 106, 209; restrictions, 84

Laclau, Ernesto, 41, 50; chains of equivalence concept, 19, 23, 34–6, 37, 78–9, 193, 198

Landolt, Patricia, 121–2, 140, 170

LASPO Act (2012), 136, 177, 201

legal aid, 124, 140, 176, 177; residence requirement for, 71, 136, 138, 201

legal arguments and judgements, 25, 87, 118, 140, 162, 165; on conditionality and sanctions, 44–5, 149–51; on CTC two-child limit, 102–3, 157–9; discrimination and, 177–9; ECHR articles and, 200–1; fairness and, 43–4; human rights and, 41–2, 69–70; on lone parents and benefit cap, 105, 155–7; on mental health and disabilities, 104, 152–4; on MIR rules, 107–8, 125–6; on support for asylum-seekers, 112–13, 114, 116, 129–32; on Zambrano carers and children's rights, 109–10, 111, 127–8, 163

legality critique, 24, 25, 26, 134, 137, 142; implementation of policies, 41–5; morality and, 123, 126, 128, 129, 132–3; term usage, 21–2

liberal competition state, 74, 75, 94, 97

Lockwood, David, 68, 74, 100, 140, 192, 206; civic expansion concept, 58, 66, 72, 88, 205; civic stratification concept, 20, 35, 49, 57, 59, 61, 64, 77; on conflict and discontent, 76, 208; on moral resources, 58, 65, 74, 87, 122, 193; on universal human rights, 69 lone parents, 64, 207; benefit cap and, 43, 61, 102, 105, 154, 155–7, 159, 202; conditionality and, 104–5, 148; discrimination and, 178–9

low-paid work, 6, 82, 101–2

'low-skilled' workers, 51, 86, 90, 93, 107; COVID-19 and, 65, 68, 209–10, 212

'make work pay' policy, 31–2, 39–40, 101–2, 105–6

margins, contestable, 99, 100, 119; asylum policy and, 115–16; boundary problems and, 24, 95, 96, 117; migration policy and, 110–11; welfare policy and, 105–6

market economy, 5, 29–30, 49

Marshall, T.H., 57–8, 77; social citizenship model, 19–20, 23, 53, 55–6, 70, 75, 167, 171

Mau, Steffen, 75

May, Theresa, 17, 93

Mayblin, Lucy, 76, 134, 164

mental health problems, 40, 104, 106, 152–3, 159, 175; destitution and, 87, 185, 186, 199

Mezzadra, Sandro, 170

migrant rights, 14, 20, 58, 89, 206; access to benefits, 108–10; citizenship rights and, 23, 51, 53, 57, 69, 71–2; granting or denial of, 57, 77, 162–3

Migration Advisory Committee (MAC), 85–6, 107, 108, 161

migration policy. *See* immigration policy

minimum income requirement (MIR), 62, 65, 70, 136, 163, 172, 204; concessions on, 129; criticism of, 197, 199, 202; discrimination and, 178; legal challenges to, 107–8, 110,

125–6; lowering of, 210–11; salary and skill thresholds, 106–7, 210

Mische, Ann, 144, 160

MM and DM v SSWP, 104, 152, 175

MM and Ors v SSHD, 107–8, 126, 216n2

moral economy, 26, 47, 49–50, 166; from above and below discourses, 25, 64, 119, 124, 128–9, 132–3, 135–6, 138–41; all economies as, 23, 30, 68, 74, 120, 191; alternative, 205–6, 212; of austerity Britain, 31–3, 51; Booth's concept, 29–30; composite, 203; Fassin's concept, 21, 25, 74, 119–20, 121, 201; political discourse and, 16, 19, 20; as a practice, 190–1; re-embedding, 31–3; Sayer's concept, 74; systemic approach, 121; Thompson's concept, 5, 29, 120, 190; of welfare and migration, 9, 74–5

morality critique, 24, 25, 137, 140, 206, 212; agency and, 142; fairness and, 32–3, 34, 79–80, 132, 193; human suffering/flourishing and, 45–9, 50, 201–3, 206; legality and, 123, 126, 127–30, 132–3; sociological approaches, 16, 28–9, 98; term usage, 21–2

moral resources, 20, 66, 67, 72, 93; Lockwood's notion of, 58, 65, 74, 87, 122, 193

moral sentiments, 35, 74, 120, 191; activation of shared, 64, 88, 122, 140

moral standing, 41, 49, 64, 86, 129, 205; agency and, 165–6; of claimants, 151–2, 153, 161; erosion of, 35, 67, 68, 71, 139, 193, 194–5, 208; granting of rights and, 67, 72; informal, 24, 77, 95; of migrants, 68, 88–9, 93, 124, 195; public

Index

perceptions of, 66, 87–9; of target groups, 26, 36, 73, 95, 122–3, 140, 209, 212

Munch, Richard, 83, 94, 100, 116–17, 161, 191; on battlefields of change, 21, 22, 24, 97–9, 117; on liberal competition state, 74, 75, 97; on political rhetoric, 89, 192, 197

National Asylum Support System (NASS), 15

National Audit Office (NAO), 173, 185

National Health Service (NHS), 8, 27, 138, 162, 173, 208–10

National Referral Mechanism (NRM), 164–5

nation-state, 54–5

Neilson, Brett, 170

neoliberalism, 49

New Labour, 12, 13, 15, 80

non-citizens. *See* citizen/non-citizen divide; undocumented migrants

non-European Economic Area (EEA) migrants, 3, 6, 8, 25, 52, 81, 124; conditionality and controls, 57, 62, 83, 119; fiscal costs and contributions, 85–6; NHS workers, 8, 210; visas and income requirements, 106–8, 124, 172, 194; Zambrano carers, 109–10, 127–8

no recourse to public funds (NRPF), 14, 15, 124, 172, 205; COVID-19 and, 211, 212; discrimination and, 179; effect on children, 111, 182–3, 204; guidance on, 129, 140, 200; ten-year route to settlement and, 106, 128, 176, 199

normativity, 98, 119, 147, 149; citizenship and, 20, 53, 55; morality critique and, 21–2, 28, 30. *See also* social norms

Nussbaum, Martha, 47

Nzolameso v City of Westminster, 178

O'Brien, Charlotte, 12, 109, 163

Osborne, George, 4, 32, 33, 67

out-of-work benefits, 81, 84, 88, 93, 172, 199

Oxfam, 38, 47

Palmer, Ellie, 42

Parliament, 43–4, 85, 130, 140, 159, 213n4

permanent residence, 61, 63, 83, 84, 107, 108

Polanyi, Karl, 29

political discourse, 4, 20, 25–6, 75, 177; analysis and application, 191–3; Cameron's party speeches and, 17, 24, 67, 78–81; forms of contestation, 21–2; moral economy and, 16, 19–20, 85; policy and, 5, 17, 26, 85, 88, 95, 98, 191, 195–7

post-national society, 19, 23, 56, 57

poverty: child, 3, 38, 40, 183; food, 29, 45–7, 58–9, 130, 183; relative and absolute, 6. *See also* destitution

practical reason, 143, 145, 159–60

public perceptions, 11, 26, 72, 86, 163, 196; COVID-19 and, 210, 212; of moral standing, 66, 87–9; of reality, 4; Windrush migrants and, 138, 140, 207

public transportation, 209

racialization, 8, 14, 63, 90

rationality critique, 24, 25, 26, 50, 86, 206, 212; asylum support policy and, 129, 132, 133, 136; boundary-drawing and, 138; legality and, 123, 125–6, 127, 129, 137, 139, 200; morality and, 45,

50, 140; and purposive rationality, 143, 146, 159; term usage, 21–2; welfare–migration–asylum complex and, 198–9; welfare reform and, 37–41, 49

referendum on EU membership, 3, 6, 17, 73, 161–2, 198; voting results, 89–93, 94, 95, 215n17, 215n19

Refugee Action, 112–13, 129–30, 132

Refugee Council (RC), 21, 134

regime of rights, 35, 57, 65–6

Reilly and Hewstone v SSWP, 44, 175

Reilly and Wilson v SSWP, 44–5, 149–50, 159, 175

rent, right to, 62, 71, 137, 162, 174, 200

responsibility, 99, 127, 194–5; culture of, 23, 31, 58, 98; fairness and, 33, 79–81, 193, 196, 202; moral, 135; of parents and caregivers, 104–5, 110, 126, 156, 158; personal or individual, 103, 117, 142–3, 161, 207; welfare reform and, 82–3, 147–8

rough sleeping. *See* homelessness

RR v SSWP, 151, 159

sanctions: for failure to comply, 5, 60, 82, 100–1, 147, 151, 172; intensification of, 12–13; legal challenges to, 44–5, 69–70, 149–51, 200; poor understanding of, 199; regime, 44, 101, 103, 106, 151, 175, 197, 200; welfare conditionality and, 3, 40–1, 58, 88, 102, 147–8, 184

Sanneh and Ors v SSWP, 109, 127, 163, 172, 179

Sayer, Andrew, 74, 143, 149, 159

self-employment, 7, 209, 213n3; 'false', 6, 82

SG and Ors v SSWP, 43–4, 103, 155–6, 179, 180

Shutes, Isabel, 10, 11, 96

sick pay, 7, 209

single parents. *See* lone parents

Skeggs, Beverley, 148–9

social division, 7, 97–8

social inclusion, 75, 77, 94, 171; citizenship and, 16, 53, 55–7, 167, 187, 189, 192, 203, 206

social norms, 74, 75, 119, 146, 191

social rights, 96, 97, 98, 167, 189, 192; citizenship and, 18, 19–20, 53, 55–6, 59, 70; contraction of, 16, 23, 116; entitlement to, 57, 78; erosion of, 94, 99, 189; human rights and, 67; of migrants, 3, 9–11, 83

social security, 12, 42, 87, 108, 109; entitlements, 70, 214n11; individualized model of, 109, 202

Social Security Act (1966), 14

Social Security Advisory Committee (SSAC), 38, 39, 40, 87

socio-economic systems, 5, 20, 30, 49, 68, 74, 191

sociological approaches, 51, 159, 160–1; to citizenship, 53; to morality, 16, 28–9, 34–5, 98

solidarity, 11, 47, 75, 93, 97, 100, 117

sovereignty: national, 77; parliamentary, 70, 71, 200, 206; state, 19

stigmatization, 41, 48, 158; receipt of a right and, 58, 65, 195, 208

stratified rights, 61, 99, 106, 112, 171, 179, 196. *See also* civic stratification

Stuart, Ben, 89, 90, 92

Stubbs, Joshua, 89, 90, 92

suicide, 184–5, 205

symbolic violence, 13–14

Syrian refugee crisis, 15, 96, 111. *See also* asylum-seekers; failed asylum-seekers

system of control, 119, 124–5, 136, 138, 140, 203–4; denial of rights and, 169, 196; errors and, 175. *See also* immigration controls

tax credit (TC), 31, 48, 60, 81, 86, 89, 102

taxpayers, 12, 18, 35, 58, 79, 88; burden of, 38, 107, 129, 194; defence or protection of, 18, 98, 117, 160, 189, 193; fairness to, 33, 34, 43, 100, 104, 112, 147, 155, 182, 196

Taylor-Gooby, Peter, 7, 33, 38, 85

Teather, Sarah, 167

Thompson, Edward P., 5, 23, 29, 64, 120, 190

topology: meaning of, 26, 170–1, 203; of welfare–migration–asylum complex, 172–3, 179, 180, 186–7

trafficking, 164–5, 166

unaccompanied minors, 4, 112, 116, 131, 134, 216n6

UN Convention on the Rights of the Child (UNCRC), 44, 70, 105, 114, 126, 134; legal judgements and, 180–2, 200, 201

under-occupancy penalty (bedroom tax), 38–9

undocumented migrants, 4, 8, 25, 71, 80–1, 142, 185; COVID-19 and, 211; failed asylum-seekers as, 113–14, 133, 164, 166, 194, 198; hostile environment for, 4, 8, 16, 25, 62, 124, 137–8, 173–5, 194–5, 205. *See also* citizen/non-citizen divide

unemployment, 68, 100, 170, 208, 211; benefits, 37, 40; domestic, 5, 23; EU referendum and, 90–1; rates, 3, 6, 7

Universal Credit (UC) system, 6, 40, 41, 82–3, 147, 174; conditionality and sanctions, 102–3, 151;

COVID-19 and, 4, 7, 38, 47, 102, 148, 208–9; design flaws, 183, 201, 205; eligibility and requirements, 13, 85, 100; payment waiting period, 5, 172, 184; rollout of, 32, 102, 175, 183; zero-hours contracts and, 7, 33, 209, 213n4

universal principles, 70, 205–6

universal rights, 53, 57, 65, 67, 69–71, 77

Upper Tribunal (UT), 151–2

Vaisey, Stephen, 28, 98

value-added tax (VAT), 38

values, 49, 119–20, 149, 159; competing, 36, 198; conflict, 92, 95

visas, 62, 106–7, 112, 194, 211

Webster, David, 47, 101

welfare chauvinism, 11

welfare–migration–asylum complex, 5, 22, 24, 167, 188, 195; administrative errors and access to justice and, 175–7; as a composite system, 203–5; destitution and, 183–6; discrimination and, 177–9; hostile environment and, 173–5; modes of control and, 171–2, 195; morality critique, 201–3; rationality critique, 198–9; topology of, 26, 172–3, 186–7; treatment of children and, 180–3

welfare policy, 81, 105, 117; agency and, 144–6, 159–60, 161–6; changes, 6, 24, 25, 32, 33, 60, 82–3, 94, 147–8, 215n7; design and implementation, 21–2, 42, 50, 59, 161; domestic welfare and migration link, 51–2; fairness and responsibilities agenda, 80, 82, 83, 193; frame of analysis, 16–18. *See also* benefit cap; conditionality; 'make work pay' policy

welfare reform, 7, 13, 18, 35, 160–1, 174; Brexit and, 5–6, 24, 73; destitution and, 183–6; fairness and, 43–5, 107, 171, 199; moral mission of, 16, 19, 23, 29, 80, 123; policy adjustments, 82–3, 145–8; rationality critique, 37–41, 49; rights and, 41–2, 69, 194; stratifying elements, 60–1, 83

Welfare Reform Act (2012), 17, 31, 82, 100, 147, 167

Welfare Reform and Work Act (2016), 31, 38, 82, 147, 167

welfare rights, 6, 8, 15, 58, 68; contraction of, 17, 129; for domestic claimants, 12, 24, 93; migrants and, 61–3, 108–10

welfare system, 26, 75, 76, 97, 109, 146; administrative failings of, 175–7; claimant 'activation' and, 143, 170; control and, 51–2, 196; cuts, 4, 5, 38, 45–6, 72, 102; dependency, 33, 58–60, 80, 81, 85, 100, 101, 204; desert and, 169; perversities of, 205, 207; radical restructuring, 3, 31, 82, 189; 'scaremongering', 6, 174; spending, 35, 37, 189, 211. *See also* domestic welfare; guaranteed minimum

Windrush scandal, 63, 173, 185, 203, 216n9; destruction of records, 137, 177, 198; public sympathy and, 138, 140, 207

women, 61, 156, 160, 184, 199; discrimination, 42, 155–6, 178–9, 204; domestic workers, 63–4, 66

Work and Pensions Committee (WPC), 6, 38, 39, 46, 102, 174, 183–4, 211

Work Capability Assessment (WCA), 39, 70, 148, 197, 202; administrative errors, 175; criticism of, 103–4, 152–3, 159

work incentives, 12, 31, 39, 102, 148, 183, 212; behavioural change and, 103, 142, 187; misdirected, 154; single parents and, 104, 155, 156, 157, 202

working-age benefits, 7, 37, 82, 86, 91, 172; freeze on, 5, 18, 32, 46, 60; main types, 215n11

Working Tax Credit (WTC), 7, 32, 60, 102, 104

workless households, 40, 43, 52, 102, 104, 147, 214n8

Work Programmes, 39, 44, 60, 101, 200, 215n2; sanctions and appeals, 101, 175

Work Related Activity Group (WRAG), 13, 103–5, 148, 152, 153, 194

Wright, Sharon, 13, 143–5, 150, 152

Zambrano carers, 111, 139–40, 172, 199, 204–5; benefit tourism and, 128, 163, 166, 183, 194; discrimination and, 179; on S17 support, 109–10, 127, 179, 182, 185; treatment of children and, 181, 183, 198, 201

zero-hours contracts, 6, 39, 82, 157, 209, 213n4; refusal of, 7, 33